# Computers, Internet, and Cellphones MADE EASY for SENIORS®

## Publisher's Note

This book is intended for general information only. It does not constitute medical, legal, or financial advice or practice. The editors of FC&A have taken careful measures to ensure the accuracy and usefulness of the information in this book. While every attempt has been made to assure accuracy, errors may occur. Some websites, addresses, and telephone numbers may have changed since printing. We cannot guarantee the safety or effectiveness of any advice or treatments mentioned. Readers are urged to consult with their professional financial advisors, lawyers, and health care professionals before making any changes.

Any health information in this book is for information only and is not intended to be a medical guide for self-treatment. It does not constitute medical advice and should not be construed as such or used in place of your doctor's medical advice. Readers are urged to consult with their health care professionals before undertaking therapies suggested by the information in this book, keeping in mind that errors in the text may occur as in all publications and that new findings may supersede older information.

The publisher and editors disclaim all liability (including any injuries, damages, or losses) resulting from the use of the information in this book.

*If any of you lacks wisdom, you should ask God, who gives generously to all without finding fault, and it will be given to you.*

*James 1:5*

FC&A Publishing®
103 Clover Green
Peachtree City, GA 30269

Produced by the staff of FC&A

ISBN 978-1935574651

# TABLE OF CONTENTS

# THE GOLDEN AGE OF TECHNOLOGY

We live in a golden age of technology. This is a statement that can probably be claimed by any generation – we all think that we are always living at the peak of technological development. However, with the pace of change in the world of computing and digital technology – with new devices, new gadgets, new apps, and new operating systems – almost every year could be described as a new golden age!

Just because digital technology is moving so fast does not mean that you have to let it leave you behind. It is easy for anyone to take command of their digital devices and use them to enhance and improve their lives in numerous ways. All it takes is a bit of confidence, and the information in this book, and you will soon feel that you are at the forefront of the digital revolution.

## User specifications – you are in control

When looking at computing hardware (desktop computers, laptops, tablets, and smartphones) and software (apps and operating systems that are the engines for the hardware) you will hear a lot about specifications and system specifications. These are the features of the hardware and the requirements for the software to operate effectively.

But what about the user specifications? When deciding the range of digital technology that you need, it is important to decide what you want it for, rather than being persuaded to buy the latest (usually most expensive), all-singing, all-dancing device, and then wondering how you are to make the best use of it.

So before you buy a new computer, laptop, tablet, or smartphone (or upgrade your current one), make a list of what you want to do with your digital devices. This could include:

- Surfing the Web with desktop, laptop, and mobile Web browsers.

- Communicating with family and friends using email.

- Speaking to your grandchildren using video chatting.

- Managing and editing your photos so that you can create high-quality photo collections.

- Buying and listening to music, throughout your home and also on the go.

- Researching vacation options and doing your organizing online.

- Protecting yourself in the digital world.

- Using word processing and spreadsheet apps.

- Keeping organized with calendars, reminders, address books, and notes.

The good news is that all of these things can be done with an inexpensive desktop or laptop computer, a tablet, and a smartphone. You don't even have to have all of them, but as we will see, you may just want to have a range of options to give yourself maximum flexibility. The first thing to do is to create a list of what you want to do with the technology, and then you can acquire the best devices for your needs. Don't let eager sales people persuade you to buy something you don't need.

## Operating system

Operating systems are the engines that run the device on which they are installed. Without an operating system it would be very hard to get any sense out of your desktop computer, laptop, tablet, or smart-phone, without an in-depth knowledge of computer programming.

There are two main types of operating systems: those for PCs and laptops, and those for mobile devices such as tablets and smart-phones. The choice for PCs and laptops is between Windows 10 and macOS High Sierra for Apple computers (Macs). Windows 10 is available on a wide range of hardware devices, since Microsoft licenses Windows to be used by different computer manufacturers. Apple chooses not to do this, with the result that macOS is only available on Mac computers and laptops.

The operating systems used in this book are:

- Windows 10 Fall Creators Update.
- macOS High Sierra.
- iOS 11, for Apple's mobile devices, (iPhone, iPad, and iPod Touch).
- Android 8.0 Oreo, that runs on smartphones and tablets from a range of different manufacturers.

Although these are the latest versions of the respective operating systems, many of the functions and processes will be the same for earlier versions of the software.

## Hardware/Software cycle

One of the most frustrating features of the world of technology is the hardware/software upgrade cycle. This is the seemingly never-ending race to develop new hardware devices, that then need more advanced software, and software that then only runs on the latest hardware devices. For instance, Windows 10 won't run on some desktop computers because the graphics card is too old to support all of the features of the operating system. Similarly, the latest version of Apple's mobile operating system, iOS 11, will only run on the iPhone 5s and later. So, if you have an iPhone that is older than this and want to use iOS 11, you will have to upgrade your phone. If you always want to have the latest devices, you will regularly be prompted to update the apps that are on them; and in order to use the latest apps, you will need the latest devices. The reason for this is obvious. Companies want you to keep upgrading your hardware and software as it generates money for them. However, there is a valid argument to say that if you are happy with the devices and software that you have, and they do everything that you need, then stick with them, rather than entering into the hardware/software upgrade cycle.

---

### HIGH-TECH HEALTH

Looking at a monitor or screen for too long can lead to eye strain and headaches. To avoid this, make sure that your eyes are tested for screen use and, if it is recommended that you wear glasses or contact lenses for screen use, then do so. Ensure that the brightness on your monitor is adjusted to what feels best for you (either too bright or too dark could cause eye strain) and take regular breaks so that you are not looking at the screen for long, uninterrupted periods.

---

# Quick fix for mistakes

We all make mistakes when we are using computers, but there is a fantastic keyboard shortcut that can be used to save yourself from any mishaps you have made by undoing previous actions. Deleted a file or removed some text by mistake? No problem. Press Ctrl+Z (Command+Z on a Mac) and the damage is repaired. Keep doing this to go back multiple steps. For an iPhone, if you make a mistake while typing, shake the phone and tap the **Undo** button. It's that easy.

# Do get your back up

Backing up content on your computer, laptop, tablet, or smartphone is one of the most important housekeeping tasks that you can perform. Imagine that you are working on a literary masterpiece and your computer dies and won't turn on. (Rule No. 1 of computing: bad things sometimes happen with computers, and usually at the most inconvenient time.) In a lot of cases it is possible to retrieve data from a computer that seems to be damaged beyond repair, but storing items in the cloud is also an excellent option. Cloud computing services store your content in large computers (known as servers) so you can retrieve it if you lose it from your device. However, it is still also a good idea to have a physical backup of important items, and this can be done with an external hard drive or USB flash drive, both of which can be connected to a computer with a USB cable.

## Top 10 websites for seniors

For most topics that are covered on websites, there are usually versions or sites that are tailored specifically to seniors. Search for a topic online and add "for seniors" to view the options. In the meantime, here are 10 sites to get started with.

1. AARP (formerly the Association of Retired Persons) at *aarp.org*. This contains a wide range of content relating to seniors. It includes topics such as health, work, retirement, travel, money, entertainment, and food. There is a subscription fee, but a lot of the content on the site can be viewed without membership.

2. Social Security Administration at *ssa.gov*. The official US government site that covers Social Security, including information on retirement and Medicare.

3. SeniorLaw at *seniorlaw.com*. A legal site that is tailored specifically for seniors and their families. It covers areas including elder law, Medicare, guardianship, estate planning, and trusts.

4. Buzz 50 at *buzz50.com*. For seniors who want something a bit more tailored to their needs than Facebook or Twitter, this is a social networking site for the over 50s, with chat rooms and discussion forums.

5. Evergreen Club at *evergreenclub.com*. This site provides a network of low-cost, comfortable bed and breakfast accommodations throughout the US and Canada, for travelers over 50. There is a $75 annual membership, for which you get access to over 2,000 private homes in the network. After the membership fee, costs are $20 a day for two people.

6. National Institute on Aging at *nia.nih.gov*. Another official government site that provides a wealth of information about health issues. Type a keyword into the Enter a Health Topic space on the homepage to see all of the related content.

7. Work Force 50 at *workforce50.com*. Aimed at the 50+ workforce, this site has a directory of available positions that can be searched for using the range of search tools, including a Quick Job Search by State option.

8. Senior Planet at *seniorplanet.org*. A site that promotes Aging with Attitude, with articles and resources covering subjects including news, health, dating, senior style, travel, and entertainment.

9. ElderTreks at *eldertreks.com*. This is a site aimed at the adventurous over 50s, with small group tours to exotic locations around the world. With more than 30 years of experience, they organize adventures in over 100 countries.

10. SeniorCupid at *seniorcupid.com*. More than just a dating Website, this provides mature singles with forums, blogs, chat, and, of course, dating options.

---

**BRIGHT IDEA**

When entering website addresses, there is no longer any need to enter the site's prefix, e.g. www. Just enter the name of the site and press Enter. Or press Ctrl+Enter (Command+Enter on a Mac) to add .com.

---

# Keeping up with technology

So there is a lot to think about in the digital world, but none of this should be seen as intimidating. The technology is there to work for you, rather than the other way around. Computers, tablets, and smartphones are devices that can improve your life if they are used properly and effectively.

The golden age of digital technology is well and truly upon us so, with the help of this book, mine some golden nuggets of your own and open up a wealth of new opportunities in the digital world.

# 2 CHOOSING THE RIGHT HARDWARE FOR YOU

## Understanding the specifications

Hardware is the first step for any journey into the world of computing and technology, but it can be easy to be put off by the array of jargon and specifications (specs) that you are faced with. This can undoubtedly be rather daunting, so it is important to understand a bit about these items before you look at buying a new computer, laptop, tablet, or smartphone, or upgrade from your current one. It is important to work out what you want from a device, but the good news is that almost everything on the market today has a spec that will easily meet most everyday computing tasks.

Some of the specifications to look for are:

- **Processor.** This determines the speed at which operations are performed on the device. The quicker the processor, the faster the device should work. The speed of processors is usually measured in gigahertz (GHz), and the higher the number, the faster the processor.

- **Memory (RAM – Random Access Memory).** This determines how quickly operations can be performed on the device by managing the operating system and any apps that are being used. In some ways it can affect the speed of the device more than the processor. If you have several apps open at the same time, this can slow down the device if you do not have enough memory, as it is trying to perform too many operations at the same time. Memory is usually measured in gigabytes (GB) – look for a minimum of 8GB.

## BRIGHT IDEA

If you are going to spend money on upgrading one item on your computing device, whether it is a PC, laptop, tablet, or smartphone, make it the memory, as this will ensure that the overall performance and operation of the device is improved.

- **Storage.** This relates to the physical storage on your device in terms of how much content can be saved onto it. This is measured in gigabytes, and, more commonly now, terabytes. Additional storage (and for backing up your content) can be added with an external hard drive, which attaches using a USB cable and can provide terabytes of additional space. Also, since external hard drives are usually portable, it is a good way to transfer content from one compatible device to another.

## A CLOSER LOOK

Data on computing devices is measured in bits (binary digits). This is the smallest unit of digital data and has a value of either 1 or 0. Larger units of data are multiples of bits as follows:

Byte = 8 bits

Kilobyte (KB) = 1024 bytes

Megabyte (MB) = 1024 kilobytes

Gigabyte (GB) = 1024 megabytes

Terabyte (TB) = 1024 gigabytes

To translate that into the real world of computing: a plain text email would consist of approximately 2KB, while a one hour movie, with suitable compression, would be about 4GB.

- **Graphics card.** Also known as a video card or a display card, this is a device which interprets graphical elements within the computer and then shows them on the display. They are most widely used for playing games on computers, but they also have an important function in displaying other graphical elements of the operating system and its apps.

- **Ports and slots.** PCs and laptops in particular have a range of ports and slots around the body of the device, which can be used to connect peripheral devices. These include: USB slots, for connecting devices with a USB cable, such as a USB flash drive for storing files on; an Ethernet slot, for connecting to the Internet with an Ethernet cable; a DVD/CD player and/or writer, for playing media DVDs and CDs or for copying information. Mac desktops and laptops also have a Thunderbolt slot, which is similar to USB but faster. DVD/CD drives are becoming less common on laptops, but an external one can be used with a USB cable if required.

---

**A CLOSER LOOK**

The latest version of USB is USB 3.1 and the latest version of Thunderbolt is Thunderbolt 2. Thunderbolt 2 has approximately twice the transfer speed of USB 3.1. If you have a USB 3.1 port, it will still be able to use devices using earlier versions of USB.

---

- **Connectivity.** This refers to the method for connecting to other networks or devices. The two main ones to look for are Wi-Fi and Bluetooth. The latest version of the Wi-Fi standard is known as 802.11ac (the 'ac' is the part that changes when there is a new standard available). The latest version of Bluetooth is Bluetooth 5.0.

> **A CLOSER LOOK**
>
> Bluetooth is a wireless technology for sharing data over short
> distances (up to approximately 400m for Bluetooth 5.0).
> It was developed in Sweden, and the name and Bluetooth logo
> come from a 10th century Nordic king, Harald Bluetooth.

- **Battery.** For laptops, tablets, and smartphones, battery life is an
  important issue. Every computer user wants a battery that lasts
  as long as possible, but the time it takes to charge a battery can
  also be an important issue. Look at the spec for battery life for:
  talk time (on a smartphone); standby; surfing the Web; and
  playing videos and music. Also, look to see if there is a fast-
  charging spec, e.g. the time it takes for up to 50% of the
  battery to be charged. When using a laptop, try to keep it
  plugged into the main electricity supply to save the battery.
  This can also be done with tablets and smartphones, but it
  means you cannot move around with them.

- **Operating system.** The operating system is the software that
  gets your computing device up and running, and enables the
  apps to function. The latest versions of major operating systems are: Windows 10 Fall Creators Update; macOS High
  Sierra; iOS 11; and Android 8.0 Oreo.

> **A CLOSER LOOK**
>
> When looking for the specs for specific devices, look at the
> manufacturers' websites and review the technical specs that
> they have there. Also, websites such as *cnet.com*, *pcmag.com*,
> *zdnet.com*, and *pcworld.com* regularly review new devices.
> They keep archived reviews so that you can look at the specs
> for any devices that you are thinking of buying and compare
> them with other similar models.

# Apple vs Microsoft

Both Apple and Microsoft have devoted fans of their devices and software, and they support them with as much fervor as any football, baseball, or hockey fan. Although they both have advantages and disadvantages, the products from either company will serve you well in the developing world of digital technology. A few points to consider when looking at products from Apple and Microsoft:

- Apple products are undoubtedly more expensive compared to most comparable items from Microsoft. For instance, a 12-inch MacBook costs $1,299 from the online Apple Store. A comparable Windows 10 laptop could be bought for approximately $500.

- Apple users often claim that using a Mac is more intuitive than a Windows PC. In reality, there is not really a huge difference in using an iMac with macOS High Sierra or a PC with Windows 10. Most people adapt to what they are using, and their favorite operating system is frequently the one that they used first on a computer.

- Security is a significant issue for all computer users, and this is one area where there is a more marked difference between Apple and Microsoft. The architecture for Apple's desktop and laptop computers is based on a system known as UNIX, which is a robust system considered to have good security in the world of computing. Apple products are not immune to attacks from hackers, but there tend to be fewer than those aimed at Windows devices.

As with many passionate arguments, there is no definitive answer to the question, "Which is better, Apple or Microsoft?" Whichever you choose, both will do an excellent job in meeting all of your computing needs.

# iOS vs Android

In terms of mobile computing devices, the same arguments for Mac vs Windows are deployed between fans of Apple's iOS and the

Android operating system. As with PC and laptop operating systems, if you get used to using one, you will probably be happy with it. The main points about iOS and Android are:

- Android is open-source which means manufacturers can customize it on their devices. This results in dozens of different varieties of Android – Android on a Samsung smartphone will look different to the same version on a HTC device. Each manufacturer can customize the way Android looks and also add their own apps to the standard ones (produced by Google, who owns Android).

- iOS is produced solely by Apple and only appears on their devices, i.e. the iPhone, iPad, and iPod Touch.

## Windows 10 PCs

Several companies produce good quality Windows 10 PCs which will easily meet your computing requirements. The days of all PCs being a separate monitor and hard drive (usually in a tower format) have passed, and there are some models which are a more convenient all-in-one design, with the monitor and hard drive contained as one unit. However, the monitor with separate hard drive is still alive and well, and this should be a less expensive option than the all-in-one models.

When looking for a PC, look for a minimum specification of:

- 2GHz processor.
- 8MB of memory (RAM).
- 512GB of storage.
- 2 USB ports, but the more the better.

## Windows 10 laptops

Laptops have, quite rightly, grown in popularity as people want their computing to be more mobile, and they are now a genuine option as a replacement to having a desktop PC. One of the main considerations when choosing a laptop is size. This is determined by the screen size and will depend on how you are going to use it:

- If a laptop is mainly going to be used in the home for tasks such as surfing the Web or watching movies, as large a screen as possible is best, in the range of 17-inches (measured diagonally from corner to corner).

- If you want a laptop to use on the go, then a small screen size is best to increase portability. Look for a model with a 13-inch or 15-inch screen.

One of the main differences between a desktop PC and a laptop is that a laptop uses a trackpad for moving the cursor on the screen rather than a mouse (although a mouse can still be attached to a laptop, either with a USB cable, or wirelessly). Before you buy a laptop, try to use it physically first, even if you eventually buy it online. This will give you a chance to assess its size as well as the feel of the keyboard and the trackpad.

# iMacs

The iMac is Apple's flagship desktop computer. The current model of iMac is essentially a (very stylish and high-quality) monitor, which also contains the hard drive. The latest models of iMacs feature 21.5-inch and 27-inch screens, with high-quality Retina 4K displays. There is also an iMac Pro, with a Retina 5K display.

The main drawback of the iMac in relation to Windows 10 PCs is the price, with the 21.5-inch model starting at $1,099.

---

**A CLOSER LOOK**

Another desktop option for a Mac computer is the Mac mini. This is just a hard drive, with no monitor, mouse, or keyboard. It can be attached to an Apple or a third-party monitor. Starting at $499, it is an excellent option for a first venture into the world of Apple desktops.

# MacBooks

The Apple range of laptop computers are known as MacBooks. In keeping with the usual Apple design ethos, they are sleek and stylish, but expensive compared to comparable Windows 10 laptops. The currently available MacBooks are:

- **MacBook.** This is the smallest of the MacBooks. It has a 12-inch screen (measured diagonally), 8GB of memory, either a 1.3GHz or 1.4GHz processor, and either 256GB or 512GB of storage.

- **MacBook Air.** This is the thinnest of the MacBooks (and one of the thinnest laptops on the market at a maximum height of 0.68 inch). This model has a 13.3-inch screen, 8GB of memory, a 1.8GHz processor, and either 128GB or 256GB of storage.

- **MacBook Pro.** For more intensive computing, the MacBook Pro is a good option. It comes in two models, 13-inch and 15-inch, and packs enough punch to easily be a desktop replacement. There are two models for both sizes of MacBook Pros with 8GB of memory, either 2.3GHz or 3.1GHz processor, and a range of storage covering 128GB, 256GB, or 512GB.

---
**CAUTION**

Some of the elements of MacBooks are configurable, i.e. processors can be upgraded to be faster, memory can be upgraded to be quicker, and storage can be upgraded to be larger. However, it is best to have this done in an Apple Store, or by an authorized Apple dealer, as you could invalidate the warranty if you do it yourself.

---

# iPads

The iPad is Apple's tablet computer, and there are three main models:

- **iPad.** This is the original size of iPad, measuring 9.7-inches. Some previous versions were known as iPad Air, but it has now reverted to just iPad. There are two versions with either 32GB or 128GB of storage.

- **iPad mini.** For those who like their tablets a bit smaller, the iPad mini has this area covered. At 7.9-inches, it is small enough to fit in a bag or a large pocket, but large enough to provide a full iPad experience. The current model is the iPad mini 4 and has 128GB of storage.

- **iPad Pro.** The iPad Pro is the largest and most powerful iPad in the range. It comes in two sizes: 10.5-inch and 12.9-inch. They have a range of 64GB, 256GB, or 512GB of storage. The iPad Pro can also be used with the Smart Keyboard and Apple Pencil – an external keyboard and a stylus that can be used to increase productivity when using the iPad Pro.

## iPhones

In a mere 10 years, the iPhone has become so widespread that it is impossible to go down a sidewalk without seeing someone peering at, or tapping on, their iPhone.

---

**BRIGHT IDEA**

The iPhone has a screen of fantastic size and quality. However, if you are using it one handed, it can be difficult to hold the phone and stretch to reach items at the top of the Home screen. There is a simple solution: double-tap (not double-click) on the Home button and the icons on the Home screen will generously move halfway down the screen so that they can be accessed easily with one hand.

---

The latest models of iPhone are:

- **iPhone 8 and the iPhone 8 Plus.** Both models, released in September 2017, have a durable and stylish glass body, the camera has been enhanced from the previous model, it has improved lighting options for taking high-quality portrait photos, and it supports wireless charging. It runs on iOS 11, Apple's latest mobile operating system.

- **iPhone X (pronounced 10).** To celebrate the 10th anniversary of the iPhone, Apple also announced another model in September 2017, the iPhone X. This is Apple's most sophisticated iPhone to date (with an equally sophisticated price tag of $999) with a 5.8-inch Super Retina screen display that goes virtually to the edge of the phone's body, Face ID technology for unlocking the phone just by looking at it, emojis that can be animated with your own facial expression (known as animojis), and wireless charging.

### A CLOSER LOOK

Wireless charging does not, unfortunately, mean that the iPhone 8 and X do not have to be connected to anything. In reality, it has to sit on a charging mat (bought separately) that is connected to the household power. So, although the iPhone is not connected with a wire, the charging mat still is. The Apple version of the charging mat is the AirPower mat.

# Android smartphones and tablets

Unlike the iPhone and the iPad, there are several manufacturers who produce Android smartphones and tablets, so there is a greater diversity in terms of appearance and pre-installed apps. Manufacturers of Android devices include:

- Google. Since they own Android, their devices usually have the latest version of Android installed on them.

- Samsung. They produce a large range of handsets for Android, including their latest flagship model, the Galaxy S8.

- Sony.
- HTC.
- LG.
- Lenovo.

For a detailed look at the latest Android smartphones and tablets, check out the website at *android.com*.

# What not to do with your smartphone

Smartphones and cellphones are undoubtedly wonderful things and they can improve our lives in numerous ways. However, there is also the danger that we can misuse them, in ways that are bad manners or a danger to our health. To avoid your smartphone causing you, or people around you, any unnecessary annoyance or injury:

1. Don't use your phone while driving. Is anything really that important that it can't wait? If you try calling or texting while driving, you are not only putting yourself at risk, but also other road users. If you have to use your phone, pull over safely and attend to it while you are stationary. Also, using your phone while driving is illegal in at least 39 states.

2. Don't text and walk. Not only is this more likely to result in an inaccurate text message, you risk injuring yourself or other pedestrians. If you have to text, find a spot where you are not in the way of anyone else, stop walking, and then compose your text.

---

**CAUTION**

In July 2017, Honolulu, in Hawaii, passed a law (the Distracted Walking Law) to become the first city in the world to ban people from looking at their phones, or other digital devices, while crossing roads. First time offenders face fines of $15-$35, while repeat offenders can be fined up to $99.

3.  Don't use your phone crossing the road. It seems too obvious, but every day there are countless people who walk across busy roads, heads down, looking at their phones.

4.  Don't talk loudly and for prolonged periods around other people. If you do need to make a call in these circumstances, make it as short as possible, and tell the person that you will call them back at a more suitable time.

5.  Don't use your phone in the cinema or theater. If you have paid to see a movie or a show, then concentrate on that and enjoy it. Turn your phone off rather than just putting it on vibrate – looking at brightly lit screens can be just as annoying for other people as the phone ringing or buzzing.

6.  Don't keep your phone on at night. If your phone is turned off at night, the chances are you will get a better night's sleep since your mind will be free from anything that may be happening on your phone.

7.  Don't discuss any important details on your phone in public, e.g. online banking details or debit or credit card numbers. It is perfectly possible to conduct financial transactions on your phone, but if other people are nearby, they could gain access to important personal details.

8.  Don't have the keyboard sounds activated if you are texting around other people. The keyboard "clicks" can be extremely annoying, so turn them off in your phone's Sounds settings.

9.  Don't use your phone in a restaurant if you are having a meal with other people. It's just rude. Even if others are using their phones, take some time just to enjoy your surroundings rather than tapping away at a screen.

10. Don't let your phone take over your life. Let your phone work for you, not the other way around.

## MONEY-SAVER

Cellphone plans come in three main versions: *standard*, for regular users of their cellphone, for calls, texts, and surfing the Web (this is usually a contract for a specified period of time, e.g. 12 months); *monthly no-contract*, where you only pay each month for features that you want; and *prepaid minutes*, where you pay upfront for a number of minutes and then use them as you want. A standard contract is the best option if you use your cellphone a lot, but look for a contract that gives you unlimited calls, texts, and data (for Web browsing), if possible. However, if you want to leave the contract early, there is usually an early-termination fee – but you don't always have to pay it! Contact your carrier and try the following:

- Be polite, ask nicely, and keep asking. A pleasant approach can get you a long way, and if you start the conversation off on the right footing, then they may be more likely to look on your request favorably. If the person you speak to is not willing to give you what you want, call again and talk to someone else, or try and speak to someone higher up the management chain.

- Give a good reason for wanting to cancel your contract. Don't be too creative, but saying you are moving abroad to live with your family may be a good starting point.

- Try to trade the remainder of your contract to someone else. There are websites that specialize in doing this, and although there is usually a fee of $20 to $25, this will be a lot less than an early-termination fee. Try the website *celltradeusa.com*, who also offer short-term cellphone plans, or *trademycellular.com*, who match up individuals who want to leave a contract with those who want to take one on.

- Switch to a contract from a smaller carrier. They may be so keen to get new business that they will pay the early-termination fee, in effect buying out your contract. Try Virgin Mobile or Boost Mobile to see what they can offer.

# Printers and scanners

A printer is an important addition to your digital hardware, whether you want to print out some family photos, a page from the Web, or a hard copy of a letter. As with most things in the digital world, there are different types to consider when looking for a printer.

- Laser printers. These are generally for printing in black and white. (There are color laser printers but these are expensive.) They are fast and print documents to a high quality.

- Inkjet printers. These can be used for color documents and also photos, for which photo-quality paper is the best option. For inkjet printers, the ink is placed onto the paper using nozzles connected to the ink cartridges.

- Wireless printers. These can connect to your Wi-Fi network, so they don't have to be physically connected to your computer. The printer can then be accessed from a device that is connected to the same Wi-Fi network. Some wireless printers are also designed to work specifically with mobile devices, i.e. you can print to them directly from your smartphone or tablet.

---

**A CLOSER LOOK**

Most modern printers are "plug-and-play." This means that your computer will generally recognize them and provide the correct software (drivers) to enable them to work. If your printer is not recognized, add it in Settings > Devices > Printers & scanners and click on the **Add a printer or scanner** button (Windows 10); or System Preferences > Printers & Scanners and click on the + button (macOS High Sierra).

---

# Saving ink

The most expensive part of the printing process is undoubtedly the ink. The black and color cartridges for an inkjet printer can cost almost as much as the printer itself, so it pays to try and save as much ink as possible.

1.  Only print what you need.

2.  For inkjet printers, use separate color cartridges for each color. If one color runs out, you only have to replace one cartridge.

3.  Use a bookmarklet app when printing Web pages. This will ensure that only the Web page content is printed and not ads and banner content. There are a number of options, which can be downloaded for free from their respective websites. Once they are downloaded, they reside on your browser displaying a button for printing Web content. Two to look at are PrintWhatYouLike at *printwhatyoulike.com* and PrintFriendly at *printfriendly.com*.

4.  When printing in black and white, go to your printer settings and select Grayscale, rather than Black. This prevents the printer from using any color to produce black, which can save a lot of ink. Also, use the Draft option (if there is one) rather than High Quality.

5.  Ignore your printer if it says it is out of ink. Just keep printing until it actually runs out – you could save up to 40% of your ink. Sometimes a gentle shake can free up some more ink, too. In some cases, there is a sensor on the side of the printer cartridge that claims the printer is out of ink. Cover this with a small piece of black tape to disable it, and keep using your printer.

---

**BRIGHT IDEA** ─────────────────────

For inkjet printers, the nozzles can get blocked, which results in poor performance in terms of streaks and faintness. Solve this, and extend the life of your cartridges, by running the head cleaner function. Check your printer's manual (or online help) for how to access this, which will be through the printer's own control panel or through the printer's app on your computer.

# The scanner in your pocket

Some printers have a function for scanning and copying documents. However, these are more expensive than standard printers and, if you do want to scan documents, you can save yourself some money by using the scanner that you already have in the form of your smartphone or tablet. There are several scanning apps that can be used with iOS 11 or Android to scan documents and save them as PDF (Portable Document Format) files. This is a transferable file format, which retains the original formatting of a document and is designed to be compatible with different devices and operating systems. Have a look at the scanning apps Scanbot, Tiny Scanner, and Adobe scan (available for both iOS 11 and Android), then start scanning and saving your important documents.

# 8 must-have hardware accessories

Every industry has its own range of gadgets and accessories and the digital industry is no different. As with most accessories, decide what you want to do and then look for an accessory, rather than buying something and then trying to find a use for it.

1.  **USB flash drives.** The USB flash drive has become virtually an indispensable accessory for most computer users. It is about the size of a packet of gum, is inexpensive, and can hold huge amounts of data. Flash drives can be used to backup content on your PC or laptop. Connect the flash drive via a USB port and it will show up as an external drive in File Explorer or the Finder. Copy and paste, or drag, files into the flash drive to store them here. Also, because of the size of a flash drive, it is easy to take it with you — for added security — since it is away from your home computer. On *amazon.com,* a 16GB flash drive can be bought for $8.49, and a 64GB one costs $21.99. This is more than large enough to backup or transfer your photos, documents, and music. If not, just buy a larger one.

2. **USB hubs.** USB devices are some of the most common ones that you will connect to your PC or laptops, including flash drives, digital cameras, external hard drives, and smartphones. Sometimes there are not enough USB ports on your PC or laptop, and this is where a USB hub is useful. It contains multiple USB ports (usually about 8), and attaches itself by a single USB connection, thereby giving you multiple ports for your accessories.

3. **External hard drive.** A step up from a USB flash drive in terms of storage is an external hard drive. Like a flash drive, it connects via a USB port and can contain large amounts of data, up to 2TB for $69.99 on Amazon. These are excellent for storing the same type of content as a flash drive, but they can also be used to backup your whole Windows 10 or macOS High Sierra system. For Windows this is done through Settings > Update & security > Backup; for High Sierra it is done with the Time Machine backup app.

4. **Phone covers and screen protectors.** Smartphones are valuable devices, so why risk breaking the phone or its screen? For a few dollars, you can protect both. A phone cover can be used to cover the back and sides of the phone (some, with a fold-over cover, also protect the front of the phone). This not only provides protection if it is dropped on the ground, it can also make it easier to hold. Smartphone bodies are very sleek, but they can sometimes feel a bit slippery, particularly if you are holding them in one hand. A cover, particularly a rubber one, gives extra grip so it doesn't slip out of your hand. A screen protector is a piece of clear, hardened plastic that is attached to the screen of the phone. If the phone is dropped, the screen protector may break, but the screen of the phone should be protected.

5. **Mobile battery pack.** To avoid your smartphone or tablet running out of battery when you are away from home, carry a mobile battery pack with you. This is a device that you can

charge before you leave home and then plug into your smartphone or tablet to charge it on the go.

6. **Spare phone charger.** Sometimes you are out and about, forget your phone charger, and your phone battery runs out. This can be, at best, an annoyance or, at worst, a considerable inconvenience if you need to make an important call or tell someone where you are. To avoid this, buy a spare phone charger and always keep this in a jacket pocket or bag. Keep your other one at home.

7. **Wireless mouse and keyboard.** With a wireless mouse and keyboard you can position yourself where you like and, most importantly, where you are most comfortable. These devices generally connect via Bluetooth and have to be "paired," i.e. the device has to recognize the accessory so that it can work properly. Ensure that Bluetooth is turned On before you start using a wireless mouse or keyboard.

8. **Docks and stands.** There is a range of options on the market in terms of docks and stands, for smartphones in particular. Docks can be used to charge the device – the dock is plugged into the electricity supply and the device is then attached to the dock to charge it. Some tablets have cases that also double as stands. If you want to watch a movie or read a book, the cover folds out to form a stand to support the tablet.

# 3 GETTING A GRIP ON APPS

On its own, an operating system would be of limited use. You could turn on your computer or mobile device, but then not really do much with it. If the operating systems are the engines of computers and digital devices, the apps that can be used with them are the gas that enables them to spring into life and become vital companions for entertainment, communication, organization, research, photography, and much, much more.

App is short for "application" and is just a modern name for what was traditionally called a program.

In terms of your own computing devices, there are three main types of apps to consider:

- Pre-installed apps.

- Apps from an app store.

- Third-party apps.

## Pre-installed apps

These are the ones that will be installed on your device when you buy it. In terms of Apple devices, all of the apps will be standard-ized. If you buy an iMac, it will have the same apps as for a MacBook, as these come with the operating system, macOS High

Sierra. With a Windows 10 PC or laptop, there will be a range of standard Microsoft apps, but there will probably also be some apps that have been installed by the manufacturer of the device itself. For instance, if it is a Hewlett Packard (HP) computer, it may have a range of HP apps in addition to the Microsoft ones.

Similarly with tablets and smartphones, the iPhone and iPad will have the same range of apps, using iOS 11, as the hardware and software is only produced by Apple. However, since Android phones and tablets are produced by a range of manufacturers, they have some generic apps as well as those produced by the handset manufacturer, i.e. Samsung, HTC, or Sony.

## Apps from an app store

Apps are big business and all of the main players — Apple, Microsoft, and Google — have their own app stores for downloading more apps to your devices. There are thousands of apps available, covering almost every subject imaginable. If you can't find an app for one of your hobbies or interests, then it will be a very niche topic! The idea behind app stores is that, for a specific type of device, you will have a related app store. For instance, on Apple devices, apps are downloaded from the Apple App Store; on a Windows 10 device, it is the Microsoft Store; and for devices using Android, the Google Play Store is used. In each case, you will need a (free) account with the relevant service, but this can be created when you first start using your device. Once you have a user account, you will have a whole world of apps at your fingertips.

## Third-party apps

While it is possible to find and download apps that are not pre-installed or come from your device's linked app store, this is not generally recommended. The reason for this is security. If you use an app from a non-verified source, there is more chance that it could contain a virus or malware (malicious software) that could do great harm to your device. This is not to say that apps from recognized app stores are immune from viruses, but there is less of a risk than from a third-party site.

## Downloading new apps

Downloading new apps is a great way to expand a device's functionality. It also offers a huge range of options for enhancing your hobbies and interests. Whatever device you are using, there will be a comparable app store for finding more apps:

Wherever you get your apps from, the process is similar:

1.  Access the appropriate app store from the related app on your device. (**Microsoft Store** for Windows, **App Store** on an Apple Device, and **Google Play Store** for Android.)

2.  The app store will open at its homepage, which includes links to other sections of the store, not just apps. For instance, the **Microsoft Store** has links to Home, Apps, Games, Music, Movies & TV, and Books; the **App Store** has links to Today, Games, Apps, and Updates; and the **Google Play Store** has links to Home (apps), Games, Movies & TV, Music, Books, and Newsstand.

3.  Tap on the **Apps** option in the relevant app store.

4.  Swipe up the screen to view the items on the homepage, which are generally the most recently released and bestselling apps.

5.  All of the app stores also have a **Top Charts** section, where the top free, top paid-for, and top grossing apps are displayed.

6.  Each store has a Search box, which is usually the best starting point for searching for apps.

7.  Click or tap on an app in which you are interested. This will take you to a

page displaying general details about the app, reviews, and details about what is new in the latest version.

8. Click or tap on an app. For paid-for apps you will have to enter your account details (Apple ID, Microsoft Account, or Google Account) before you can download the app.

9. New apps are downloaded to the next available Home screen on a tablet or smartphone, the Start Menu for a Windows 10 PC or laptop, or to the Applications folder and the Launchpad screen on a macOS computer. Click or tap on the new app to open it.

# Managing apps

Apps can be updated by their creators at an alarming rate. It sometimes seems like you have just installed an updated version, when there is another one released. At times, this is to release a new version of the app, complete with new features. However, in many cases, the releases are to fix minor bugs in the app or to update any security issues. Therefore, it is important to update your apps when you can, if only to ensure that they are as secure as possible. Each platform deals with updating apps differently.

### Updating Windows apps

By default, apps on a Windows 10 PC or laptop are set to install updates automatically. However, this can also be customized to suit your own needs.

1. Access Settings > Update & security and click on the **Windows Update** option in the left-hand panel.

2. Under the **Update settings** heading, click on **Advanced options**.

3. Select the required options under the **Choose how updates are installed** heading.

4. If you do not want constant updates to be installed, drag the **Pause Updates** button to Off to pause them for up to 7 days.

Pause Updates

Temporarily pause updates from being installed on this device for up to 7 days. When updates resume, this device will need to get the latest updates before it can be paused again.

 On

5. In the main Windows Update window, click on the **Restart options** button.

⚙ Restart options

Schedule a time

We'll finish installing updates when you tell us to:

On

Pick a time:

| 12 | 00 | AM |

Pick a date:

6. Drag the **Schedule a time** button to On to select a specific time at which you would like automatic updates to be installed.

7. Some apps require the PC or laptop to be restarted before the updates take effect. This is particularly true for updates to Windows 10. Drag the **Show more notifications** button to On to see regular alerts about when your system is going to restart. These will also be available in the Action Center.

ACTION CENTER       Clear all

○ Cortana

Trust this device
To get messages from your other device,  ∨
Sunday

✉ Mail
Your iCloud account setting are out-of-date.
9:55a

To manage individual apps with Windows 10:

1. Access Settings > Apps and click on the **Apps & features** option in the left-hand panel.

2. Under the **Installing apps** heading, click in the box and select an option for where you want to allow apps to be downloaded from. The options are **Allow apps from anywhere, Warn me before installing apps from outside the Store**, and **Allow apps from the Store only**. The last option is the most secure in terms of the threat of downloading apps containing viruses or malicious software.

Apps & features

Installing apps

Choose where you can get apps from. Installing only apps from the Store helps protect your PC and keep it running smoothly.

Allow apps from anywhere

Warn me before installing apps from outside the Store

Allow apps from the Store only

3. Under the **Apps & features** heading, click on an app and click on the Advanced options

button to view details about the app.

---

**BRIGHT IDEA**

If you click on an app under the **Apps & features** heading, there will be an **Uninstall** button. Click on this to uninstall the app. However, there is also a quicker way to do this: click on the Start button, right-click on an app on the Start Menu, and click on the Uninstall button.

---

## Setting default apps

Certain file types and functions can have default apps specified for them, i.e. if you double-click on an image file, the default image editor/viewer will open it. To do this:

1. In the Settings > Apps section, click on the **Default apps** option in the left-hand panel.

2. If an item does not have a default app, click on the **Choose a default** button.

3. Click on the app you want to use as the default for this function.

4. If a function already has a default app allocated to it, click on the item and select another app, if required, or tap on the **Look for an app in the Store** option, to find another suitable app in the Microsoft Store.

## Updating macOS apps

On a macOS High Sierra computer or laptop, apps can be managed through System Preferences:

1. Open System Preferences and click on the **App Store** button.

2. Check On the **Automatically check for updates** checkbox to enable macOS High Sierra to look for updates in the App Store.

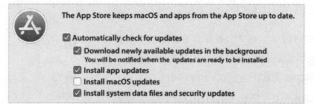

3. Check On the **Install app updates** checkbox and, if required, the **Install macOS updates** checkbox and the **Install system data files and security updates** checkbox.

4. Click on the **Show Updates** button to view available app updates.

5. The updates are shown under the **Updates** heading in the App Store. (This can be accessed directly from the App Store icon on the Dock too.)

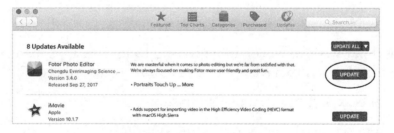

6. Click on the **Update All** button to install all of the available updates, or the **Update** button next to specific apps.

---

**A CLOSER LOOK**

Available app updates are also displayed on the main Apple menu, under the App Store option. The number of available updates is displayed on the App Store button – click on it to go directly to the Updates section of the App Store.

## Updating iOS 11 apps

On an iPad or iPhone, apps can be updated in the App Store. To do this:

1. Access the App Store and tap on the **Updates** button on the bottom toolbar.

2. All of the apps that have an available update are listed. Tap on the app, or the **more** button, to view information about what the update contains.

3. Tap on the **Update** button to update a single app.

4. Tap on the **Update All** button to update all of the available apps.

---

**A CLOSER LOOK**

Updating a lot of apps can take a considerable amount of time. However, this happens in the background and you can continue using your iPad or iPhone as normal.

---

If you don't want to worry about having to update apps manually, there is an option to have it all done automatically for you:

1. Access Settings > Apple ID button.

2. Tap on the **iTunes & App Store** option.

3. Drag the **Updates** button to On to enable automatic downloads of updates to your apps. (This can also be accessed from Settings > iTunes & App Stores).

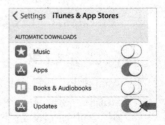

## Updating Android apps

On Android devices, apps can be updated automatically from the Play Store, and individual apps can also be managed from within the device's settings. To specify how apps are updated:

1. Tap on the **Play Store** app.

2. On the Play Store homepage, tap on this menu button, to the left of the Google Play Search box.

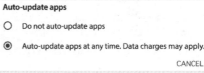

3. Towards the bottom of the menu, tap on the **Settings** button.

4. Tap on the **Auto-update apps** option.

5. Select how you want apps to be updated, either **Do not auto-update apps** or **Auto-update apps at any time. Data charges may apply.** (Data charges may apply if you are using a cellular network to download app updates.)

To update apps manually:

1. Access the Play Store main menu as above and tap on the **My apps & games** button.

2. Tap on the **Updates** tab. At the top of the page is a message relating to the security information for your Play Store apps, following the latest security scan. Tap on this button to perform another scan.

3. Tap on the **Update** button next to a specific app to update it.

4. Tap on the **Update All** button to update all of the apps that have a new update.

5. If Auto-update has been selected for your Android apps, there shouldn't be any items waiting to be updated.

Information for individual apps on an Android device can be viewed through the Settings app:

1. Access Settings > Apps.

2. Tap on an app to view its details.

3. Tap on an item to view details about it, e.g. **Storage**, to see how much space the app is taking up.

4. If you want to stop using the app, but leave it on your device, tap on the **Disable** button.

5. If the app is frozen, or not behaving as expected, tap on the **Force Quit** button to close it. Open the app again from the Home screen or the **All Apps** section to see if this has fixed the problem.

# 8 app and website categories to keep an eye on

### Genealogy

One hobby that has been greatly enhanced by the Internet is research into family history. What used to take hours of painstaking research in records' offices and libraries can now be done from the comfort of your own home with a few clicks.

Genealogy websites vary in the type of information that they store and also the costs, but most of them offer a free trial or a basic plan with which you can view a certain level of information. If this looks promising, and you want to look further into your family history, paid-for options provide the potential for much greater detail.

Some genealogy options include:

- **Ancestry.com.** This is the world's largest genealogy site, with over 10 billion historical records covering, births, deaths, marriages, census records, military records, and much more. There is also a DNA option for revealing your ethnic mix and distant ancestors. There is a 14-day free trial and then different subscription options: U.S. Discovery for $99 for 6 months, or $19.99 monthly; World Explorer for $149 for 6 months, or $34.99 monthly; or All Access for $199 for 6 months, or $44.99 monthly.

- **MyHeritage.com.** This can be used to create your family tree. There is also an option for taking a DNA test to help trace your heritage. Basic searches can be undertaken for free, and a reasonable amount of research can be done in this way. There is also a range of monthly subscription options, ranging from $6.25 a month to $13.95 per month, or a discounted annual option for $167.

- **FamilySearch.org.** This popular site allows you to search records and family trees. It also has access to the FamilySearch Wiki, where people can add their own family tree information, with a view to creating a global family tree. You can also upload family memories to the site, such as photos, audio records, and documents, to create a unique family album. The site is free, but you have to register with an email address and password.

- **Genealogy and Family History (USA.gov).** This is an official United States government website that provides records relating to ancestors and descendants, and includes U.S. Census Data and Statistics. There are links to State archives, the Nationwide Gravesite Locator, The Statue of Liberty – Ellis Island Foundation (which has 51 million passenger records of people who entered the United States through this port), and the National Archives and Records Administration.

- **GenealogyBank.com.** This site covers over 7,000 US newspapers from 1690, and can be used to find names, births, marriages, obituaries, and local news. Search for your ancestors' names to see if they appear in the newspapers, covering over 300 years. There is a 30-day free trial, and you can also send people a gift membership for $69.95 for a full year's access.

## Banking & finance

With a range of banking and financial services now available online through apps and related websites, there have never been more ways to manage your bills, finances, and bank accounts.

Some of the options for online banking and finance are:

- **Online banking.** This is essentially online access to your bank account. It can be accessed from the bank's mobile banking section of their website, or from their mobile banking app. The websites usually have more account information when you log in, but the app is an excellent way to keep an eye on your finances when on the move. Both methods require a username and a password to access your account.

> **A CLOSER LOOK**
>
> Bills can also be paid with an online bank account. To do this, you will need the recipient's account details, and then you can set up a transfer payment from your account. Make sure that you enter the recipient's details correctly to ensure the payment is made to the correct account.

- **Stocks and shares.** If you have any investments in the form of stocks and shares, these can be managed through online options. Most major banks have share dealing services, so that you can buy and sell shares through an investment account. Shop around to see which ones offer the best value in terms of fees for managing the account or for performing share transactions.

- **Financial management apps.** Keeping track of your personal and household expenses can be a chore, but help is at hand with financial management apps. These are apps designed to keep track of your income and expenditures. This can be broken down into different categories such as Clothing, Fuel, Housing, and Travel. Some of these apps can be quite complex, but free financial apps will meet most people's needs and be easier to use. Search for "financial management" or "money management" in the Search box of your app store.

- **Credit checks.** Getting a credit check is not only a good way to see your credit history and how credit worthy you are, it can also be a good way to guard against identity theft. If you notice something unusual has happened to your credit score, this could indicate that someone is making fraudulent purchases using your details. Some options to look at include Experian at *experian.com*, Equifax at *equifax.com*, Free Credit Check at *freecreditcheck.com*, Credit.com at *credit.com* and Check My File at *checkmyfile.com*.

## Food & drink

Apps and websites cater to every type of food and drink imaginable, and it may get your mouth watering just looking at some of the photos.

- **Recipes.** If there is a recipe that hasn't yet made it online, then it probably should stay that way. Recipes from around the globe are available through apps and websites, and a simple Web search can usually provide several options. Or just search for recipes for a certain ingredient and see what is suggested.

- **Restaurant reviews.** As with most services, there are plenty of reviews for restaurants, cafes, bars, etc. These are either on the establishment's own site, or on a travel review site such as TripAdvisor. Make sure you look at the full range of reviews to get a balanced view of the establishment. Some restaurant sites and apps will also allow you to book a table through their online service.

- **Healthy eating options.** Eating healthy doesn't mean that you can't enjoy food and drink. There are numerous sites dedicated to a healthy diet. They also usually have some information about general fitness and health.

- **Delivery.** Most food delivery services now have an online presence. So if you feel like ordering a pizza, there should be an app that will let you select your favorite meal with a few taps.

## Photos & videos

Digital photography has transformed the way we take and use photos. We can now take hundreds or thousands of photos on a smartphone or a tablet and upload them for everyone to see online. The three main categories of apps and sites for enhancing our digital photography experience are:

- **Photo management sites.** These are sites that enable users to upload their photos and then invite other people to view them. Two of the main ones are Instagram and Flickr.

- **Photo editing apps.** These range from performing sophisticated editing effects, such as adjusting the exposure, to fun apps that can customize photos in a range of weird and wonderful ways.

- **Printing sites.** Printing photos at home on a color printer can be expensive. A much cheaper option is to use an online service. Upload your photos to the site, specify the size and number of photos that you want, and then sit back and wait for them to be delivered. Most photo printing sites also offer a range of photo gifts such as mugs, calendars, and computer mouse pads.

## Entertainment

Online entertainment has been an enormous success on the Internet with hundreds of companies offering online content through apps or websites. Most major TV networks have an online presence where you can usually catch up on TV shows that you have missed. The major players such as Netflix, Hulu, and Amazon Prime Video not only have huge libraries of content, but they also produce their own original shows, too.

## Technology

Apps and websites about technology may not be as exciting as those for movies and TV shows, but they can provide valuable information about what is currently happening in the fast-moving world of digital technology. As a starting point, keep an eye on the websites of your devices' manufacturers, e.g. Microsoft, Apple, and Google, and also review sites such as *pcmag.com*, *pcworld.com* and *macworld.com*. Plus, there are forums that discuss issues and problems relating to all areas of technology. Search the Web with a particular query. It is almost certain that someone else will have had the same issue and there will be a discussion thread somewhere about it that will be available in the search results.

## Social media

As social media has grown out of online technology, it is only natural that it can be accessed easily through websites and apps. Both methods can be used to access your social media accounts. You could log in to your Facebook account through a browser on a PC or laptop, or you could use an app on a mobile device. (Apps are generally quicker as you can get to the login page in one tap.)

## Sports

Keeping up with your favorite sports team can be done faster than it takes them to score a home run, a touchdown, or a three-point field goal. Options include:

- **Just search for a result.** Results for most major sporting events are available online, and you don't even have to go looking for them. Just enter a request such as, "Show me the latest Braves result" into a Search engine, and the score will be there.

- **Sports websites and apps.** Broadcasters such as ESPN and CBS have their own websites and apps, providing news, analysis, and reports on sporting events and teams around the country and the globe.

- **Team websites and apps.** A lot of teams have their own websites and apps. Search for these online or in your device's app store. This can give you a unique insight into your teams and their players.

# 4 GETTING SET WITH SETTINGS

## First stop – dive into Settings

No one likes to turn up at a party only to discover that someone else is wearing the exact same outfit. We all like to think that we have our own individual style and that we are all unique (which we are). With most things in our lives, we like to personalize them a bit, whether it is a style of drapes or a few accessories in our car. Similarly, with computing devices, there is no reason why you cannot customize your devices, so that they have the appearance that is best suited to you. This is where one of the most important functions comes into play: the Settings app.

All computing devices (whether they are PCs, laptops, tablets, or smartphones, running Windows 10, macOS, iOS, or Android) have a Settings app. These contain a huge range of options for customizing the appearance of your devices as well as settings for how they operate, such as connecting to Wi-Fi and setting security preferences. Although the Settings on your device may not be the most glamorous place to start, it is a good idea to have a look through them when you first begin using a new device. Get to know your Settings, and they will prove to be a lifelong friend.

# Accessing your Settings

Unusual in the world of computing, the Settings icon is reasonably consistent across devices and operating systems, appearing as a gear icon.

### Windows 10 Settings

When you start with Windows 10, the Settings app is located on the Taskbar at the bottom of the screen. Click on this to access the range of Settings. You can also access Settings from the Start menu:

1. Click on the **Start** button in the bottom, left-hand corner of the screen.

2. Click on the **Settings** tile on the Start menu.

### macOS Settings

The only difference on a Mac using macOS High Sierra is that the Settings are called System Preferences. However, they are the same in all but name. To access them:

1. Click on this button on the Dock at the bottom of the screen.

2. The range of System Preferences is displayed.

### iOS Settings

On an iOS device (iPhone, iPad, or iPod Touch) the Settings app sits clearly on the Home screen when you first turn it on. Tap on the **Settings** app to access the range of settings.

### Android Settings

Since Android devices can be customized by the manufacturers of the handsets, the Settings app is not always readily available on the Home screen. If it is not visible:

1. Tap on the **All Apps** button to view all of the apps on the device.

2. Tap on the Settings app to view the range of settings in the same way as for an iOS device.

Settings

**BRIGHT IDEA**

For iOS and Android devices, drag the Settings app onto the Dock/Favorites Tray at the bottom of the screen to pin it there and ensure it is readily available from any screen.

# Finding hidden settings

The number of available settings can seem a bit daunting at first, but as you start to work with them and use them to customize your device, you will soon know where to find the items that you use most frequently. However, there will always be occasions when you want to alter something and the relevant setting does not appear. The answer to this is simple: just search for it within the Settings app:

1. Open the **Settings** app. On all devices there is a Search box to look for settings.

2. Type the setting you want to find (see tip on page 43).

3. The result is displayed within the context of the Settings app, e.g. if the setting is buried deep within the Personalization section (in Windows 10), this is where it will be displayed in the search results. This is indicated by the icon next to the result.

---

**A CLOSER LOOK**

The Search boxes within Settings apps are not the most sophisticated in terms of interpreting keywords and phrases. They do not always recognize exact phrases, so it is better to search using a single word, rather than longer phrases. For instance, in Windows 10, the phrase "Turn notifications off" will not show any results. However, if you just type "Notifications" this will display the settings that are associated with Notifications.

| Turn notifications off | × |
| --- | --- |
| No results for Turn notifications off | |

| Notifications | × |
| --- | --- |
| 🖵 Notifications & actions settings | |
| 🖵 Turn app notifications on or off | |
| 🖵 Choose which apps show notifications | |
| ↻ Choose how long notifications are shown | |

---

# 11 settings to keep by your side

There are hundreds of different settings for Windows 10, macOS, iOS, and Android devices, and some of them will be looked at in the individual chapters about these operating systems and their devices. However, some settings are consistent across all devices, and you will return to them again and again. These include:

1. **Wi-Fi.** (All devices, Settings > Wi-Fi, except macOS, System Preferences > Network > Turn Wi-Fi On). This is used to connect your PC, laptop, tablet, or smartphone to a Wi-Fi network for accessing the Internet. There will be an option to connect to an available router, which will be your home network or a public Wi-Fi hotspot in an area such as an airport or a coffee shop. At home, enter the password for your router to connect to the Wi-Fi network. If this is successful, the Wi-Fi network setting will show as **Connected**.

---

**CAUTION**

Beware when using public Wi-Fi hotspots as they are not as secure as using your home network. If you are entering details for items such as online banking (either through a Web browser or a banking app), it could be possible for hackers to steal these details through the public hotspot. If the hotspot requires a password to connect to it, this makes it slightly more secure, but not much. If in doubt, do not enter any personal details into your device when you are using a public Wi-Fi hotspot. Specifically, don't use your debit or credit card for making online purchases when using a Wi-Fi hotspot, as it could make it easier for hackers to obtain your card details.

2. **Display.** (Windows 10, Settings > System > Display; macOS, System Preferences > Displays; iOS, Settings > Display & Brightness; Android, Settings > Display). This is used to determine settings including screen brightness, font size, screen resolution (for PCs and laptops), and screen timeout options for tablets and smartphones (this is the length of inactivity before the device is automatically locked).

**BRIGHT IDEA**

Turning down the screen brightness on a tablet or a smartphone is a good way to save some battery power.

3. **Personalization.** (Windows 10, Settings > Personalization; macOS, System Preferences > General/Desktop & Screen Saver; iOS, Settings > General > Wallpaper/Sounds; Android, Settings > Display/Sound). This is a range of settings which can be used to customize the look and feel of your device to your own tastes. On Windows 10 and macOS devices, you can change the color of buttons and toolbars, change the background and Lock screen, customize the Taskbar and Dock, and apply an overall color theme. On

iOS and Android devices, you can select a wallpaper background for the Home screen and Lock screen (either with system images or your own photos) and specify a range of sounds for items such as using the keyboard, the mute button, and incoming messages. If you want a unique appearance for your computing device, this is the place to be.

4. **Notifications.** (Windows 10, Settings > System > Notifications & actions; macOS, System Preferences > Notifications; iOS, Settings > Notifications; Android, Settings > Sound). All modern computing devices like to remind you about what is going on and display notifications about everything from an incoming email to a new post on your Facebook page. In general, this is a very good thing as it enables you to keep up-to-date about all of the important things in your digital world. However, it can have a downside: notifications can have a range of alert icons and sounds attached to them. This can become annoying if you are bombarded with on-screen messages, and an array of pings, dings, and rings as you are using your device. The Notifications settings are where you can take control of how these messages are used. You can select the items for which you want notifications to appear and then determine the way that they are displayed. For instance, you can turn off the sounds so that only the message appears.

5. **Software updates.** (Windows 10, Settings > Update & security > Windows Update; macOS, System Preferences > App Store; iOS, Settings > General > Software Update; Android, Settings > About device). Keeping up-to-date with the latest software releases is important for the security of your device, as updates will be issued for any potential security threats or bugs that have been identified for the operating system. Within the software updates settings there are also options for specifying whether updates are done manually or automatically. This is important if you do not like being bombarded with a lot of updates and want to take a bit more control over the

software update process. However, if you do choose to install updates manually, make sure that you check this regularly to ensure that you do not miss any important releases.

## STAYING SECURE

One very annoying notification that everyone can get from time to time is a pop-up ad in a Web browser. However, it is much easier to block these with modern defenses using an ad-blocker. In fact, most modern browsers have these pre-installed. For Microsoft Edge, click on the menu button at the right-hand side of the top toolbar and click on AdBlock to view its settings and details of ads it has blocked. For Safari on macOS High Sierra, open Safari and select Safari > Preferences from the top toolbar. Click on the **Security** tab and check On in the **Block pop-up windows** checkbox. For Safari using iOS 11, go to Settings > Safari and drag the **Block Pop-ups** button to On. For Chrome on an Android device, open Chrome and tap on the menu button to the right of the address bar. Select Settings > Site settings > Pop-ups and drag the **Pop-ups** button to Off. If you want extra protection, try the Adblock Plus browser, which can be downloaded from *adblockplus.org* and is available for all platforms.

6. **Date & time.** (Windows 10, Settings > Time & language; macOS, System Preferences > Language & Region; iOS, Settings > General > Date & Time; Android, Settings > Date & time). It is important to have the correct date and time on your device as this can affect how certain functions operate, i.e. if you have updates scheduled to be installed at specific times. The language used by the device can also be set with these settings on Windows 10 and macOS devices, while iOS and Android devices have a separate language setting.

7. **Account details.** (Windows 10, Settings > Accounts; macOS, System Preferences > Users & Groups; iOS,

Settings > Apple ID; Android, Settings > Accounts). On Windows 10, macOS, and Android devices, numerous people can have their own account so that they can log in to the device and create their own content, access their email account, etc. The account setting is where you can add new users, specify the type of account (such as a child's account, which provides less functionality), and also change the settings for your own account. On an iOS device, you can specify settings for your account such as how you use iCloud, the online backup, storage, and sharing service.

---

**A CLOSER LOOK**

iOS devices can only have one user account associated with them at one time. Android devices can have several different user accounts added to them so that different people can use the device. Each user account can be protected by a password so that no one else can access the account. On an iOS device, it has to be reset to its original factory settings for someone else to use it.

---

8. **Location Services.** (Windows 10, Settings > Privacy > Location; macOS, System Preferences > Security & privacy; iOS, Settings > Privacy > Location Services; Android, Settings > Location). Perhaps not the most glamorous member of the Settings family, this is still an important function of which to be aware. It determines which apps have permission for their location to be used by the device, usually using the GPS (Global Positioning System) sensor within the device. This is not always necessary for a lot of apps; but for some, such as the Maps app, it can be used to provide useful information in relation to your current location. It can also be used to locate missing devices, in case you lose your tablet or smartphone. Individual apps can have Location Services turned On or Off as required.

9. **Battery.** (Windows 10, Settings > System > Battery; macOS, System Preferences > Energy Saver; iOS, Settings > Battery; Android, Settings > Battery). Conserving battery use is an important issue for computing devices, particularly mobile ones including laptops, tablets, and smartphones. The battery setting can be used to conserve power by: turning the screen off automatically after a specific period of time; reducing the screen brightness; putting devices into low power mode; and limiting background activity on your device.

---

**BRIGHT IDEA** ──────────────────────────

Batteries running low or going flat on cellphones is one of the great annoyances of the digital world. Inevitably, this also happens at the most awkward moment. However, help is at hand to extend the battery charge of your cellphone, and enable you to make that important call or view your latest messages. It puts the cellphone into low power mode, by turning off all of the features it does not currently need (such as updating apps in the background) and concentrating on the important functions.

On an iPhone, go to Settings > Battery and drag the **Lower Power Mode** button to On (so that it appears green).

On an Android phone, go to Settings > Battery  > Battery Saver and drag the button to On.

---

10. **Privacy.** (Windows 10, Settings > Privacy; macOS, System Preferences > Security & Privacy; iOS, Settings > Privacy; Android, Settings > Security). It is worth taking some time looking around the Privacy settings on your device, as these can provide valuable options for increasing your digital safety and security. Some of the settings that are available will determine which apps can communicate with each other on your device. For apps such as Mail and Contacts, this makes sense as they use some shared information. However, for other apps there may not be a reason to let them communi-cate with several other apps, so you can select these and turn

off any sharing options that you do not want between apps. Also, the privacy settings have options for specifying location sharing for specific apps, or for the entire system. If you do not want items to share their location (and a range of other information), then turn location sharing Off.

---

**STAYING SECURE**

The Privacy settings also deal with online advertising and how this follows you on the Web. For Windows 10 users, you can stop online ads stalking you on the Web from within the Privacy settings. Select Settings > Privacy and click on the **General** option in the left-hand panel. Under the Change privacy options heading drag the **Let apps use advertising to make ads more interesting to you based on your app usage** to Off. (Turning this off will reset your ID.) On the same page, click on the **Manage my info that's stored in the cloud** link. This takes you to an online help page where you can further refine your privacy settings. Drag the buttons for **Personalized ads in this browser** and **Personalized ads wherever I use my Microsoft Account** to Off to limit the amount that you will be followed when you are browsing the Web.

For added security, try an app or browser that blocks Web tracking. Download Ghostery, at *ghostery.com*, to your PC or laptop's browser, or download the Ghostery Privacy browser app for iOS 11 or Android.

---

11. **Apps.** (Windows 10, Settings > System > Apps; macOS, System Preferences > App Store; iOS, Settings > [Individual app name]; Android, Settings > Apps). Individual apps can be selected within Settings to apply their own settings. Select an app to view the options.

# Troubleshooting Windows

For Windows 10 users, there is a range of very useful Troubleshooting settings that should be the starting point when something is not behaving as it should be on your PC. To access this, go to Settings > Update & security and click on the Troubleshoot option in the left-hand panel. There are options for fixing problems related to a range of issues, including:

- Internet connections.

- Sound issues.

- Printer problems.

- Software update issues.

- The dreaded Blue Screen (sometimes known as the Blue Screen of Death), when only a blue screen appears when you start your PC.

- Problems with hardware items connected to your PC.

- HomeGroup problems, when trying to use this to share files with other people.

- Keyboard and power problems.

- Issues with Windows Search.

- Problems with apps from the Microsoft Store.

Click on a category and click on the Run the troubleshooter button. The troubleshooter will analyze your PC for the selected issue and display a report on any problems, with suggestions about how to solve them. This can involve running a wizard that will go through the problem step-by-step to see if it can find a solution. The troubleshooter will not solve every issue that you have, but it is a good starting point, particularly to rule certain things out.

## Controlling sounds with settings

One of the items that can have a significant impact on your computing experience, and those near to you, are the sounds that can be produced by your device. These range from keyboard clicks when you are typing on a mobile device, to sounds for when you receive notifications or alerts. These can be useful for warning you about certain events, but they can also become annoying (particularly to other people) if your computing device sounds like a symphony orchestra, with chimes, pings, and dings every few minutes. Therefore it is a good idea to know how to control the sounds on your device.

## Windows 10

For a PC or laptop using Windows 10:

- Open the **Settings** app.

- Select Personalization > Themes.

- Under **Themes** at the top of the window, click on **Sounds** (**Windows Default**)

- The Sound window has options to apply a Sound Scheme, which allocates all of the system sounds.

- Click on an item in the **Program Events** panel and select a sound for it from the Sounds drop-down list. (Click on the Test button to hear a preview of the sound.)

- Check On the **Play Windows Startup sound** box to play this sound when your Windows 10 device is turned on.

- Click on the **Apply** button to set the new sound scheme.

- Click on the **OK** button.

---

**A CLOSER LOOK**

If you want to turn off all of the sounds on your Windows 10 PC or laptop, turn off the computer's speakers. To do this, click on the speaker icon on the right-hand side of the Taskbar on the bottom of the screen and click on the left-hand microphone icon, so that it has a cross next to it.

---

## macOS High Sierra

For an iMac, Mac mini or MacBook using macOS High Sierra:

1. Open **System Preferences**.

2. Click on the **Notifications** option.

3. Select an app in the left-hand panel.

4. Check the **Play sound for notification** On or Off, depending on whether you want to hear a notification sound or not.

## iOS 11

For an iPhone, iPad, or iPod Touch using iOS 11.

1. Open the **Settings** app.

2. Tap on the **Sounds** option.

3. Drag the **Vibrate** buttons On or Off to determine whether the device vibrates or not when sounds are played, i.e. the sound and the vibration will be activated; or only vibrates when the device is on silent, i.e. all sounds are muted.

4. Use the **Ringer and Alerts** button to specify the volume

for these items (drag it to the far left to mute all sounds and alerts).

5. Under the **Sounds and Vibration Patterns** heading, tap on the item to which you want to apply specific sounds. For instance, tap on the **New Mail** option to apply settings for what happens when a new email arrives.

6. Tap on the **Vibration** button to set a vibration effect for a new email.

7. Under the **Alert Tones** heading, tap on a sound for a new email. Select **None**, if you do not want a sound to play when a new email arrives. A preview of each sound plays when you tap on the item.

8. Repeat Steps 5 to 7 for other items such as phone ringtones, text tones, and calendar alerts. Set a different alert for each so that you can identify them by their particular sound.

| | | |
|---|---|---|
| ⬤ EE 📶 | 13:08 | ✳ 24% ▭ |
| ‹ Sounds | **New Mail** | |
| Vibration | | None › |
| STORE | | |
| Tone Store | | |
| Download All Purchased Tones | | |
| This will download all ringtones and alerts purchased using the "nickvandome@mac.com" account. | | |
| ALERT TONES | | |
| None | | |
| Aurora | | |
| ✓ Bamboo | | |
| Chord | | |
| Circles | | |
| Complete | | |
| Hello | | |

**BRIGHT IDEA**

If you are using your iPhone or iPad in public, think about turning off the Keyboard Clicks, so that it does not disturb people around you. To do this, open Settings > Sounds > swipe to the bottom of the window and drag the Keyboard Clicks button to Off.

## Android

For smartphones and tablets using Android:

1. Open the **Settings** app.

2. Tap on the **Sound** option.

3. Drag on the sliders to specify a volume level for each item, e.g. alarm volume and notification volume.

4. Tap on the **Ringtones** option for either notifications or the default alarm.

5. Tap on an option to select it and tap on the **OK** button.

6. Tap on the **Other sounds** option to select sounds for the dialing keypad, the lock screen, and touch sounds on the keypad.

# Changing your wallpaper

Changing the wallpaper, or background, on your device is an excellent way to put your own stamp on its overall appearance. This can be done with graphics and images that are included with the device's operating system, and you can also use your own photos.

### Windows 10

For Windows 10 devices:

1. Open the **Settings** app.

2. Select Personalization > Background.

3. Click in the **Background** box and select **Picture/Solid color/Slideshow**

4. For **Picture**, click on one of the picture options to apply it as your Desktop background.

5. Click on the **Browse** button to select one of your own photos as the background (from your Pictures folder). Select a photo and click on the **Choose picture** button.

> **A CLOSER LOOK**
>
> Select Personalization > Lock screen to select a background item for the Lock screen, in the same way as for the Desktop background.

## macOS High Sierra

For an iMac, Mac mini, or MacBook using macOS High Sierra:

1. Open **System Preferences**.

2. Select the **Desktop & Screen Saver** option.

3. Click on the **Desktop** tab.

4. Select one of the options in the left-hand panel. These are folders of images: Apple for the system images; and Photos for your own photos. Click on an image to select it as your Desktop background.

▼Apple
🗂 Desktop Pictures
🗂 Nature
🗂 Plants
🗂 Art
🗂 Black & White
🗂 Abstract
🗂 Patterns
🌑 Solid Colors

## iOS 11

For an iPhone, iPad, or iPod Touch using iOS 11:

1. Open the **Settings** app.

2. Select the Wallpaper > Choose a New Wallpaper option.

3. Select one of the system wallpaper options. These are **Dynamic**, **Still**, and **Live**. Dynamic photos are ones that

❮ Wallpaper    **Choose**

Dynamic     Stills     Live

All Photos
711

appear to move when you tilt the Home screen; Still is a standard photo; and Live is a small animated graphic which moves when you press and hold it on the Lock screen. (The **Live** option is not available on the iPad.)

4. Underneath the system options, select your own photos, from the **All Photos** option.

5. Once an item has been selected, tap on the **Set** button and select the wallpaper for either **Set Lock Screen**, or **Set Home Screen**, or both.

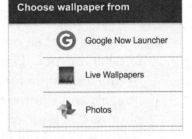

## Android

For devices using Android.

1. Access Settings > Wallpaper.

2. Select the **Wallpaper** option.

3. Select a location from where you want to select the wallpaper.

4. Tap on an item to select it.

5. Tap on the **Set wallpaper** button.

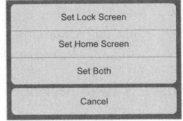

---

**BRIGHT IDEA**

Wallpaper can also be set for an Android device by pressing on the Home screen and tapping on the **Wallpapers** button at the bottom of the window. Select a wallpaper from the bottom bar, or the **My photos** option.

# 5 MASTERING WINDOWS 10

The Windows operating system, produced by Microsoft, has been around in widespread use for over 20 years and is the system with which people will be most aware. However, Windows has changed and developed over the years, and the latest version, Windows 10 Fall Creators Update, has many new features from earlier editions.

Windows 10 is the successor to Windows 8 (there was no Windows 9), which was Microsoft's first attempt to produce an operating system that could be used for both PCs and mobile devices. Unfortunately, Windows 8 was an awkward creation that failed to fully satisfy either of the groups it was looking to impress. Windows 10 was released with some of the traditional features of Windows reinstated, and it is a much more familiar environment for the PC user.

One of the features of Windows 10 is that it is updated regularly online: updated versions are produced rather than a whole new operating system. This is why there are no plans for a Windows 11. The main versions of Windows 10 so far have been:

- Windows 10 (July 2015)

- Windows 10 Anniversary Update (August 2016)

- Windows 10 Creators Update (April 2017)

- Windows 10 Fall Creators Update (October 2017)

This method enables Microsoft to keep Windows 10 as up-to-date as possible, without users having to acquire a whole new operating system.

---

**BRIGHT IDEA**

If you can't wait to see the latest version of Windows 10, you can sign up in **Settings** to get the beta (test) versions, before the finalized version is released to the general public. Since it is a test version, there may be bugs and some rough edges, but these should be ironed out with each subsequent beta release. To sign up for this, go to Settings > Update & Security, click on the **Windows Insider Program** option and click on the **Advanced Options** button in the main window. Under the **Get Insider Preview builds** heading, click on the **Get started** button. Click on **Next** and **Confirm** in the next two screens and then click on the **Restart now** button. When your computer restarts, go back to Settings > Update & security > Windows Insider Program and select how you would like the beta versions of Windows 10 delivered, under **What pace do you want to get the new builds?** This will determine how often you receive updates.

---

To view your current version of Windows:

1. Right-click on the **Start** button.

2. Click on the **System** option.

3. The version of Windows 10 will be displayed on the **About** page. It will be identified by a version number, i.e. 1703, rather than the marketing name.

---

**A CLOSER LOOK**

One regular feature of Windows that is harder to find in Windows 10 is the Control Panel, where numerous settings for the system can be applied. A lot of these have been moved to the Settings app in Windows 10, but the Control Panel is still a useful resource. It used to be accessed from the Start Menu, or by right-clicking on the Start button and clicking on Control Panel. However, in Windows 10 it is slightly hidden away under Windows System > Control Panel on the left-hand side of the Start Menu. To make it easier to access, right-click on it and click on **Pin to Start** and More > Pin to taskbar.

# Beginning with the Start Menu

The Start Menu has been a familiar feature throughout most of the history of Windows and, in Windows 10, it has been enhanced so that it contains more features, making it the ideal place to begin getting to know Windows 10.

The Start Menu is accessed by clicking on the **Start** button in the bottom, left-hand corner of the screen.

### Shut down, Restart, and Sleep

Before looking around the Start Menu, it is useful to know how to turn off your PC from here. This may sound simple, but it is not immediately obvious when first looking at the Start Menu. To access the options for turning off your PC:

1.  Click on the **Start** button.

2.  Click on the Power button.

3.  Click on one of the options –
    **Sleep, Shut Down, or Restart**. Sleep puts the PC into a state of hibernation, but when it wakes up (press any key or move the mouse cursor to do this), you will be able to continue using your PC from where you left off.

> **A CLOSER LOOK**
>
> The Shut Down options can also be accessed by right-clicking on the Start button. This also gives you an option to Sign out, which can be used if other people have a user account set up on the same PC.

## Accessing apps

As with all operating systems, apps are the items that you want to get your hands on to start making good use of your device. With Windows 10, the Start Menu is the place to view all of the available apps and also start managing them so that you always have the ones you want at your fingertips.

There are two areas for viewing apps on the Start Menu. The left-hand side contains an alphabetical list of all of the apps on your PC.

The right-hand side contains a range of colored tiles, relating to each app. This can be customized so that your favorite apps appear here.

> **BRIGHT IDEA**
>
> Click on the button at the top of the Start Menu to expand the items on the left-hand side so that they have a full textual explanation.
>
>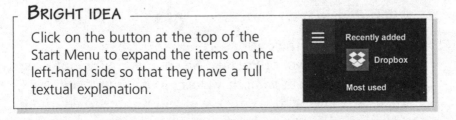

To view all of the apps on the Start Menu:

1.  Use the scroll bars to move through the list of apps.

2.  Click on a letter heading on the Start Menu, e.g. A.

3.  This displays an alphabetical list. Click on one of the letters to go to that section.

4.  Click on an app on the Start Menu to open it.

The items that appear above the Start button are shortcut buttons to certain functions, e.g. File Explorer, Settings, etc. These can be customized so that you have your favorite items here:

1.  Access Settings > Personalization and click on the **Start** option in the left-hand panel.

2.  Towards the bottom of the main **Start** window, click on **Choose which folders appear on Start**.

3.  Drag the buttons On or Off for the items which you want to appear on the Start Menu, above the Start button.

## Pinning items

When looking through the Start Menu, you may think that there are a lot of apps to manage here. The good news is that you can take the ones that you use most frequently and "pin" them to convenient locations so that they are easily accessible:

1.  Access the Start Menu and navigate through the alphabetical list until you find the required app.

2.  Right-click on the app to access its contextual menu (this is a menu that is specific to the item that is currently being accessed).

3.  Click on the **Pin to Start** option to keep the app on the Start Menu. It will be pinned as a colored tile in the right-hand side of the Start Menu.

4.  Click on the **More** button and click on **Pin to taskbar**. This pins the app's icon to the bottom Taskbar.

5.  Click on an app's icon in the tiled area of the Start Menu, or the Taskbar, to open them directly from these locations.

> **A CLOSER LOOK**
>
> To remove items from the Taskbar or the Start Menu, right-click on them on the Start Menu and select **Unpin from Start**, or **Unpin from taskbar**. You can also right-click on the apps where they have been pinned, i.e. the tiled area of the Start Menu or the Taskbar, and use the same commands to unpin them from here.

## Working with tiles

The tiles area of the Start Menu was first introduced with Windows 8, and it has been refined in Windows 10. Because of the size and colors of the tiles, it is a good way to view and access the apps you use most frequently.

Tiles are organized in groups. Tiles can be moved within the same group and also moved to other groups.

1.  Click and hold on a tile and drag it to another area within a group. The other tiles move to accommodate the new tile.

2.  Click and hold on a tile and drag it into another group, in the same way as for moving it within its own group.

Tiles can also be resized, so that your favorite ones are more prominent:

1.  Right-click on a tile.

2.  Click on the **Resize** button.

3. Select an option, from **Small**, **Medium**, **Wide** or **Large**.

4. The tile is resized accordingly, with the other apps in the group moving to accommodate the new size of tile.

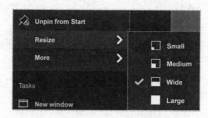

---

**BRIGHT IDEA**

Right-click on a tile and click on the More > Turn Live Tile on option. This will enable the tile to display graphical, real-time information on the app. This works with apps such as the Photos app and the Contacts app, where items from these apps are displayed on the tiles. However, it is particularly effective with apps such as the Weather, News, and Sports apps, as they can display the latest headlines which update whenever there is new information. But one word of warning: if you have a lot of Live Tiles activated on the Start Menu, it can be a bit overwhelming for lots of tiles to display animated information and move constantly.

---

Tile groups can be moved and also renamed, so that you can create your own customized layout. To rename a tile group:

1. Click on the tile heading.

2. Drag over the current title to highlight it.

3. Type the new title.

4. Click outside the title box or press the Enter button on the keyboard to apply the new title.

To move a tile group.

1. Move the cursor over the title bar and press and hold on this button at the right-hand side of the title bar.

2. Drag the title bar to a new location.

3. All of the apps within the group will be moved with the title bar.

# Working with the Taskbar

The Taskbar is the row of icons along the bottom of the screen in Windows 10. It is an invaluable asset, which you will use regularly whenever you are on your PC.

The Taskbar consists of two sections. The main section contains icons which are shortcuts to apps. This is where you should pin your favorite apps from the Start Menu. Some apps are also placed on the Taskbar by default: the Edge browser, File Explorer, the Microsoft Store, and Settings. When apps are opened, they appear on the Taskbar until they are closed, unless they have been pinned to the Taskbar, in which case they remain visible on the Taskbar even after they have been closed.

**A CLOSER LOOK**

To close an item on the Taskbar, right-click on it and click on **Close** window. If it has not been pinned to the Taskbar, the app's icon will disappear.

The right-hand side of the Taskbar consists of the Notification area, with a range of system icons for quick access to various functions.

As with most things in Windows 10, it is possible to customize the Taskbar so that it looks and works in the way that you want:

1. Access Settings > Personalization and click on the **Taskbar** option in the left-hand panel to access the Taskbar settings.

2. Drag these Taskbar buttons On or Off to determine the appearance and operation of the Taskbar. If it is locked using the **Lock the taskbar** option, it cannot be resized from the bottom of the screen. If it is not locked, it can be resized by moving the cursor over the top of the

Taskbar

Lock the taskbar

On

Automatically hide the taskbar in desktop mode

Off

Automatically hide the taskbar in tablet mode

Off

Use small taskbar buttons

On

Taskbar and dragging upwards. If the Taskbar is hidden, it only appears when the cursor is moved over its location.

3.  Click in the **Taskbar location on screen box**, and select the area where you want

| Taskbar location on screen |
| --- |
| Bottom ∨ |

the Taskbar to be located. The options are **Left**, **Top**, **Right** and **Bottom**.

---

**A CLOSER LOOK**

In the Taskbar settings, click in the **Combine taskbar buttons**, then use the drop-down list to specify what happens to icons when the Taskbar becomes full. The options are: **Always hide labels** – each app appears on the Taskbar as a single item, regardless of how many windows are open within the app. **When taskbar is full** – apps with more than one open window collapse into a single button on the Taskbar, to save space. When the cursor is moved over the app icon, all of the open windows for that app are displayed as thumbnails above it. **Never** – all open windows for an app are displayed, e.g. if there are two open Word documents, there will be two Word icons on the Taskbar.

---

To customize the items that are located in the Notification area of the Taskbar.

1.  Access the Taskbar section within Settings > Personalization > Taskbar and click on **Select which icons appear on the taskbar**, under the **Notification area** heading.

2.  Drag the buttons On or Off for the items that you want on the taskbar. (The same process can

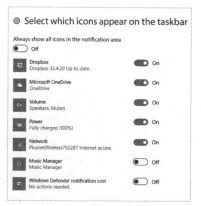

65

be done for **Turn system icons on or off**, under the **Notification** area heading.)

3. Click on an item in the Notification area to access it, e.g. the volume for PC's speakers.

---

**BRIGHT IDEA**

Drag the **Show badges on taskbar** buttons to On in the Taskbar settings window to display badges on items when there is an update or a notification, e.g. if there is a new item in the Mail app, or the Action Center for notifications, a badge will appear on the relevant icon on the Taskbar indicating the number of new items.

---

# Customizing Windows 10 with Settings

The Settings for Windows 10 enable you to create your own working environment. To use Settings within Windows 10:

1. Click on the **Settings** app on the Taskbar.

2. The main categories are displayed in the Settings window.

3. Click on a category to view the items within it.

4. Click on items within a category to look deeper within that category.

5. Click on this back arrow button to move back to the previous page.

6. Click on the **Home** button to go back to the main Settings window.

**A CLOSER LOOK**

Take some time to explore the Windows 10 Settings. Even if you do not use a lot of the settings initially, it helps to know what they do and where they are if you need them later.

# Working with File Explorer

File management is an important part of working with a PC. As you create more and more content, it is good to know where to find it and organize it. With Windows 10, file management is done with the File Explorer.

There are several elements to File Explorer:

**Navigation pane.** This is a pane at the left-hand side that contains the locations and folders on your PC. Click on an item to show its contents in the main window.

---

**A CLOSER LOOK**

Right-click in a clear area in the Navigation pane to access a menu for specifying which items appear here. The choices are for, **Show libraries**, **Show all folders** and **Expand to current folder**.

| | |
|---|---|
| ✔ | Show libraries |
| | Show all folders |
| | Expand to current folder |

---

**Address bar.** This appears at the top of File Explorer. It displays the actual location of the item that is currently selected, or the location being viewed, e.g. Libraries > Documents > Writing.

**Ribbon (also known as the Scenic Ribbon).** This is the bar of controls that can be used at the top of the File Explorer window to apply a range of commands to the selected item or content being viewed.

**Command bar.** This contains the Ribbon menus: File, Home, Share, View, and Manage.

**Main window.** This displays the contents of the item selected in the Navigation pane. For instance, if the Pictures folder is selected in the Navigation pane, this is what will be displayed in the main window. If it contains more folders (sub-folders), these will be in the main window and can be investigated by double-clicking on them. Numerous levels of folders can be investigated in this way.

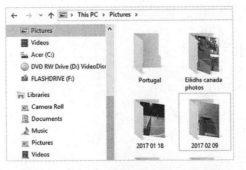

## A CLOSER LOOK

It is possible to check how much storage you have used up, and have left, through File Explorer. To do this, open File Explorer and right-click on your PC's hard drive (usually the C: drive) in the Navigation pane and select **Properties** from the menu. Click on the **General tab** to view the amount of **Used space** and **Free space** in the Properties window.

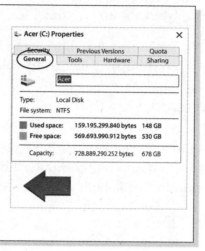

## File Explorer locations

The items in the Navigation pane are links to different locations within your PC. These include:

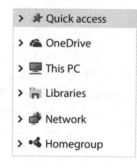

- **Quick Access.** This is a collection of the most recent files and folders that have been created or edited on your PC.

- **OneDrive (if set up).** This is Microsoft's online backup and sharing service. Files can be saved here and then accessed from another device, if you are signed in with your Microsoft Account. This can also be accessed online from *onedrive.live.com* (again, login with your Microsoft Account).

- **This PC.** This contains links to all of the areas on your PC, including the hard drive, C: drive.

- **Libraries.** This is a location that collates relevant content from different places on your PC. It is not a physical folder in the same way as those under **This PC**, but it displays items that are in those locations.

69

- **Network.** This displays any network connections that have been set up on your PC.

- **Homegroup.** This is the Windows 10 function for sharing content between compatible computers.

## Around This PC

The content on your PC is stored in, logically enough, the **This PC** location in the Navigation pane of File Explorer. This contains details about your computer's hard drive, the C: drive usually, and a number of default folders. These include:

- Desktop.

- Documents.

- Downloads.

- Music.

- Pictures.

- Videos.

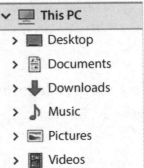

This is where your content will be stored, and apps will try to store items in the correct folder depending on the content. For instance, if you create a new Word document, when you first Save it, the default suggested location will be This PC > Documents. Of course, you can navigate to a different location and save it elsewhere, but the default folders are designed to contain the appropriate content.

The **This PC** folders can contain numerous sub-folders, which you can create to store and manage files and documents for different topics. To create a new folder:

1. Access the **This PC** folder in the File Explorer Navigation pane.

2. Select one of the default folders underneath the main **This PC** folder, e.g. **Pictures**.

3. Right-click in a clear area in the main File Explorer window.

4. Select New > Folder from the menu.

5. The new folder is created, with the name **New folder** highlighted. Type a new name for the folder and press **Enter** on the keyboard.

6. New folders can also be created in the required locations by pressing Ctrl+Shift+N, to create a new, blank folder as above. Right-click on a folder and select **Delete** from the menu to remove it.

---

**A CLOSER LOOK**

If a folder in the File Explorer Navigation pane has a small right-pointing arrowhead to the left of it, click on the arrowhead to expand the folder. The arrowhead becomes down-pointing and the folder's contents are displayed below it.

---

## Browsing in Libraries

Another location within the Navigation pane is the **Libraries** location. This can be displayed, or hidden, by right-clicking in a clear area of the Navigation pane and checking the **Show libraries** option On or Off. The **Libraries** location contains similar folders to those in **This PC**:

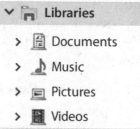

- Documents.

- Music.

- Pictures.

- Videos.

The difference between the **Libraries** folder and those under **This PC** is that **Libraries** displays items from more than one location. It is not a physical folder, in the way that those in **This PC** are, but it acts as a shortcut to similar content in different locations. For instance, the **Libraries** Documents folder can display documents that are held in the **This PC** Documents folder, and also the Public

71

Documents folder and the OneDrive Documents folder (if this has been set up).

If you want a Libraries folder to display items from more locations, this can be done from the Navigation pane of File Explorer:

1. Under the Libraries folder, right-click on the required folder and select **Properties** from the menu.

2. In the Properties window, the locations from which content is being accessed in the Libraries folder is displayed.

3. Click on the **Add** button to add more locations to be shown in the specified Libraries folder (these do not have to be covering the same type of content as the folder title, but it makes sense to keep them the same).

4. Click on the **Include folder** button to add this location to the Libraries folder.

## Finding files in File Explorer

One of the main functions of File Explorer is clearly to help you find files on your PC. If you have a good idea of where the files are, this can be done by navigating through the file structure in File Explorer, starting with the Navigation pane. However, there is a quicker, full-proof way of finding any file on your PC:

1. Open **File Explorer** and select a location in the Navigation pane. For instance, if you are looking for a Word document, select the **Documents** location. For a photo, select the Pictures location, and so on. If you are not sure where the file is located, select **Libraries**.

2. Click in the Search box to the right of the Address Bar. The Search box will also display the location over which you are searching, e.g. **Search Documents**, **Search Pictures** etc.

3. Enter the name of a file you want to find. Initially, this can just be a keyword if you can't remember the exact filename.

4. Search results are displayed in the main File Explorer window.

5. If required, refine the search keywords/phrase to narrow down the results.

6. The column to the right of the filename displays the actual folder path.

| Search Results in Documents > | | | | vandome | ✕ |
|---|---|---|---|---|---|
| Name | Date | Size | Folder path | | |
| Chapter Seven. iPad... | 9/30/2017 2:36 AM | 20 KB | C:\Users\Nick\Documents\FCA | | |
| Chapter Nine. Clou... | 9/29/2017 11:00 PM | 15 KB | C:\Users\Nick\Documents\FCA | | |
| Chapter Three. App... | 9/29/2017 7:43 PM | 14 KB | C:\Users\Nick\Documents\FCA | | |
| Chapter Two. Choo... | 9/29/2017 7:19 PM | 20 KB | C:\Users\Nick\Documents\FCA | | |
| Chapter One. Golde... | 9/29/2017 7:12 PM | 13 KB | C:\Users\Nick\Documents\FCA | | |
| Chapter Eight. Andr... | 9/29/2017 6:06 PM | 13 KB | C:\Users\Nick\Documents\FCA | | |
| Chapter Six. Hands ... | 9/29/2017 12:09 AM | 13 KB | C:\Users\Nick\Documents\FCA | | |
| Advertising bullets t... | 9/27/2017 11:33 PM | 5 KB | C:\Users\Nick\Documents\FCA | | |
| Chapter Four. Getti... | 9/26/2017 9:16 PM | 748 KB | C:\Users\Nick\Documents\FCA | | |
| VANDOME_Work-f... | 9/15/2017 9:48 PM | 16 KB | C:\Users\Nick\Documents\FCA docs | | |
| VANDOME_Work-f... | 9/15/2017 9:48 PM | 16 KB | C:\Users\Nick\Documents\FCA docs | | |

## Unwrapping the Ribbon

The Ribbon area of the File Explorer is where a range of commands can be applied to folders and files that are selected in the File Explorer. The elements of the Ribbon are accessed from the tabs on the Command bar at the top of the File Explorer:

- **Home.** This contains options for editing functions, including Copy, Paste, Move to, Copy to, Delete, Rename, selection options, and Properties. Select an item, or items, in the main File Explorer window and apply one of the options in the Home section of the Ribbon.

- **Share.** This contains options for sharing selected items, including the **Share** button for sharing to a variety of apps, such as Mail, Messaging and social media, Email, Burn to disc (if your PC has a DVD/CD writer), and Print. There are also options for sharing to the Homegroup if it has been set up.

- **View.** This determines the appearance of the items in the main File Explorer window. It includes the size of the file icons and whether the file name extensions are shown, e.g. .docx for a Word document.

- **Manage.** Depending on the item that is selected in the File Explorer, there is also a **Manage** option. This can be used to manage the selection, e.g. if a Libraries item is selected, there is an option to **Manage library**, which determines how the content is collated by the Libraries folder.

## Customizing the File Explorer

As with other elements of Windows 10, the File Explorer can be customized to a certain extent.

- To determine what is displayed in the Navigation pane, click on the **View** tab on the Ribbon and click on the **Navigation pane** button. Click the **Navigation pane** options On or Off (On is with a check symbol showing) to show or hide the Navigation pane. Click on the **Preview pane** button to display previews of selected items in the main File Explorer window. Click on the **Details pane** button to display file details of selected items in the main File Explorer window.

- In the main File Explorer window, files can be shown in different formats. To do this, click on the **View** tab on the Ribbon and select one of the options. These are: **Extra large icons**; **Large icons**; **Medium icons**; **Small icons**; **List**; and **Details**. Move the cursor over one item to see a preview of how it will look in the main window. Click on one of the options to apply it.

- Files in the main window can be sorted according to different criteria at the top of the window in **Details** view, e.g. **Name**, **Date** created or modified, **Type**, **Size**, etc.

Click on one of the headings to sort the files according to the heading, e.g. alphabetical for Name, ascending or descending for Size.

- At the top of the File Explorer, click on this button to customize the items that appear on the Quick Access toolbar at the top of the File Explorer. This also has an option to move this toolbar below the Ribbon, and also **Minimize the Ribbon**.

- In the **View** section of the Ribbon, click on the **Options** button at the right-hand side to specify a range of **Folder Options**. This includes options for how folders open and also the number of clicks that can be used to open items.

To change the categories that are shown at the top of the main File Manager window, e.g. Name, Date, etc, right-click on any of the category headings to view all of the available options. Check items On or Off as required.

---

**A CLOSER LOOK**

Click on the down-pointing arrowhead when you move the cursor over one of the headings in the main File Explorer window to select a filter for the files in the folder currently being viewed. For instance, for **Date modified** you can select a date range and only files modified within that range will be shown.

---

# Selecting items

When working with File Explorer, there will be times when you may want to select more than one item. This could be to open multiple items at the same time (select them all and double-click on one of the files to open them all in their default app), copy them all, or rename them all (see **Renaming items**). There are a number of ways in which multiple files (and folders) can be selected:

- To make a sequential selection, click on the first file to select it. Hold down the Shift key on the keyboard and click on another file. All of the files between the two selected files will also be selected.

- To select a non-sequential group of files, hold down the Ctrl key and click on all of the files that you want to select.

- Drag the cursor over a group of files that you want to select. This can only be done with a sequential group.

- If you have made a selection and want to add a sequential selection to it, hold down the Ctrl key to select the first file of the new sequential selection, then hold down the Ctrl+Shift keys and click on the last file of the new sequence. This method can be used to combine sequential and non-sequential selections.

Selections can be made in any of the File Explorer views. The **Large icons** view is a good one if you want to see the files, such as for photos. The **Details** view is a good one for quickly being able to select a lot of files.

## Copy, Paste, Cut, and Move

Copy and paste is probably one of the most useful functions on a PC, enabling you to move items around. This can be done with a range of items:

- Pieces of selected text.

- Files such as Word documents and photos.

- Folders, containing numerous files.

CAUTION

If you copy an item and then copy another one before you paste or move it, the second item will be the one that is pasted or moved, not the initial one.

Because it is such a common and useful operation, there are several ways in which items can be copied:

- If an item is selected, such as a piece of text within a Word document, press Ctrl+C on the keyboard. The selection is then copied onto the Clipboard, ready to be pasted into a new location.

- Select an item, right-click on it, and select **Copy** from the menu that appears.

- Select an item in File Explorer, right-click on it, then select **Copy**.

- Select an item in File Explorer, click on the **Home** menu from the Command bar, and click on the Copy button in the Ribbon area.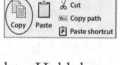

- Select an item in the main File Explorer window. Hold down Ctrl on the keyboard and drag the selected item over another location within the Navigation pane. As you drag the item, a tooltip will appear with the words "**Copy to...**" indicating that the item can be copied to the location to which you have dragged it. Release the mouse to copy the item here.

**A CLOSER LOOK**

An item can be copied into its original location within File Explorer, but it has "Copy" added to the original filename.

Once an item has been copied, actions can be applied to it. The most common one is Paste.

- Once an item has been copied, move to the target location (this can be another part of the same document, another location within File Explorer, or another folder) and press Ctrl+V on the keyboard.

- Move to the target location in File Explorer, right-click in a clear area (so as not to select something else by mistake), and select **Paste** from the menu that appears.

- In File Explorer, move to the target location, select the **Home** menu from the Command bar, and click on the **Paste** button in the Ribbon area.

Instead of **Copy**, **Cut** can also be used in the same way. Select **Cut** instead of **Copy** (or select Ctrl+X on the keyboard), in which case the item is removed from its original location. It is only reinstated when it is pasted into a new location.

---

**A CLOSER LOOK**

To **Move** an item (rather than copy and paste it), drag it from File Explorer to a new location, but without holding down the Ctrl button.

---

## Quick Access

One of the locations in File Explorer is the Quick Access folder. This displays the latest files that have been created, opened, or edited. This is an excellent way to view items that you have worked with recently. To view items in the Quick Access folder:

1. Click on the **Quick Access** folder in the Navigation pane.

2. The latest files are displayed in the main File Explorer window.

3. Double-click on an item to open it (in the same way as for any other file in File Explorer).

4. Right-click on a file or folder and select **Open file location** to view where the item is saved within your file structure.

# Adding items to Quick Access

In addition to displaying all of the recently created and used files, the Quick Access section can also have folders added to it, so that you can see the latest items in specific folders. For instance, you can add the **Pictures** folder so that you can see the latest photos that you have added to your PC. To add a folder to Quick Access:

1. Navigate to a folder within the Navigation pane of File Explorer.

2. Right-click on the folder and select **Pin to Quick access**.

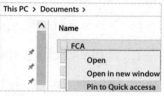

3. The folder is added under the main Quick Access heading in the Navigation pane.

4. To remove an item from Quick Access, right-click on it in the Quick Access folder and select **Remove from Quick access** from the menu.

5. Once an item has been added to the Quick Access folder, it appears with a pin icon to the right of its name.

---

**BRIGHT IDEA**

Folders can also be added to the Start Menu in this way. Right-click on them in the Navigation pane of File Explorer and select **Pin to Start** from the menu. A new tile is added to the Start Menu and the folder can be accessed directly from here.

---

Items can also be added to the Quick Access folder by navigating to them in the main File Explorer window. Click and hold on the item and drag it over the Quick Access folder in the Navigation pane.

# Renaming items

When adding items to your PC, they may not always have meaningful names. This is particularly true of digital photos that have been downloaded from a camera or a smartphone. These tend to have file names that are a combination of numbers and letters, based on the device on which they were captured, e.g. IMG_3018.jpg. To rename individual files:

1.  Navigate to the required file in the main File Explorer window.

2.  Right-click on the file and select **Rename** from the menu.

3.  The file name is highlighted in blue. Type the new name and press the Enter button on the keyboard.

Files can also be renamed by clicking on them once to select them, then clicking on them again about a second later to highlight the filename in blue as above, and then overtyping it. However, if the second click is too soon after the first one, it is interpreted as a double-click and the file will be opened.

---

**BRIGHT IDEA**

There is a simple trick to renaming a group of files just by changing the name for one file. This can be done for two files or two hundred. Select all of the files in a folder that you want to rename. Press F2 at the top of the keyboard. The last file is highlighted in the same way as for renaming a single file. Type the new name for the file and press the Enter button on the keyboard. The same filename is added to all of the selected files, with a numbered suffix after the filename. This does not give much flexibility in terms of unique file names, but it is a good option for items such as vacation photos, so that they are named New York (1), New York (2), etc.

# Working with windows, in Windows

Giving its name to the operating system, the windows that contain content in Windows 10 are an essential part of your computing experience. They are very flexible in terms of how you can display them and manage them, enabling you to work more quickly and efficiently.

## Moving and resizing a window

Windows are definitely not fixed items. They can be moved around and resized to display them the way you want:

- Click and hold on the Title Bar at the top of a window, and drag it around the screen. Release to place it as required.

- Use the control buttons in the top, right-hand corner of a window to, from left to right, minimize a window (onto the Taskbar), expand the window to full screen, and close the window.

- Drag a window to the top of the screen to expand it to full screen.

- Move the cursor over any window border until it turns into a double-headed arrow, and drag to resize the window horizontally or vertically.

- Move the cursor over any window corner, and drag to resize the window horizontally and vertically at the same time. (Hold down the Shift key while you are doing this to resize the window proportionally, i.e. the same amount horizontally and vertically at the same time.)

- Drag a window to the left-hand or right-hand side of the screen to enable it to fill half of the screen. Any other open apps are minimized in the other half of the screen. This is known as multitasking. Click on an app on the Taskbar, or click on one of the minimized thumbnails to expand it in the opposite side of the screen from the other app. Open another app and drag it into one of the corners of the screen to add it to a quarter of the screen. Do the same for a fourth app. Each app can then be accessed independently of the others.

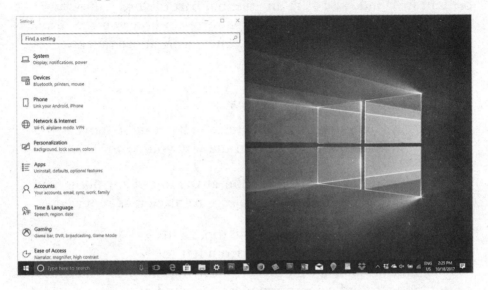

# Viewing the Action Center

One of the items that can be accessed from the Taskbar is the Action Center. This contains a range of quick action buttons for turning functions on or off, as well as the Notification Center, which can display a range of alert messages. To use the Action Center:

1. Click on this button at the right-hand side of the Taskbar.

2. Click on these buttons at the bottom of the Action Center to turn the items On or Off, or access them directly, e.g. open the Settings app (**All settings**).

3. The top of the Action Center contains notifications that have been set to appear here.

The items in the Quick actions section of the Action Center can be customized in Settings:

1. Access Settings > System > Notifications & actions.

2. Press and hold on the **Quick actions** buttons and drag them into new positions to change the order in which they appear in the Action Center.

3. Click on the **Add or remove quick actions** option.

4. Drag the buttons On or Off for the items you want to appear in the Action Center.

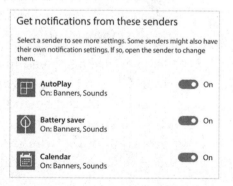

To specify the notification items that appear in the Action Center:

1. Access Settings > System > Notifications & actions.

2. Under **Get notifications from these senders**, drag the buttons On or Off to specify which apps you want to allow notifications from. When there is a new item or an alert from an activated app, the notification will appear in the Action Center.

3. Click on a specific item to select options for how the notification operates, i.e. whether it appears as a pop-up banner and a sound, in addition to being in the Action Center. (If desired, the notification can also be selected here not to appear in the Action Center.)

> **Caution**
>
> Do not set too many notifications, otherwise you may feel you are being bombarded with messages and alerts.

# Emailing with Windows 10

## Using Mail

Email was one of the first "killer apps" on the Internet (an application that helped to create mass adoption of the Internet because of its usefulness), and it remains one of the most popular ways to keep in touch with family and friends. Windows 10 comes with the Mail app, which can be used to manage all of your email needs. To use the Mail app:

1. Click on the **Start** button and select the **Mail** app. (This is a good app to pin to the Start Menu and the Taskbar.)

2. The left-hand panel of the Mail app contains links to email accounts and folders. Click on an account name and the **Inbox** button.

3. Messages are displayed in the middle panel. Click on a message to view its content in the right-hand panel. (Drag the middle bar to change the proportion of the window used by the middle and right-hand panels.)

4. Use buttons above a message to **Reply** to the message; **Reply all** to reply to everyone who was included in the original email; **Forward** the message to someone else; **Archive** it; or **Delete** it.

> **CAUTION**
>
> If there are a number of recipients included in an email, think carefully before using **Reply all**. Do all of the recipients really need to see your reply? It could just lead to an avalanche of emails, with all of the recipients then replying to all, too.

## Creating an email

To create a new email:

1. Click on the **New mail** button to start a new email.  + New mail

2. Enter a recipient in the **To** box. (If the recipient and their email address are already in your Windows 10 address book, the People app, they will appear as an option as you begin to type their name. Click on their name to add them in the **To** box.)

3. Enter a title for the email in the **Subject** box.

4. Enter the body text for the email below the Subject box.

5. Click on the **Format** tab at the top of the Mail window to select options for font size, color, alignment, and pre-formatted styles for the text of the email. (Before formatting text, drag over it with the cursor to select it.)

6. Click on the **Insert** tab to add any attachments (see page 86) and click on the Send button.

## Adding photos and attachments

Email is a great way to share photos with family and friends, and photos can be added with a few clicks:

1. Compose a new email as above.

2. Click on the **Insert** tab on the top toolbar.

| Format | **Insert** | Options |
|--------|------------|---------|
| 📎 Files | ⊞ Table | 🖼 Pictures ⮑ Link |

3. Click on the **Pictures** button (you can also insert files, tables, and links to websites).

4. Navigate through File Explorer to find the required image and click on the **Insert** button.

5. The selected image is inserted into the body of the email.

> ⌐ BRIGHT IDEA ─────────────────
>
> When adding any attachments, add the attachment first before you write the text of the email. Many emails have been sent with the words, "Hi, take a look at the attached photo," with no attachment in sight.

## Adding your signature

At the bottom of an email is a default message saying **Sent from Mail for Windows 10**. However, you can amend this so that it always sends your own unique message, signature, or none at all. To do this:

1. Click on the **Settings** icon at the bottom right of the left-hand panel.

2. Click on the **Signature** option.

3. The default text is displayed.

4. Type your own text.

5. The new signature will be added to all outgoing emails. (If a new email is already open, it will still show the previous signature. All new ones will show the new signature.)

## Adding email accounts

Most of us have a web-based email account these days: Gmail, iCloud, Yahoo!, Outlook.com (including Hotmail and MSN), etc. Other email accounts can be created via the company that provides your Internet access, Internet Service Provider (ISP). This will generally include the company name, e.g. *jane_brown@verizon.com*.

Regardless of how many email accounts you have, it is possible to view all of them through the Mail app in Windows 10:

1. Open the **Mail** app.

2. Click on the **Accounts** button.

3. Click on the **Add account** button.

4. Select the required account from the list. (If you have an email account from your ISP, click on the **Other account** button and use the email details provided by your ISP.)

5. Enter the account details, e.g. email address and password, and follow the selected wizard.

6. When the account has been added, it will appear under the **Accounts** heading in the left-hand panel. Click on the account name to view the emails within it.

## Dealing with junk email

Junk mail, or spam, is one of the great scourges of modern computing. It usually comes in two forms:

- Unsolicited junk mail from spammers trying to sell you something or, worse, trying to trick you out of your personal financial details.

- Marketing junk mail from companies or websites with which you have registered to buy items online.

In Windows Mail (and most other email apps) there is an option to train the app to recognize junk email and, over time, it will start to move it directly into your junk folder without you having to do anything. To mark items as junk:

1. Open your **Inbox**.

2. Right-click on the item you want to mark as junk.

3. Select **Move to Junk**.

There are some tips that can be used to try and limit the amount of junk mail you receive, and protect yourself from the spammers:

1. Never reply to junk email from spammers, even to try and unsubscribe. All this does is confirm to them that it is an active email address, and just encourages them to send more spam. (Marketing emails can usually be unsubscribed from if it is a company you have done business with online.)

2. Never reply to any offers in junk email from spammers, particularly of a financial nature. For instance, if an email says, "Your account with XX has been locked. Please click here to enter your details and unlock your account." **Never, ever, click on these types of links.**

3. Check the email address. Some spammers produce a generic title to appear in the From box in their emails, e.g. Microsoft or Apple. To check if this is genuine, click on the sender's title to view the actual email address that is associated with it. If it is spam, the address will bear no similarity to the named organization.

4. Check the spelling and grammar in the email. If there are a lot of obvious spelling and grammatical mistakes, then it is likely spam.

5. Use a "junk" email address for online transactions. This is an active email address (best created with a web-mail service such as Gmail) that you can use when registering with online retail sites. This way, you can still have access to details about your purchases, but any marketing emails will be sent to this account and not to your personal one used for communicating with family and friends. (Even if you select not to receive any marketing material from an online retailer, you probably will. If not from the company themselves, then from someone who has bought email addresses from them.)

6. Use an email filter. Check in the Settings section of your email account for specific security settings relating to spam and make sure that your privacy settings are as robust as possible.

7. Make your email address harder to guess. Some spammers work by trying to guess email addresses, e.g. *john_smith@ gmail.com*. To try and avoid this, insert numbers and symbols into your email address, e.g. *john_smith8458$@gmail.com*. Even though this may look a bit complicated, once family and friends have it in their address books, they will not have to remember it.

8. Use spam-blocking software. There is a range of spam-blocking software on the market. Search using this phrase on the Internet and research the options carefully before you settle on one product.

9. Report spam to the Federal Trade Commission at *spam@ uce.gov*. Forward the unwanted spam message to this email address. Include the name of your email provider and the sender's email provider, if you can tell this from their email address.

10. If problems with spam persist, consider changing your Internet Service Provider, as they may not have sufficient defenses in place.

> **BRIGHT IDEA**
>
> Keep on top of your Inbox by dealing with emails as they arrive. Once an email has been answered or dealt with, delete it or archive it if you want to keep a record of it. (Use the Archive button on the top toolbar when viewing an email.)

# Video chatting with Skype

Skype is the Windows 10 app that can be used for video calls to family and friends, over the Internet. It is free to make video (and voice) calls to other Skype users.

Skype is owned by Microsoft and should come installed with Windows 10. If not, it can be downloaded from the Microsoft Store.

# 6 HANDS ON WITH MACOS HIGH SIERRA

## An Apple a day – around the Apple menus

When you first open up macOS High Sierra, the first items to become familiar with are the Apple menus. These are contained on a Menu bar at the top of the screen. The Apple menus consist of:

- **The Apple menu.** This is the menu accessed from the Apple symbol. It contains access to System Preferences, the App Store for updating software, and options for turning off or sleeping your Mac.

**A CLOSER LOOK**

From the Apple menu, click on the **About This Mac** option to view a range of details about your Mac, including the version of the operating system (**Overview**), information about the **Display** being used, and details for the amount of **Storage** and **Memory** in your Mac.

- **Finder menu.** This is the menu for customizing the appearance and operation of the Finder.

- **File menu.** This is the menu for applying actions to individual files that have been selected in the Finder.

- **View menu.** This is the menu for specifying how the windows, folders, and files appear in the Finder.

- **Edit menu.** This is the menu for applying a range of editing functions to selected files in the Finder. These include the standard Cut, Copy, and Paste options.

- **Go menu.** This can be used to move to different areas of the Finder and different sections of your Mac.

- **Window menu.** This is the menu for organizing the appearance of currently open apps.

- **Help.** This contains help files and links to online help resources.

## Off, restart, and sleep

Turning computing devices off should be one of the simplest tasks but, since they all operate in different ways, there is no standard command to turn them off. This is true for macOS High Sierra, which has its own method of accessing the Off function (it's not complicated but, like anything, it's only easy once you know how):

1. Click on the **Apple** menu.

2. The options are at the bottom of the menu.

3. Click on **Sleep**, **Restart**, or **Shut Down**.

| Sleep |
| Restart... |
| Shut Down... |

## macOS settings – System Preferences

The macOS High Sierra settings are known as System Preferences, and they can be accessed from this button on the bottom toolbar, the Dock.

1. Click on an item to view its options.

2. From a specific section, click on the back button to move back to the previous window, or click on the grid button to go back to the System Preferences Home screen.

# Pull up to the Dock

The Dock in macOS High Sierra is one of the most useful items that you will use on your Mac. By default, it is located along the bottom of the screen, and remains there regardless of what apps are open and being used. Different items can be added here and content from apps can be accessed directly from the Dock. The Dock has a narrow dividing line towards the right-hand side. Items to the left of the dividing line are apps, that can be opened by clicking on them; the items to the right of the dividing line are open documents that have been minimized, the Trash icon, and Stacks that have been added (folders that have been added to the Dock).

### Customizing the Dock

The first step to customizing the Dock can be done from System Preferences:

**Dock**

1. Open **System Preferences** and click on the **Dock** option.

2. Drag the **Size** slider to change the overall size of the Dock. The icons on the Dock increase or decrease in size accordingly.

3. Check the **Magnification** box to On to enable apps on the Dock to be magnified when the cursor is moved over

them. Drag the **Magnification** slider to specify the degree to which this can be done.

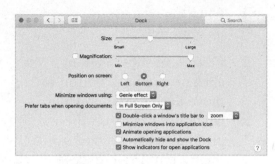

4. For **Position on screen**, select whether the Dock appears at the **Left**, **Bottom**, or **Right** of the screen (the default position is **Bottom**).

5. For **Minimize windows using** option, click in the drop-down box to select

how you would like windows to be minimized onto the Dock. The **Genie effect** option, shrinks it onto the Dock like a genie disappearing into a bottle.

## Adding and removing items

Items can be added to and removed from the Dock so you have exactly what you want there. To do this:

1. Open the **Finder** and access the **Applications** folder in the Sidebar.

2. Click and hold on an app and drag it onto the Dock to add it here.

3. If an app that has not been added to the Dock is opened, it appears on the Dock while it is in operation, with a small dot underneath it. Click on the dot to access its menu. Select Options > Keep in Dock to add the app to the Dock once it has been closed.

4. To remove an app, drag it away from the Dock until the **Remove** tag appears. Release the app here to remove it.

## Creating Stacks

Whole folders can also be added to the Dock, by dragging them from a Finder window, and these are known as Stacks. Once a Stack has been added, it appears to the right of the dividing line. Click on the stack to view all of the files within it. Click on a file to open it.

## Viewing app information from the Dock

Once an app has been opened and appears on the Dock, there is a quick way to see the specific files that are open within the app and access them:

1. Click and hold on the dot below an open app to view its menu.

2. Select one of the options for working with the app, e.g. **Quit**, **Hide**, or **Show All Windows**.

3. Above the menu options is a list of the open files, with a black diamond to the left of the filename, and recently opened files. Click on a file on this menu to go to it directly.

## It's called the Finder for a reason

Macs are known to be intuitive, so it seems only logical that when you want to find something, you go to the Finder. This is the Mac file management system (equivalent to File Explorer in Windows 10). It is where you can find and view all of the elements, folders, and files on your Mac. Get to know the Finder and you will always be able to navigate around your Mac. Click on this button on the Dock to open the Finder.

The elements of the Finder are:

- Sidebar, which contains links to items on the Mac.

- Main window, which displays the content of the item selected in the Sidebar.

- The top toolbar, which contains options for customizing the appearance of the Finder.

- View options buttons, which are the options for how the items in the main window are displayed.

- The Search box.

## Using the Sidebar

Within the Sidebar is a list of folders and locations on your Mac. Click on an item in the Sidebar to view its contents in the main Finder window.

Items can be added to the Sidebar by dragging them there. For instance, if you want a particular folder of photos to be readily available, add this to the Sidebar:

1. Click on the **Pictures** folder in the Sidebar.

2. Navigate to the required folder within Pictures, in the main window.

3. Click and hold on the required item and drag it onto the Sidebar. This does not physically move the folder, it only adds a shortcut to the Sidebar, from where you can access the actual folder.

To remove an item from the Sidebar, drag it away from the Sidebar area and release it.

BRIGHT IDEA

To customize the items that appear in the Sidebar, select Finder > Preferences from the Menu bar. Click on the Sidebar tab and, under the **Show these items in the Sidebar** heading, check the required items On or Off.

The folders in the Sidebar are links to the relevant folders on your Mac. These include:

- **Recents.** This contains the most recently created, opened, or modified files.

- **Home folder.** This is a folder that will contain the username that you used when you first logged into your Mac. It contains folders for all of the content you create or use, e.g. **Documents**, **Downloads**, **Movies,** and **Music**. Some of these folders are also available on the Sidebar.

- **Applications.** This contains all of the apps on your Mac. They can be opened from here and added to the Dock by dragging them onto it.

- **iCloud Drive.** This can be used for copying documents to the iCloud Drive, where they will be backed up and can be shared with other people.

A CLOSER LOOK

New folders can be created within an existing folder on your Mac. To do this, navigate to the area where you want to create the new folder and select File > New Folder (or Shift+Ctrl+N) from the Menu bar. Type a name for the new folder and press the **Enter** button on the keyboard.

## Adding tags

If the Finder starts to get cluttered with too many items, add colored tags to them so that they are more easily identifiable.

The tags are listed at the bottom of the Sidebar. Ctrl+click on one and click on the **Rename** option to give each tag a specific name. Select items in the main window and drag them over a tag to add the tag to them. Click on a tag in the Sidebar to see all of the items with this tag.

## Customizing the main window

The items in the main Finder window can be customized using the top toolbar or the main Menu bar.

- From the Menu bar, select View > Show View Options to display a panel with options for changing the size of the icons in the main Finder window (**Icon size**), the way icons are arranged in the Finder, and the background for the main Finder window (**White**, **Color**, or **Picture**).

---

**A CLOSER LOOK**

The Finder main window uses tabs in the same way as a website, so that you can have more than one window of content open at a time. Click on this button to add a new tab – different areas of the Finder can be displayed in each tab, e.g. in one tab you might have the Recents folder open, and in another the **Music** folder.

---

# Taking off with Launchpad

Apps on a macOS High Sierra computer are located in the Applications folder within the Finder. However, there is a quick way to view all of the apps on your Mac.

1. Click on the **Launchpad** button on the Dock.

2. All of the apps are displayed. Click on the dots at the bottom of the window (or swipe from right to left with a trackpad) to view all of the apps on your Mac.

3. Drag one app over another in the Launchpad window to create a folder and help organize your apps. The folder name is based on the category of the apps. Click on the name and overtype it to give it a new name.

---

**A CLOSER LOOK**

To remove a macOS High Sierra app, click and hold on it in the Launchpad window. When it starts to wobble, click on the cross in the top, left-hand corner to remove it. Alternatively, drag an app over the **Trash** icon on the Dock and drop it in here to remove it.

---

# Organizing with Mission Control

Having lots of apps on your Mac is excellent in terms of entertainment, organization, and productivity, but it can be a bit of drawback if you have too many apps open and aren't sure where everything is. This is where Mission Control comes to the rescue, by showing everything that you have open.

1. Click on the **Mission Control** button on the Dock.

2. All of the open apps are minimized and shown as thumbnails on the Desktop.

3. Click on an app to make it the currently active one.

> **BRIGHT IDEA**
>
> To quickly scroll through all of your open apps on a Mac, press Command+Tab to see a bar in the middle of the screen with all of your open apps. Keep pressing the tab key to move between them. Release the keys to access the selected app.

# Sharing macOS accounts

macOS High Sierra is such a great operating system that it seems a shame to keep it to yourself. The good news is that you don't have to. Use the Users & Groups option to add more users:

1. Access System Preferences and click on the **Users & Groups** icon.

Users & Groups

2. Click on the **padlock** icon, and add your user password (which would have been created when you first signed in to your Mac) to enable new users to be added.

3. Click on this button to add a new user account.

4. Enter the new user's details and click on the **Create User** button.

Create User

5. In the Users & Groups window, click on the **Login Options** button.

Login Options

6. Select the **Show fast user switching menu as** option to select a way to display usernames.

Show fast user switching menu as   Full Name

7. Click on the current name at the top, right-hand side of the screen. All of the users who have access to the Mac will be listed here. Click on one to enable them to log in with their password. The session for the first user remains in place.

If they repeat this process and log in again, all of their items will be as they left them.

---

STAYING SECURE

If grandchildren are going to be using your Mac, Parental Controls can be set when a new account is created. To do this, select a user account in Users & Groups and check On the **Enable parental controls** option and click on the Open Parental Controls button. Settings can then be applied for using Apps, the Web, Stores, and Time.

# 7 IPAD, IPHONE, AND IOS 11

## Setting up

When you first start using a new iPad or iPhone, you will have the option to perform a few setup tasks. If you can't wait to get started with your new device, the good news is that you can skip a lot of these and apply them at a later date from the Settings app. The setup options include:

- **Language and country.** This can be used to set the system and keyboard language and also your geographical location. (This can also be applied in Settings > General > Language & Region.)

- **Wi-Fi.** This can be used to connect to your Wi-Fi network, for access to the Internet. (This can also be applied in Settings > Wi-Fi.)

- **Touch ID and Passcode.** This can be used to create a Touch ID, so that your iPad or iPhone can be unlocked by using your fingerprint. A passcode is also required, in case the Touch ID doesn't work, or a passcode can be used on its own for unlocking your iPad or iPhone. (This can also be applied in Settings > Touch ID & Passcode.)

- **Apple ID and iCloud.** This can be used to create your unique identifier Apple ID, for access to a range of Apple's online services, including iCloud for backing up and sharing your files and information. (This can also be applied in Settings > Apple ID > iCloud.)

- **Location Services.** This can be used to give, or deny, certain apps permission to use your location to make their services more effective, e.g. finding directions from your current location using the Maps app. (This can also be applied in Settings > Privacy > Location Services.)

- **Siri.** This can be used to set up the iOS 11 digital voice assistant, Siri. (This can also be applied in Settings > Siri & Search.)

## Connecting to Wi-Fi

The process for connecting to Wi-Fi, for access to the Internet, is the same whether it is done during the initial setup process or from the Settings app:

1. Open the **Settings** app.

2. Select the Wi-Fi option.

3. Ensure the **Wi-Fi** button is On (swiped to the right and showing green).

   | Wi-Fi | ⬤ |
   |---|---|

4. Under **Choose a Network**, tap on the Wi-Fi network that you want to connect to.

5. Enter the password for your Wi-Fi router and tap on the Join button. (The router password will be provided with the documentation that came with the router, and it may also be contained on a sticker on the router itself).

   Enter the password for "YourWirelessNetwork123"

   Cancel     **Enter Password**     Join

   Password  ●●●●●●●●●●

6. If the Wi-Fi network has
   been joined successfully,
   there will be a checkmark
   next to it, which indicates
   this is the current network
   being used.

| ❮ Settings | **Wi-Fi** | |
|---|---|---|
| Wi-Fi | | ⬤ |
| ✓ YourWirelessNetwork123 | | 🔒 📶 ⓘ |

7. Once a Wi-Fi network has been joined, you will be able to
   get online and browse the Web and send emails using Wi-Fi.

---

**CAUTION** ——————————————————

If a Wi-Fi network has a padlock icon next to it, this indicates
that it is a locked network, i.e. you need a password to join it.
Look to join only locked networks as these are more secure
than ones that have open access.

---

# Locking with Touch ID and a Passcode

Security is of paramount importance for all computer users. The
first defense in protecting your data is ensuring that your devices are
locked so that no one else can just pick them up and immediately
get access to your content. With iOS 11 on the iPad, iPhone 8, and
iPhone 8 Plus, devices can be locked with a six character passcode
and also with your unique fingerprint. Once this has been set up,
the phone can only be unlocked with your fingerprint or the passcode. To set up Touch ID:

1. Open the **Settings** app.

2. Select the **Touch ID & Passcode** option.

3. Specify what you want to use Touch ID for, e.g. unlocking
   your iPad/iPhone, paying for items with Apple's contactless
   payment system, Apple Pay, and downloading items from
   the iTunes and App Stores.

4. Tap on the **Add a Fingerprint** button. Place the finger that you want to use for Touch ID on the Home button. Lift it and replace it several times so that the sensor gets a good, complete image of your fingerprint.

5. Lift your finger from the Home button and reposition it slightly, so that the sensor can capture any areas of your fingerprint that were not covered in the previous step.

6. Enter a six figure passcode, which will be used if your Touch ID does not work.

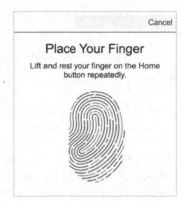

7. Verify your passcode and the Touch ID function is ready to use.

8. When the iPad/iPhone is locked, place your finger on the Home button to unlock the device with Touch ID. (This can be done with a light pressure on the Home button. You do not have to press too firmly.)

---

## BRIGHT IDEA

Ensure your finger is dry and free from dust or grease when using Touch ID, otherwise the sensor may not recognize your fingerprint. Several fingerprints can be added; so, for instance, you could add a fingerprint for each hand so that you can unlock your iPad or iPhone with either hand.

# Getting an Apple ID

An Apple ID is an important part of the Apple computing experience and can be used on any compatible Apple device: iPad, iPhone, macOS computer or laptop, and the iPod Touch music player. It is a unique sign-on identifier that gives the user access to a range of Apple services including the iCloud backup and sharing service, App Store, iTunes Store, Messages and FaceTime. An Apple ID can be created with any email address and unique password. There are several ways to create an Apple ID:

1.  During the initial setup process as shown above.

2.  When you first access any of the apps that require an Apple ID, e.g. when you first tap on the App Store icon, you will be prompted to create an Apple ID.

3.  From within the Settings app, from the Apple ID button.

4.  From the Apple Website at *https://support.apple.com/en-us/HT203993*.

The process for creating an Apple ID is similar regardless of which route you use to arrive there. Here is how you create an Apple ID using the Settings app. (This is also where you can go to view and edit your Apple ID details once it has been set up)

1.  Open the **Settings** app. Select the **Sign in to your iPhone** button. This is the first button at the top of the Settings categories.

## Settings

Q Search

Sign in to your iPhone
Set up iCloud, the App Store, and more.

2.  Tap on the **Don't have an Apple ID or forgot it** button.

3.  Tap on the **Create Apple ID** button.

4. Enter your date of birthday and tap on the **Next** button.

5. Enter your name and tap on the **Next** button.

6. Enter the email address that you want to use with the Apple ID (This can be any email address. It does not have to be an Apple one). The email address that you use will be your Apple ID username. Tap on the **Next** button.

7. Enter a password for your Apple ID. This has to be at least 8 characters long and include a number, an uppercase letter, and a lowercase letter. Tap on the **Next** button.

8. To verify your identity, enter a phone number at which you can be contacted by either **Text Message** or **Phone Call** for verification purposes.

9. Enter the six-figure verification number that is sent by the method selected in Step 8.

10. **Agree** to the Terms and Conditions.

11. Tap on the **Verify Email Address** button to complete the Apple ID sign-up process.

12. Your Apple ID is ready to use.

13. Tap on the Apple ID button (previously the **Sign in** button) in the Settings app to view details of your Apple ID account, and to also access the various iCloud options for backing up and sharing content.

**A CLOSER LOOK**

One of the iCloud options is iCloud Backup. This can be used to backup everything on your iPad or iPhone. This is a useful security feature, in case you lose your device or it stops working. Instead of losing all of the content that you have on it, you can retrieve it from the iCloud Backup by using another device, setting it up using your Apple ID. The device will be populated from the iCloud Backup. To use this, select Settings > Apple ID > iCloud and drag the **iCloud Backup** button to On.

# Favorite apps, at your fingertips

When your iPad or iPhone is turned on, the first thing you will see is the Home screen, populated with the pre-installed iOS 11 apps. A few quick tips for getting around the Home screen and working with your apps:

- Swipe from right to left to view more screens of apps.

- Tap on an app to open it.

- Press and hold on an app until it starts to wobble, and drag it onto the Dock at the bottom of the screen. This will make it available from any Home screen. Up to 12 apps can fit on the Home screen on the iPad, and up to 4 on the iPhone. If the Dock is full, an app will need to be removed before another one can be added. Apps on the Dock can be removed by pressing on them and dragging them back onto the Home screen.

- Press and hold on an app and drag it to the edge of the screen to move it to another Home screen. When it gets to the edge of the screen, hold the app here until the next screen appears automatically. Release the app at the point where you want it to be located.

- On the iPad, from any Home screen, swipe up from the bottom of the screen to access the App Switcher and the Control Center (at the right-hand side of the screen). The Control Center contains a collection of icons for commonly used features, including turning Wi-Fi On or Off, playing music, a flashlight, volume and brightness controls, and the camera.

- On the iPad, from within any app, swipe up from the bottom of the screen to access the Dock. Swipe up again to access the App Switcher and the Control Center.

- In the App Switcher, swipe from left to right to view all of the currently open apps.

- In the App Switcher, swipe an app up to the top of the screen to close it.

- Click on the Home button to return to the Home screen.

- On the iPhone, double-click the Home button to access the App Switcher. Swipe an app to the top of the screen to close it.

- On the iPhone, swipe up from the bottom of the screen to access the Control Center.

A CLOSER LOOK

When apps on the iPad and iPhone are not being used, they stay open in the background, in a state of hibernation, and use up very little battery power. Therefore, it is not essential to close them, but you may want to do this if you have a lot of open apps.

# Adding and removing apps

The pre-installed apps on the iPad and iPhone are just the beginning in terms of what you can use on your device. Click on the App Store app and browse through thousands of apps, covering every subject imaginable. Use the **Search** button on the bottom toolbar to look for specific apps or topics.

MONEY-SAVER

Some apps in the App Store are free, others cost a bit. Some of the non-free apps do have a Lite version that is free. Try these first to see if you like that app before paying for the full version. You may even find that the lite version is suitable for your needs.

CAUTION

Some free apps have an "In-App Purchases" option. This is additional content that has to be paid for after you have downloaded the free app. It is not essential to buy this content, but the app will have more limited use without it.

If you want do a bit of spring cleaning with your apps, it is easy to remove the ones you don't want:

1. Press on the app you want to remove. (This only requires a gentle press. If you press too hard on some apps, this will

activate the 3D Touch functionality, which displays a short-cut menu for the selected app. This applies mainly to the pre-installed apps.)

2. All of the apps will start to wobble slightly and an **X** will appear in the left-hand corner of the apps that can be deleted.

3. Tap on the **X** on the app you want to delete.

4. A confirmation box appears for deleting the app. Tap on the **Delete** button to remove the app.

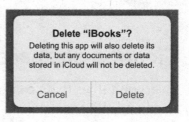

5. Apps that have been deleted can be reinstalled from the App Store. If an app was originally paid for, it is free to reinstall it. Tap on your account icon at the top, right-hand side of the App Store. Tap on Purchased > My Purchases and tap on the cloud icon next to any apps that you want to reinstall.

---

**BRIGHT IDEA**

Apps receive frequent updates to fix bugs or security issues, or to use a different design and user interface. Also, some apps refresh their content without needing a full update. This is done over Wi-Fi, or a cellular network, but can use up battery power if a lot of apps are being refreshed regularly. To ensure that this does not happen, select Settings > General > Background App Refresh > Background App Refresh and tap the Off option. Alternatively, on the first Background App Refresh page, drag the buttons to Off for specific apps that you do not want to refresh automatically.

> **A CLOSER LOOK**
>
> To free up space, iOS 11 has a clever function, whereby it can remove apps that have not been used for a period of time, without deleting any of their data. When they are reinstalled, the data is replaced. To do this, select Settings > iTunes & App Store and drag the **Offload Unused Apps** button (at the bottom of the window) to On.

# Clearing up space on the Home screen

Everyone likes their computing devices set up differently. On the iPad and iPhone, you can have numerous apps covering several Home screens (as one Home screen becomes full, another one is added to accommodate new apps). However, if you like a more organized Home screen, it is possible to create folders for specific apps, generally ones covering the same type of content.

1. Press on an app until it starts to wobble and an X appears on the app.

2. Drag the app over another, similar app.

3. A folder will be created, containing the two apps.

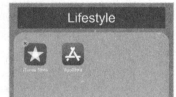

4. Tap on the title bar and type to rename the folder, if required.

5. Press the Home button to save the folder and display it on the Home screen.

6. Open a folder by tapping on it and then open individual apps within it, as required.

7. To add another app to a folder, press on it until it starts to wobble and drag it over the folder until it opens.

8. To remove an app from a folder, open the folder by tapping on it, and drag the required app out of the folder back onto the Home screen.

# 8 keyboard tips for faster typing

The iPad and iPhone have virtual keyboards, i.e. ones that appear over the screen when text or numerical data is required to be entered (although external ones can be added too). These are, understandably, smaller than for a full size PC or laptop keyboard, and the fact that there are no physical keys to press can take a little bit of getting used to. However, there are 8 ways in which you can speed up your daily typing:

1. On the iPad, swipe down on a key with a number or a symbol on it to insert that item.

2. On the iPhone, press and hold on the numbers key and swipe over one of the numbers on the top bar. The keyboard will return to the standard text keys automatically, rather than remaining on the numbers keys.

3. Double-tap the space bar at the end of a sentence to add a period and a space ready for the next sentence. (This can be turned On or Off in Settings > General > Keyboard > "." Shortcut.)

4. Press and hold on compatible letters to add accented versions. These letters include, A, E, I, O, U, C, N, S, and Z. Swipe over the required accented version to add it.

5. If you frequently use a lot of the same phrases, condense them into a few letters with Text Replacement: Settings > General > Keyboard > Text Replacement. Tap on the + symbol to add a new phrase. Type the phrase, e.g. 'Just on my way home', and enter a text shortcut in the **Shortcut** box,

e.g. "jwh." Tap on the **Save** button. Whenever the shortcut is entered, it will expand to the full phrase, once the space-bar is tapped.

6.  On the iPad, swipe upwards on the period key to add quotation marks. Swipe upwards on the comma key to add an apostrophe.

7.  On the iPad, press and hold on the keyboard button, in the bottom, right-hand corner and tap on **Undock** to enable the keyboard to be moved around the screen. Tap on **Split** to split the keyboard so that half is at each side of the screen. Press and hold on the same button and select **Merge**, or **Dock and Merge** to return the keyboard to its default position. The iPad keyboard can also be split by swiping outwards on it with two fingers. Swipe inwards on each half of the keyboard to return it to its default position.

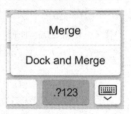

8.  Set the keyboard buttons to show an enlarged preview of each item as it is entered. This is particularly useful when entering passwords. The preview option shows clearly what is being entered for each key. To do this, access Settings > General > Keyboard and drag the **Character Preview** button to On.

---

### BRIGHT IDEA

Even if you can type quickly, it can still be a bit of a chore. A simpler option can be to just speak what text you want to appear. On the iPad and iPhone keyboard, tap on the microphone button and speak into your device. Tap on the keyboard icon once you have finished speaking and your words will appear as text. Voice typing is not always 100% accurate, particularly with unusual names or places. However, the iPad or iPhone will become more trained to your voice the more that you use it. This can be a great way to save your typing fingers.

# Doubling your iPad productivity – multitasking

Being able to do two things at once can speed up your computing experience, since you don't have to keep moving between different apps. For instance, if you want to email a family member with details of a recipe that you found on the Web, it can be frustrating if you have to keep moving between the Safari Web browser and the Mail app. The iPad with iOS 11 solves this issue with multitasking – being able to view two windows at once (known as Split View).

1. Open the first item that you want to use, e.g. the Safari Web browser.

2. Swipe up from the bottom of the screen to access the Dock. (Make sure the second app has been added to the Dock.)

3. Press and hold on the second app that you want to use and drag it to the right-hand side of the screen. When it appears as a white bar on a dark background, release it.

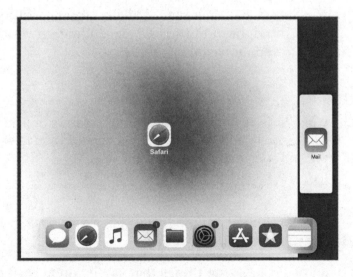

4. Initially, the second app takes up a third of the screen. Drag on the middle button to change the proportions of each app, e.g. make them 50:50.

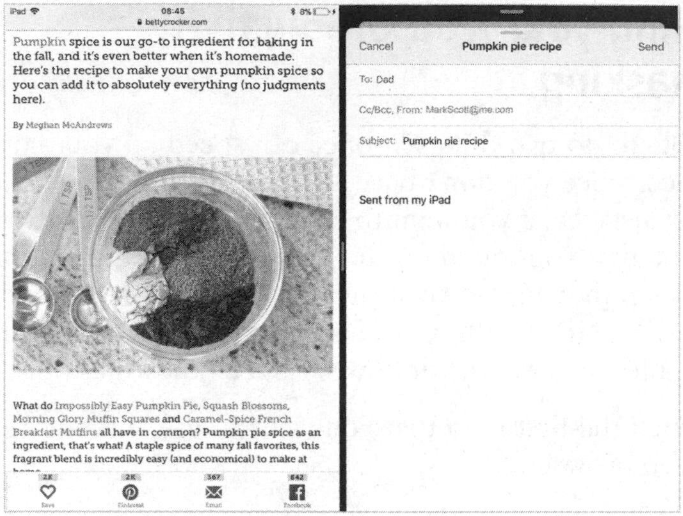

5.  Tap on each app as you want to use them. Applying an action to one app has no effect on the other one. It is easy to switch between the two apps by tapping on the one you want to be active.

6.  To close Split View, drag the middle button all of the way to the left or the right of the screen, depending on which app you want to remain visible.

---

**CAUTION**

Multitasking Split View only works on some models of iPad. Use it with iPad Pro and later, iPad 5th generation and later, iPad Air 2 and later, and iPad mini 4 and later.

---

# Making and receiving calls

Because of all of the amazing things that can be done with the iPhone, it is sometimes overlooked that it is also pretty good for making and receiving phone calls! Here's how to make a call to an existing contact with your iPhone:

1. Tap on the **Phone** app on the Dock at the bottom of the screen.

2. Tap on the **Contacts** button on the bottom toolbar.

3. Tap on a contact to view their details.

4. Tap on the **Call** button.

---

**BRIGHT IDEA**

To have all of your favorite contacts close at hand, add them to the Favorites section in the Phone app. To do this, access the person's entry in the Contacts app and tap on the **Add to Favorites** button. Select a number to be used with the favorite. The contact will then be available under the **Favorites** button on the bottom toolbar of the Phone app.

---

To make a call to a new number:

1. Open the **Phone** app and tap on the **Keypad** button on the bottom toolbar.

2. Enter the number with the keypad.

3. Tap on the green phone icon to make the call.

---

**MONEY-SAVER**

When looking for a company to provide your cellular contract for your iPhone, look for one that has as large a data allowance as possible or, preferably, an unlimited allowance. The data allowance is what is used when you access the Web or online services using your cellular network, rather than Wi-Fi. If you go over the allowance, you will have to pay extra for your data usage, so the bigger allowance the better. To check your data usage, access Settings > Cellular and look under the **Cellular Data** heading.

Answering a call on a smartphone may seem like a simple thing, but it can be a bit intimidating the first time it lights up and starts to ring. Everything seems simple once you know how:

1.  When you receive a call, the screen shows the caller's ID.

2.  Tap on the **Accept** button to take the call, or the **Decline** button to reject it.

3.  If you can't take the call, tap on the **Message** button to send the caller a text message, such as "Busy just now, will call in 30 minutes."

4.  When a call has been accepted, use these buttons on the screen to access these functions.

5.  Tap on the red phone button to end a call.

---

CAUTION

Spammers and fraudsters use smartphone numbers in a similar way to email addresses, for illicit purposes. If you receive a call from a number you don't recognize (if they are in your Contacts app, their name will appear on the incoming call screen), then do not answer. If it is someone genuine, then they will leave a voicemail message and you can call them back.

---

MONEY-SAVER

If you are using your iPhone abroad, turn off data roaming (Settings > Cellular > Cellular Data Options > drag **Data Roaming** to Off), to ensure that you don't get any nasty charges when you return home due to your phone connecting to the Web using the cellular network rather than Wi-Fi.

# Adding contacts

The iOS 11 Contacts app can be used on the iPad and iPhone for adding contact details for family and friend, including address, email address, cellphone number, and home phone number. Once these details have been added, they can be used to contact the person when using the appropriate app, e.g. if you are sending an email, start to write a person's name in the **To:** box; if they are in your Contacts app, their name will appear as you are typing. Tap on their name to add their email address automatically.

To add a contact to the Contacts app:

1. Open the **Contacts** app.

2. Tap on this button to add a new contact.

3. Enter the contact's details and tap on the **Done** button.

119

# You have mail

The iPad and iPhone are great for sending emails. They have a simple, efficient Mail app, so you can keep an eye on your messages any time. If you have an Apple ID and iCloud activated, this will display email from your iCloud account.

1. Open the **Mail** app. The **Inbox** is displayed with your emails.

2. To create a new email, tap on this button.

3. Enter the details for the email and tap on the **Send** button.

4. In your Inbox, tap on the **iCloud** button to view all of your mailboxes.

5. To create a new mailbox, tap on the **Edit** button and tap on **New Mailbox** at the bottom of the screen.

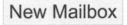

6. Enter a name for the new mailbox and tap on the **Save** button.

7. In your Inbox, tap on the **Edit** button.

8. Tap next to an email to select it.

9. Use the options on the bottom toolbar to **Mark** an item (with a **Flag,** as **Read** or **Unread,** or as **Junk**), **Move** an item to a specific mailbox (as created above), or **Trash** an item.

10. To quickly delete an item from your Inbox, swipe on it from right to left and tap on the **Trash** icon.

<br>

┌─ BRIGHT IDEA ─────────────────────────────

By default, the Mail app automatically fetches new emails from the server on which they are stored. This means that it is regularly contacting the server to see if there are any new messages, which can use up battery power. To conserve battery power, this can be turned off. Access Settings > Accounts & Passwords > Fetch New Data. Drag the **Push** button to Off. New messages can then be downloaded manually by dragging down from the top of your Inbox in the Mail app.

└──────────────────────────────────────────

## Adding Gmail (and more) to your iPad and iPhone

When you create an iCloud account with your Apple ID, this automatically creates an iCloud email account, too. However, if you have another email account, such as Gmail, you may want to be able to access this too. You could do this through the Web or the Gmail app but you can also add it to the Mail app to keep all of your emails in one place.

1. Open Settings > Accounts & Passwords

2. Tap on the **Add Account** button.

3. Tap on the email account you want to add, e.g. Google.

4. Follow the wizard and enter your sign-in details (email user-name and password) for the selected account.

5. Once the account has been added, it appears under the list of **Mailboxes** in the Mail app. Tap on an account to view the items within it, or tap on the **All Inboxes** button to view emails from all of the accounts that have been added.

| Edit |
| --- |
| **Mailboxes** |
| ✉ All Inboxes 1 > |
| ✉ iCloud > |
| ✉ Gmail 1 > |

# Text like a teenager

The younger generation never seems far away from a smartphone or tablet, sending a text about their latest activities and plans. However, there is no reason why this should be their domain, and you can quickly get up to speed with them. Before you start, one useful option is to turn on predictive text (Settings > General > Keyboard and drag the **Predictive** option to On). This gives you options of words above the keyboard (on the QuickType bar), based on what you are typing, and also what you have typed before. (The Messages app learns from your writing style and produces suggestions accordingly.)

---

**BRIGHT IDEA**

If you make a mistake when typing with your iPad or iPhone (whether it's in a text message, an email, or the Notes app), it can be fixed in a shake, literally. Gently shake your device and when the **Undo Typing** window appears, tap on **Undo**. (Repeat the process to **Redo Typing**.)

---

1. To send a text message, open the **Messages** app.

2. Tap on this button to start a new message.

3. Tap in the **To**: box to enter a recipient from the Contacts app, or type a cell number.

4. Tap in the text box at the bottom of the screen.

5. Enter text using the keyboard.

6. If predictive text has been turned on, suggestions appear in the QuickType bar above the keyboard as you type. If an item is highlighted, tap on the spacebar to accept it. If nothing is highlighted, tap on the spacebar to accept what you have typed, or tap on another word on the QuickType bar.

7. Tap on this button on the keyboard to view the range of emojis (graphical symbols).

8. Tap on an emoji to add it to a text.

9. Tap on this button to access the App Drawer, for adding additional content.

10. Press and hold on this button to access **Bubble** and **Screen** effects.

11. Tap on the **Bubble** tab and select an option for displaying the text. This determines the size of the text and the method by which it appears on the recipient's screen, e.g. **Gentle** is small text with a subtle effect, while **Loud** is larger text with a more pronounced effect.

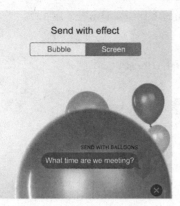

12. Tap on the **Screen** tab and select an animated background effect for the text, including fireworks, balloons, or confetti.

13. Tap on this button to add a photo to the message (either from the Photos app, or by taking one with the camera).

14. Tap on this button to send a message.

---

**CAUTION**

To ensure all of the effects in the Messages app are displayed properly, the recipient has to have an iPad or iPhone with iOS 10, or later, installed on it.

---

**BRIGHT IDEA**

Another option for messaging is the third-party WhatsApp app. This can be downloaded from the App Store, for iPhone. This is an excellent messaging option as it enables group messaging, so that a group of people can all see the same messages and interact with them.

---

# Making a video call

What is better than phoning your family and friends? Being able to see them while you are talking to them! The iPad and iPhone have a pre-installed app, FaceTime, for this. Third-party apps, such as Skype, are also available. These apps can also be used to make voice calls, free of charge over Wi-Fi, with other people using the same apps. To make a FaceTime call:

1. Open the **FaceTime** app.

2. Enter a name, email address, or number to call, or tap on the **+** button at the top of the window to select someone from the Contacts app.

   Edit    Video    Audio    +
   Enter name, email, or number

3. Tap on a contact to call them.

4. Tap on the **Accept** button if someone makes a FaceTime call to you.

5. Tap on this button to end a FaceTime call.

# Never be late again

Technology should work for us, and one way to do this is to use it to make sure that we are always reminded about important dates, events, or activities. On the iPad and iPhone there are two options for this:

### Using the Reminders app

1. Open the **Reminders** app.

2. Tap on the **Reminders** button. Enter text for the reminder and tap on the **i** symbol.

   | Reminders | 0 |
   | --- | --- |
   | | Done |
   | + Order books today | ⓘ |

3. Drag the **Remind me on a day** button to On.

4. Tap on the **Alarm** button and add a date and time for the reminder.

5. Tap on the **Done** button. The reminder will appear on your iPad or iPhone on the specified date and time.

   | Details | Done |
   | --- | --- |
   | Order books today | |
   | Remind me on a day | ◯ |
   | Wednesday, Apr 11, 2018, 11:30 | |
   | Sun Apr 8    08    15 | |
   | Mon Apr 9    09    20 | |
   | Tue Apr 10    10    25 | |
   | **Wed Apr 11    11    30** | |
   | Thu Apr 12    12    35 | |

## Using the Calendar app

1.  Open the **Calendar** app.

2.  Tap on this button to add a new event.

3.  Enter the details for the event and tap on the **Alert** button.

    | Alert | None > |
    | --- | --- |

4.  Enter a date and time in the same way as for the Reminders app and tap on the **Add** button.

> **CAUTION**
>
> Ensure that notifications are On for the Reminders and Calendar apps so that you see and hear the alerts at the specified date and time. Do this in Settings > Notifications, tap on Reminders and Calendar under **Notification Style** and drag the **Allow Notifications** button to On. Apply other options as required, such as showing the notification on the Lock screen and selecting a sound to accompany the notification.

# Small, but perfectly formed – the Notes app

Taking notes may not be the most exciting thing that you do on your iPad or iPhone, but the Notes app has such an effective simplicity that even the most basic list can be a satisfying task. Notes can be added to iCloud, so that you can access them on different devices. Start it on your iPhone when you are out and about, and finish it at home on your iPad. Some of the functions of the Notes app are:

1.  To start a new note, tap on this button.

2.  Double-tap on a piece of text to select it and apply these commands from the toolbar. (Tap on the arrow

    < iCloud      Done

    Milk

    | Cut | Copy | Paste | Replace... | ▶ |

to access more options for **Bold/Italics/Underlining**, **Look Up**, for a definition, **Share**, and **Indent**.)

3. Tap on this button to add formatting to selected text. (Or select the formatting first, and all subsequent text will take on this formatting.)

4. Tap on this button to add a checkbox before a piece of text. This is a great option as it enables you to check off items as they have been completed, giving great satisfaction.

5. Tap on this button to access additional options, including scanning a document to include it in the current note, adding a photo or video, or adding a sketch (which allows you to create a handwritten item to add to the note).

6. Tap on this button to add a sketch directly on the note.

7. Tap on this button on the top toolbar to share the note (to the left of the **Done** button).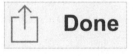

8. Tap on this button on the top toolbar to enable someone else to add to the note. Invite them through email, text message or social media.

9. Tap on the **Done** button (in Step 7) to complete a note. The latest note appears at the top of the notes list. Tap on one to view it and edit it as required.

---

**BRIGHT IDEA**

Use the Notes app to make a shopping list and then check off the items as you buy them. This way you should never forget anything again.

# Finding a lost device

Losing your iPad or iPhone can be both frustrating and worrying, as you may not be able to contact people or do any of the tasks that you normally rely on your devices for. Worse still, if an iPad or iPhone is stolen, there is the added worry of someone being able to potentially access your content. But the good news is that help is at hand with the Find iPhone function. (This works the same for iPads.) It tracks your device, using GPS to identify its location, and you can also lock or reset a stolen device remotely. To do this:

1. Access Settings > Apple ID > iCloud.

2. Tap on **Find My iPad/iPhone** and drag the **Find My iPad/iPhone** button to On.

3. Go to the online iCloud website at *icloud.com* and login with your Apple ID details.

4. Click on the **Find iPhone** icon and re-enter your Apple ID details.

5. All of the devices using this Apple ID will be displayed (as long as they are turned on).

6. Click on a device to view its details.

7. Click on the **i** symbol to access options for managing the device.

8. Click on the **Play Sound** button to request the device plays a sound (useful if you have lost the device in your home).

9. Click on the **Lost Mode** button to lock the device remotely with a passcode (which will be required to unlock it).

10. Click on the **Erase iPhone** button to delete all of the data from it. (Only use this if you are worried that the device has fallen into the wrong hands.)

# Using Apple Pay

Paying for items with a smartphone may seem like science fiction, but digital payment with your Apple devices is well and truly here and becoming firmly established in stores and malls around the country. Apple Pay can be used with debit or credit cards, but it has to be supported by your bank or card issuer. It can then be set up on your iPhone in a few simple steps. (Apple Pay can also be set up on an iPad, but this is for online purchases, rather than in-store ones.) To use Apple Pay, Touch ID and a passcode have to be in place. Touch ID is used to activate Apple Pay when paying for items.

1. Tap on the **Wallet** app and tap on the **Add Credit or Debit Card** option.

2. Add your credit or debit card details, either manually, or by using the iPhone's camera to capture its details. (If you do this, double-check that the camera has done this accurately.)

3. You will be asked to verify your details, which you can choose to do through a verification code sent to your phone by text or by phone call.

4. Complete the Apple Pay wizard to add it to the Wallet app.

5. When you pay for items, hold the iPhone up to the payment terminal and use Touch ID by pressing the Home button.

---

BRIGHT IDEA

Always have an alternative method of payment, just in case Apple Pay doesn't work for any reason.

---

---

**TROUBLESHOOTING**

If your iPhone or iPad freezes or won't turn on and you can't access anything on the screen, try a Force Restart. For the iPhone 8, press and release the Volume Up button, then press and release the Volume Down button, and then pressing and holding the On/Off button until the Apple logo appears. For the iPhone 7, press and hold the On/Off and Volume Down buttons for approximately 10 seconds, or until the Apple logo appears. For the iPhone 6 and earlier, and iPads, press and hold the On/Off button and the Home button for approximately 10 seconds, or until the Apple logo appears.)

---

# Putting it back together – resetting

Things do not always go smoothly with digital devices, but the iPad and iPhone have several options if you run into trouble:

1. Access Settings > General > Reset (at the bottom of the window) to access options for resetting the device.

2. Tap on the **Reset Home Screen Layout** option to restore the Home screen apps to their default layout.

3. Tap on the **Reset All Settings** option to reset the device settings, but retain data or media that has been created.

| ‹ General | **Reset** |
|-----------|-----------|
| Reset All Settings | |
| Erase All Content and Settings | |
| Reset Network Settings | |
| Reset Keyboard Dictionary | |
| Reset Home Screen Layout | |
| Reset Location & Privacy | |

4. Tap on the **Erase All Content and Settings** option to reset the device to its factory settings (i.e. remove all content, Apple ID details and downloaded apps, and return it to its original condition, before it was used). Only use this as a last resort if

the device is not working properly, and make sure that you have backed up its content, using iCloud Backup. Try **Reset All Settings** before using **Erase All Content and Settings**.

## The iOS lifesaver

It's not often that you would put your life in the hands of your iPhone, but there is a function that could prove to be a genuine lifesaver. The **Emergency SOS** option can be used to call emergency services, even if you are unable to unlock your iPhone. Instead, press the On/Off button five times rapidly to call the emergency service in your area. To specify settings for this:

1. Access Settings > Emergency SOS.

2. Drag the **Auto Call** button to On.

---

HIGH-TECH HEALTH

Emergency contacts for Emergency SOS, and information about your own medical history, can be added to the Health app, under **Medical ID**. When you call Emergency SOS, the contacts under Medical ID will also be notified and sent your current location.

---

## Staying safe and dry

iPads and iPhones are expensive devices and it is important to take a few steps to try and ensure that they don't get damaged, or stolen:

- Consider the physical security of your device, as much as its online security. When you are out and about, particularly in crowded areas, keep your iPhone in a zipped or buttoned pocket, preferably inside a jacket. **Never keep it in an open**

**back pocket**. If you are on vacation, be careful of people on mopeds or scooters, as this is a common method of relieving unsuspecting tourists of their phones, particularly if they are preoccupied trying to cross a busy road.

- Use a cover and a screen protector in case the device is dropped. Screen protectors are pieces of hardened plastic that are designed to fit over specific models of phones. They cost between $5 to $10 and could be one of the best investments you make.

- Water is the enemy of any electronic device, so try and avoid it with your iPad and iPhone at all costs. However, if your device does get wet, don't try and turn it on, as this could cause it to short circuit. Instead, place it in a bag of rice for at least 24 hours to try and draw out any moisture that has gotten inside it.

# 8 ANDROID MOBILE DEVICES

## The issue with Android

Android is a mobile operating system for tablets and smartphones and it is the main alternative to Apple and iOS 11 when using one of these devices. However, there is one main difference with Android and iOS 11: Android is an open source operating system, which means that it can be used on a range of different handsets, from different manufacturers, while iOS 11 can only be used on Apple devices. This results in two issues with Android:

1. There are numerous different versions on the market. As newer handsets appear, manufacturers general stop upgrading earlier models to the latest version of Android. So the Samsung Galaxy S8 will be able to run the latest version of Android (8.0 Oreo), while the Galaxy S5 is only able to run version 6.0 Marshmallow. (Some older handsets using Android will only be able to run versions as far back as 4.0, or earlier.) In general, this does not affect the functionality greatly, as many of the Android features are standardized across different versions. However, it does mean that if you always want to have the latest version you may need to buy a new handset more frequently than you would perhaps like.

2. Manufacturers can customize Android, to a certain extent, on their handsets. This does not change the core functionality of the operating system, but it does allow them to place their

own interface, known as a "skin", on the handset, creating a different visual appearance between manufacturers. For instance, Android on a Samsung smartphone will look different to Android on a Sony smartphone, but they will both be using the same fundamental operating system.

---

**A CLOSER LOOK**

Some manufacturers also use a simplified version of Android on their handsets. These do not include all of the features of the operating system, but they still have the basic functionality of Android powering them. One example of this is the range of Jitterbug phones that run on a customized version of Android (it is not part of the naming convention used by the full version). The Jitterbug is aimed at the senior market and, because Android can be customized, it has large buttons and icons, and also simplified menus. In association with the company GreatCall, the Jitterbug also has a range of health services for you and your family.

---

# Android and Google

Android is owned by Google, who bought the company that developed it in 2005, and there is generally a new version every each. Each version is numbered, and it also has the name of a type of candy or confectionery, named alphabetically for each version, e.g. 6.0 Marshmallow, 7.0 Nougat, and 8.0 Oreo. Since Google also produce smartphone handsets and tablets, it is understandable that these are the first models to get the latest version of Android. So the Google Pixel 2 smartphone is the first phone to using 8.0 Oreo and the Google Pixel C is the same for tablets.

Although Google makes the latest version of Android available to manufacturers when it is released, it can take several months for compatible handsets to be updated to this version. This update cycle is different for each manufacturer and depends on a number of factors, such as the length of time it takes to prepare the software for their range of handsets, and, in some cases, whether they have new handsets about to be released that they want to be the only one in their range running the latest version of Android.

Google is the only company that uses a "pure" version of Android, i.e. there are no "skins" used as an overlay on top of the operating system. So, if you want to see what Android 8.0 Oreo looks like in its purest form, the Google Pixel 2 smartphone is the place to look.

## Google Account

When you first start to use an Android device, you will be prompted to create a Google Account. This can also be done from the Settings app (a gear icon on most Android devices).

1. Access Settings > Accounts and tap on the **Add account** button.

2. Tap on the **Google** option.

3. Tap on the **More options** button and follow the wizard to create a new Google Account.

Use your Google Account to access functions such as the Play Store, Play Movies & TV, Play Music, and Gmail. Access your online Google Account at *myaccount.google.com*.

## Knowing your version

If your phone is not running Android 8.0 Oreo, it will not significantly alter your Android smartphone experience, although obviously it has the latest features. It is always useful to know what version of Android your smartphone is using and this can be checked within the Settings app:

1. Tap on the **Settings** app (or All Apps > Settings).

2. Tap on the **About device** option

3. The version of the operating system is located under the **Android version** section.

# Updating Android

It is always best to keep your Android smartphone or tablet as up-to-date as possible in terms of the version that is being used. This is because updates can be issued to fix bugs and also any security issues that may arise. These will usually be incremental updates, e.g. 8.1, 8.1.1, 8.2 etc. but there may also be updates to the latest version of Android, if your smartphone or tablet supports this.

To look for updates to Android.

1. Go to Settings > About device.

2. Tap on **System Updates**.

3. If there is an update to Android, this will be displayed here.

# Around the Home screen

The Home screen is the starting point for an Android smartphone or tablet. This contains the Google Search box, the Favorites Tray at the bottom of the screen, and any apps that the manufacturer has added to the device.

### Finding all apps

The full range of apps on your Android smartphone or tablet can be viewed from the **All Apps** button.

1. Tap on the **All Apps** button.

2. Swipe up and down to view all of the apps on the device.

## Adding apps to the Home screen

From the All Apps section, apps can be added to any of the Home screens on your device:

1. Access the **All Apps** section and press and hold on the app you want to add to a Home screen.

2. A minimized version of the Home screen appears over the All Apps section. Drag the app to the required position to add it here on the Home screen.

3. Drag the app to the side of the Home screen to move to the next available one and add the app here.

## Using the Favorites Tray

The line of apps at the bottom of the screen on an Android device is known as the Favorites Tray. This is where you can keep the apps that you use most frequently, making them available from any Home screen. Apps can be added to and removed from the Favorites Tray as required:

1. To remove an app from the Favorites Tray, press and hold on it on the Favorites Tray. Drag it onto a Home screen until gray outline appears. This indicates that the app can be placed here.

2. To add an app to the Favorites Tray, press and hold on it on a Home screen, or in the All Apps section, and drag it onto the Favorites Tray.

137

## Creating folders

Instead of having dozens of apps on your Home screens, folders can be used to tidy it up.

1. Press and hold on an app and drag it over another one.

2. Drop it on top of the second app to create a folder.

3. Tap on a folder to view its contents.

4. By default, it is called Unnamed folder. Tap on this to give it a more meaningful name.

**BRIGHT IDEA**

Drag a folder onto the Favorites Tray to access more apps here.

## Adding widgets and wallpaper

In addition to apps being added to the Home screen from the All Apps area, widgets can also be added here, and the wallpaper can be customized, too. Widgets are small apps that usually perform one specific task, such as showing the time or being shortcuts to your email or contacts. To add widgets:

1. Press on an empty area of the Home screen until the **Wallpapers**, **Widgets** and **Settings** options appear at the bottom of the screen. Tap on the Widgets option.

2. Swipe up and down to view the widgets.

3. Press and hold on a widget to pick it up. Position it on a Home screen in the same way as for an app. Widgets are usually larger than app icons and so need more space on a Home screen.

138

To change the background wallpaper:

1. Access the same bottom toolbar as for adding widgets, and tap on the **Wallpapers** button.

2. Tap on one of the background designs at the bottom of the window to preview it in the main window.

3. If you want to keep this as the wallpaper, tap on the **Set wallpaper** button. If not, tap on another background to preview it.

4. To use your own photos as the background, tap on the **My photos** button on the bottom bar. Select a photo and tap on the **Set wallpaper** button.

## Settings and Quick Settings

Android smartphones and tablets have the usual array of Settings for mobile devices, and they also have a Quick Settings section for the items you are likely to use most frequently.

To access Settings:

1. Tap on the **Settings** app.

2. Tap on a settings category to view the items within it.

3. Tap on this button to view a sidebar of all of the settings. Tap on one to access it.

4. Tap on the back arrow to move to the previous page, if more than one level has been accessed within a setting, tap on the back arrow until you return to the Settings homepage.

To access the Quick Settings:

1. Swipe down from the top of the screen, to access the **Notifications** area and the **Quick Settings** icons.

2. Tap on the gear icon to access the full range of Settings.

3. Tap on this button to view the expanded Quick Settings.

4. Tap on a setting to activate or deactivate it.

5. Tap on this button to Edit the Quick Settings area.

6. Drag items from the bottom panel to the top panel, to add them as a Quick Setting. Drag an item from the top to the bottom to remove it from Quick Settings.

7. Tap on the back arrow to return to the Quick Settings area.

# Managing Notifications

Notifications for Android devices can be displayed for a range of apps, such as emails, social media updates, available updates for your apps, and low battery warnings.

Notifications can be viewed by swiping down from the top of the screen. If notifications are available, their icons will be visible in the top, left-hand, corner of the screen. Swipe a notification from right to left to remove it, or tap on the **Clear All** button at the bottom of the notifications to remove them all.

Specifying what appears in the Notification area can be done through the Settings app:

1. Open the Settings > Apps and tap on a specific app. Tap on the **Notifications** button for the app.

2. Drag the buttons On or Off to: **Block all** notifications for this app; **Show silently**, so that the notification does not make a sound or vibrate; and **Override Do Not Disturb**, so that the app can display a notification even if Do Not Disturb is On (Settings > Sound > Do Not Disturb).

Notifications can be accessed from the Home screen and also if any app is open. They are also displayed on the Lock screen when the Android device is locked.

> **BRIGHT IDEA**
>
> If the battery is running low on your Android device, this will be flagged in the Notifications area. Tap on the battery notification to select **Battery saver** mode for saving power.

# Locking an Android device

An Android device has a Lock screen that is activated after a specific period of time. This can be determined in Settings > Display > Sleep and then selecting a period for inactivity, after which the device will go to sleep and the Lock screen will be activated. However, by default, the Lock screen can be unlocked simply by swiping on it, which is in no way secure. To make sure that other people don't have access to your Android device you can secure the Lock screen with a password, a PIN, or a pattern. To do this:

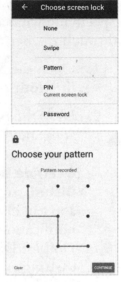

1. Access Settings > Security > Screen lock.

2. Select one of the screen lock methods:
   **Pattern**, **PIN**, or **Password** (but not Swipe).

3. The Pattern option can be used to create a unique pattern by drawing on a 3x3 grid (horizontally, vertically or diagonally) and tapping on the **Continue** button. Repeat the pattern and click on the **Confirm** button.

4. The PIN option can be used to create a numerical code of 4 characters.

5. The Password option is the most secure method for locking the screen. It must be at least 4 characters and can include, letters, numbers, symbols and special characters. Try and make a password at least 8 characters long.

6. Once the screen lock method has been set, this is required to unlock the Android device from the Lock screen.

---

**A CLOSER LOOK**

Once a screen lock method has been set, you will be prompted to select how notifications display their information on the Lock screen. This is an added security feature in case you want to prevent other people from viewing notifications when your device is locked. This can be set to **Show all notification content**, **Hide sensitive notification content** or **Don't show notifications at all**.

# Using Google Feeds

Google Feeds is a Google service that is available on Android devices. It enables you to select a range of topics and then view cards containing the latest information about the topics. For instance, you could select cards for weather, sports, and news, and see all of the latest updates in one place. Some of the cards are also generated from information in your Google Account, such as your browsing history.

---

**STAYING SECURE**

To view the information that Google stores about your activity within your Google Account, sign in to your account at *myaccount.google.com*. Click on the **Personal info & privacy option** on the homepage and click on the **My Activity** option. This displays a range of information related to your search and browsing history and any other activity in your Google Account, such as the topics that you have added for Google Feeds. There is also an **Activity controls** option in the left-hand panel, which can be used to specify a range of settings for your Google Account activity.

---

To use Google Feeds:

1. Tap on the **Google** app.

2. Initially the Google Feeds page is empty. Tap on the **Turn On** button.

3. Tap on the **Set Up** button.

SET UP

4. Tap on the **Yes, I'm in** button.

YES, I'M IN

5. Tap on the **Menu** button.

6. Tap on the **Customize** option.

7. Tap on the **Follow topics** button to add subjects that you want to see information about. These show main categories. Tap on a category as required. These show suggestions based on your location or previous search preferences.

8. Use the **Search** box at the top of the window to search for specific items. Tap on items to add them to your Google feeds.

9. Tap on the **Following** option to view items in your Google Feeds

10. Tap on the **Google** app at any time to view your Google Feeds homepage (or press and hold the Home button).

11. Tap on the **Menu** button for a card to view its options.

12. Select the **Customize** option as in Step 6 to further customize what appears in your Google Feeds. Swipe to the bottom of the page to access options for topics including, Places, Cooking, Flights, and Travel.

---

A CLOSER LOOK ────────────────────

To turn off Google Feeds, tap on the Menu button in Step 5 and tap on the **Settings** option. Select the Feed option and drag the **Enable the feed** button to Off.

---

# Adding apps

In addition to the pre-installed apps on an Android smartphone or tablet, there is a huge range that can be added from the Google Play Store. (A Google Account is required to access the Play Store. This should have been setup when you first started using your Android device.)

1. Tap on the **Play Store** app to access the store.

2. Tap on these buttons at the top of the window to access the related categories: **Games**, **Movies & TV**, **Books**, **Music** and **Newsstand** (magazine and newspapers). The Home button displays the most popular and most recently released apps. (If you have previously downloaded apps from the Play Store, the items displayed here may contain suggestions based on these downloads.)

3. Tap on these buttons on the Home page to access specific categories of apps.

4. Use the **Google Play Search** box at the top of the window to search for specific apps.

5.  Tap on the button to the left of the Search box to access a menu containing shortcuts to the other areas of the Play Store and also details of your Google Account (tap on the **Account** button).

6.  To download apps, tap on one to view its details.

7.  Review the details about the app and tap on the **Install** button to download it.

8.  The app is added to the next available Home screen.

# Removing apps

Apps can be removed from an Android device, if you no longer want to use them, or you have too many on your Home screen. They can be removed from the device or just removed from the Home screen.

1.  Press and hold on an app you want to remove.

2.  Drag the app over the **Remove** button. This removes the app from the Home screen, but it is still available from the All Apps section.

3.  Drag the app over the **Uninstall** button to remove it from the device.

4.  If the app is a pre-installed one (or a system one, e.g. Play Store), only the **Remove** option is available.

CAUTION

Apps cannot be removed from the All Apps section, it has to be done from a Home screen.

# Android phones for calls

In addition to all of the other useful functions that an Android phone has, it still handles the basics with ease. The most fundamental one is taking and receiving calls. (The Phone app is one that is customized by different handset manufacturers, but the general function is the same.)

## Receiving a call

1. When you receive an incoming call, these buttons will be displayed.

2. Swipe the left-hand green phone icon from left to right to take the call.

3. Swipe the right-hand red phone icon from right to left to reject the call.

4. Tap on the **Reject call with message** button to send the caller a text message instead of answering the call, e.g. "Can't talk right now, will call you in an hour."

## Making a call

1. Open the **Phone** app and tap on the **Keypad** button at the top of the window.

2. Type a number with the keypad and tap on the green phone icon to make a call.

3. To call someone in your address book, open the Phone app, tap on the **Contacts** button on the top toolbar, and tap on a name in your contacts.

4. Tap on this icon to make a call to the selected contact.

# Adding contacts

Once contacts have been added to your address book, you can call, text, or email them directly from their entry in the Contacts app, as long as these details have been entered.

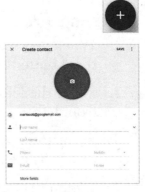

1. Tap on this icon to open the **Contacts** app.

2. Tap on this icon to add a new contact.

3. Enter the details for the contact, e.g. name, cell phone number, home phone number, email address, and address. Tap on the camera icon to add a profile picture for the contact.

4. Tap on the **Save** button to save the details and add this person as a contact.

---

**BRIGHT IDEA**

When entering a new contact or editing an existing one (tap on the pencil icon on the top toolbar of someone's entry to edit it), tap on the **Ringtone** button to assign a specific ring-tone for this contact. If you do this with all of your most regular contacts, you will be able to recognize who is phoning you just by the ringtone.

---

If someone phones or texts you, and they are not already in your contacts, they can be added directly from the Phone app. To do this:

1. Open the **Phone** app and tap on the **Log** button on the top toolbar.

2. Tap on the **Menu** button on the top toolbar.

3. Tap on the **Select** option and tap on a number to select it.

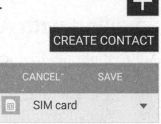

Select

4. Tap on this button on the top toolbar.

5. Tap on the **Create Contact** option.

6. Enter the person's details (the phone number will already have been inserted), select where you want to save the details, i.e. on the phone or the SIM card, and tap on the **Save** button.

# Messaging with Android

Since Android is not tied to one handset manufacturer, it can accommodate a wide variety of messaging and texting apps. Most manufacturers include a default messaging app. Others can be downloaded from the Play Store, including popular ones such as Messenger, WhatsApp, Go SMS Pro, and Viber. Whatever app you use for messaging, the process is similar.

### Sending a message

1. Open your messaging app.

2. Tap on the **New Message** button.

3. Enter the cell phone number of a recipient in the **Name or number** box.

4. Type the message in the **Type a message** box.

5. Tap on this button to access the range of emojis (graphical symbols) to add to the message.

6. Tap on this button to access additional content that can be added to the message, including photos, voice clips, and videos.

7. Tap on this button to send the message.

## Emailing with Android

Android phones frequently come with a dedicated email app. However, since Android is owned by Google it is only logical that the Gmail app is included on Android phones. Even if you don't have a Gmail account, other email accounts can be added here, so all of your emails can be managed through the Gmail app. For more details about Gmail, see Chapter Ten.

## Setting up new users

Unlike an iOS 11 device, where only one user can have an account on a specific device, Android devices allow for multiple people to have accounts on the same device. This gives them great flexibility, particularly as each user can lock their account with a password. To add a user to your Android device:

1.  Swipe down twice from the top of the screen to and tap on the **User** icon at the top of the window.

2.  All of the users on the device are displayed. Tap on one to open that user's account.

3.  Tap on the **Add user** button to add a new user (if there is more than one account on the device, this has to be done from the account that was first created, i.e. the one belonging to the device's owner).

4. In the **Add new user?** panel, tap on the **OK** button.

> **Add new user?**
>
> When you add a new user, that person needs to set up their space.
>
> Any user can update apps for all other users.
>
> CANCEL    OK

5. The new user account is created, and the new user then has to be set up. Tap on the **Continue** button.

> **Set up new user**
>
> You've been added to this tablet
>
> **Important:**
>
> • The tablet's owner can uninstall your apps or remove your space
>
> • Any other user can accept updated app permissions
>
> • Only share this tablet with people you trust
>
> Continue
>
> Cancel and remove new user

6. If the user already has a Google Account they can sign in with it, using their email username and password.

7. If the user does not have a Google Account, tap on the **More options** button and tap on the **Create account** button.

> **Google**
>
> **Sign in**
>
> with your Google Account. Learn more
>
> Email or phone
>
> Forgot email?
>
> More options          SKIP

8. Follow the **Create a Google Account** wizard to create an account that can be used with the new user.

---

**CAUTION**

You can skip the account setup process, but this means that the user won't have access to the Play Store for downloading content, and other Google services. If a Google Account is not setup at this point, it can be added from Settings > Accounts > Add account.

# Using Android Pay

We are becoming an increasingly cashless society, with digital payment becoming more popular and widespread. With an

Android device, you can join the digital payment world, using Android Pay, with a compatible debit or credit card, providing the card's issuer supports Android Pay. Once this has been setup you can use your Android device to pay for items in stores that support this type of contactless payment. To use Android Pay.

1. Ensure the Android device is protected by a Lock screen password or PIN (Settings > Security > Screen lock)

2. Tap on the **All Apps** icon.

3. Tap on the **Android Pay** app.

4. Tap on this button to add a card to Android Pay.

5. Enter details of a debit or credit card, either manually (**Add manually** button), or by taking a photo of the card with the Android Pay app (check the details if you use the photo option). This includes the card's number, expiration date, and three-figure security number.

6. Enter your name, contact phone number, and address and tap on the **Save** button

7. **Accept** the Terms & Conditions.

8. Verify the card with a verification code sent via a text message to the phone number in Step 6 and tap on the **Submit** button.

9. The device is now setup for Android Pay. To do this, unlock the device with the Lock Screen password or PIN and hold it up to the retailer's contactless payment terminal.

10. To delete a card from Android Pay, open the Android Pay app, tap on the card and tap on **Remove card** at the bottom of the page.

# 9 THE FORECAST IS CLOUDY

## What is cloud computing?

One of the great computing developments in the last ten years has been cloud computing. This is not some sinister piece of technology that will appear and ruin your barbecue in the backyard with a shower of rain, but rather a system that gives you peace of mind about the content you have created and stored on your devices. Some of the things that can be done with cloud computing are:

- Storing your content so that it is preserved if you lose it from your device, i.e. backing it up.

- Storing your content so that you can access it from another device, or from the Web.

- Storing your content so that you can share it with family and friends.

Cloud computing is essentially a large computer (known as a server) where you can store your content. If the worst does happen and your computer stops working, you can retrieve your content from the cloud. Simple.

## The cloud service will choose you

As with apps, Apple, Microsoft, and Google all have their own cloud services, accessed through a free user account. Once the cloud service is set up, you can specify what items you would like to be stored there, and it will be done automatically so that you don't have to worry about it.

Another great thing about cloud computing is that, because you are linked to it through your user account rather than a specific device, you can access the content from any other compatible device, and also from the Web. For instance, it you are using the Apple cloud service, known as iCloud, you can take a photo on your iPhone, then view and edit it on your iMac, and send it to someone from a Web browser from the online site at *icloud.com* (even if you are using a non-Apple device to access the Web).

## Setting up iCloud

For Mac and iOS 11 users, iCloud is the invisible, but powerful, force that helps you store and share the content on your Apple devices. It enables you to:

- Back up all of the content on your device.

- Back up content from specific apps.

- Access content that has been created on one device, and edit it on another.

- Share items with family members.

- Share photos directly from the Photos app.

---

**A CLOSER LOOK**

By default, you get 5GB of free iCloud storage. This can be upgraded to 50GB for $0.99 a month; 200GB for $2.99 a month; and 2TB for $9.99 a month.

---

Once you have an Apple ID, an iCloud account is automatically created too. This is linked to your Apple ID. You can then specify how you would like iCloud to operate:

1. Open the **Settings** app.

2. Select the **Apple ID** button.

3. Tap on the **iCloud** button.

4. The iCloud window displays how much storage you have used and has options for specifying which apps use iCloud. Tap on the **Manage Storage** button to see how much storage specific apps are using and also change your storage plan. See tip on following page.

5. Drag the buttons to On or Off for the items you want to store in iCloud. Items that are stored in iCloud are then available on other compatible Apple devices. For instance, if you specify that you want Notes to use iCloud, any items that you create here will be stored in iCloud – you can create a Note on your iPhone and then pick it up and continue with it on your iPad.

6. Once iCloud has been set up, you can leave it alone without worrying about it, and items will still be saved and stored here, giving you peace of mind to get on with other things.

---

**A CLOSER LOOK**

Within the iCloud settings it is also possible to set up Family Sharing. This can be used to invite up to six family members to share content via iCloud, including apps, music, and books that you have downloaded from the iTunes Store. To enable photos to be stored and shared in iCloud, select Settings > Photos and drag the **iCloud Photo Library** button to On.

---

# Using iCloud Drive and the Files app

In addition to storing items such as notes, calendars, address book, and Safari browser settings, iCloud can also be used to store documents and photos. Documents are stored in the Files app, which is part of iCloud Drive. This is set up in the iCloud section of Settings:

1. Access Settings > Apple ID > iCloud and drag the **iCloud Drive** button to On.

2. Once iCloud Drive has been activated, the apps that can use it are displayed below the iCloud Drive button. Drag the buttons to On for the items you want to use iCloud Drive. (These will be the apps whose content is stored in iCloud Drive.)

To access items in iCloud Drive:

1. Open the **Files** app.

2. Under **Locations**, tap on the **iCloud Drive** option.

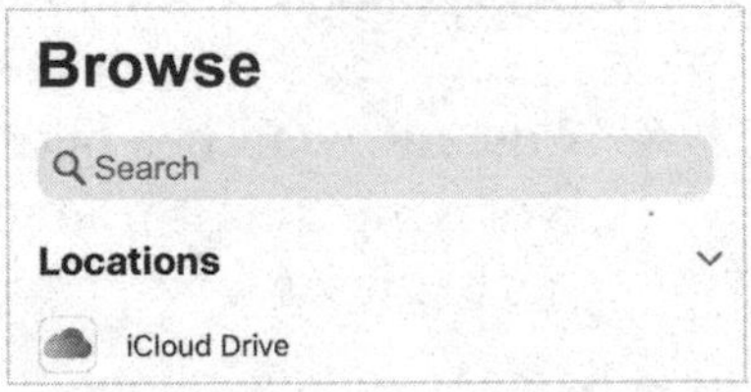

3. Folders specific to the items selected to appear in iCloud Drive are available in the Files app.

4. Tap on a folder to view its contents and open any files within it.

5. Tap on this button to add a new folder within the Files app. This will appear when creating content in a related app. for example, if you create a "Recipes" sub-folder within the main Pages folder of the Files app, it will be available when you next open the Pages app.

6. Tap on the **Select** button at the top of the window and tap on a file to select it.

7. Use the bottom toolbar to **Share** a selected item, **Copy it**, **Move it** to another folder, or delete it into the **Trash**.

8. When content is created in an app that has been enabled to work with iCloud Drive, the content will appear in the Files app. This can also be accessed from another Apple device, via iCloud and the Files app.

## Setting up iCloud with macOS High Sierra

For macOS High Sierra users, iCloud can be set up in a similar way as on an iOS 11 device:

1. Click on the **System Preferences** app on the Dock.

2. Click on the **iCloud** option.

3. Select items for iCloud in the same way as for iOS 11.

---

**A CLOSER LOOK**

When saving files in apps that support iCloud Drive, such as Apple's word processing app, Pages, there is an option to save the file directly into the iCloud Drive so it can be accessed by other devices. It can also be stored in iCloud for the specific app, e.g. saving a Pages document to iCloud means that it will be available directly from the Pages app on another Apple device.

iCloud Library
✔ Pages — iCloud
iCloud Drive

Recent Places
YourName ⇧⌘H

---

# Using OneDrive

For Windows 10 users, the cloud service is known as OneDrive. Items can be saved here from your Windows 10 PC or laptop and then opened on another Windows 10 device, or accessed online at *onedrive.live.com*. By default, you get 5GB of free storage in OneDrive. This can be upgraded to 50GB for $1.99 a month.

## Setting up OneDrive

You need a Microsoft Account to use OneDrive. Once you have this, you can set up OneDrive.

1. Click on the **Start** button and click on the **OneDrive** tile on the Start Menu.

OneDrive

2. In the **Set up OneDrive** window, enter your Microsoft Account email address and click on the **Sign in** button.

3. Enter your Microsoft Account password and click on the **Sign in** button.

4. Click on the **Next** button.

5. Select the folders that you want to use with OneDrive by checking on the boxes next to them. Click on the **OK** button.

6. The OneDrive folder is added to the Navigation pane in File Explorer.

7. Click on the **OneDrive** folder to view the items within it.

## Adding items to OneDrive

Once OneDrive has been set up, files can be added to it in two ways:

- By saving or copying files into the OneDrive folder in File Explorer on your Windows 10 PC or laptop.

- By uploading them to your online OneDrive folder at *onedrive.live.com*.

For both methods, files added in one location will be available in the other location, e.g. if you save a file into the OneDrive folder on your computer, it will be available in the online OneDrive folder, and vice versa.

To add files to the OneDrive folder in File Explorer.:

1. Create a document and select File > Save from the Menu bar.

2. Click on the **OneDrive** folder at the top of the Navigation pane in File Explorer.

3. The OneDrive folders are displayed in the main window. Double-click on the folder where you want to save the file.

4. Click on the **Save** button.

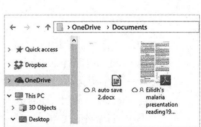

---

**CAUTION**

If you save a copy of a new file directly into the OneDrive folder, save a copy onto your PC or laptop too, using the File > Save As command from the Menu bar. This is because OneDrive is an online resource so, if anything happened to it, you would lose any files that are not also saved on your computer. OneDrive is an excellent option for backing up your files, but make sure that this is not their only location.

5.  To copy an item into the OneDrive folder, right-click on it in File Explorer and select the **Copy** option.

6.  Navigate to the required location in the OneDrive folder, right-click on an empty space, and select the **Paste** option.

To add files to the online OneDrive folder:

1.  Access **OneDrive** at *onedrive.live.com*.

2.  Enter your Microsoft Account password and click on the **Sign in** button.

3.  Click on the **Upload** button on the top toolbar and click on the **Files** or **Folder** options, depending on what you want to upload.

4.  The File Explorer will open. Navigate to the required folder, click on an item to select it and click on the **Open** button to add it to OneDrive.

New files can also be created in the online OneDrive folder, by clicking on the **New** button on the top toolbar and selecting what type of document you want to create, e.g. Word, Excel, or plain text document.

> **A CLOSER LOOK**
>
> If you create a new document in the online OneDrive folder, this can be done with Word Online even if you don't have Word installed on your PC or laptop. However, if you then want to open it on your computer, you will need a version of Word (or Excel and Powerpoint, for spreadsheets or presentations), or a compatible word processing app that can open Word files.

## OneDrive settings

OneDrive has its own range of settings, which can be accessed from the Notification area of the Taskbar (at the right-hand side).

1. Right-click on the **OneDrive** icon and click on the **Settings** option.

2. Click on the **Settings** tab for General settings and notification settings.

3. Click on the **Account** tab.

4. Click on the **Choose folders** button to specify which folders are used with OneDrive (in the same way as for setting it up in the first instance).

5. Check the files On or Off, then click the **OK** button.

---

**A CLOSER LOOK**

If the OneDrive icon is not on the Taskbar, open Settings > Personalization > Taskbar and under **Notification area**, click on the **Select which icons appear** on the taskbar option. Drag the **Microsoft OneDrive** button to On.

## Sharing with OneDrive

As well as being a useful online backup facility, OneDrive can also be used to share files with family and friends:

1. Go to your online OneDrive at *onedrive.live.com*.

2. Open a folder and click on the items you want to share. (Click on the circle in the top, right-hand corner to select items.)

3. Click on the **Share** button on the top toolbar.

4. Select what you want people to be able to do with the file, e.g. allow them to edit it, or set a date by which it will no longer be available.

5. Select a method for sharing the item (click on the **More** button if all of the options are not showing).

6. For the method of sharing, enter the details, e.g. an email address and a message, and click on the **Share** button.

7. The recipient will receive a message that you have shared an item in OneDrive with them, together with a link to view it online, and edit it, if you have given this permission.

---

**BRIGHT IDEA**

OneDrive (and other cloud services) is a great option for saving documents with important information that you want to be able to access on the move when you have access to the Internet. This should not include details such as passwords or usernames for online accounts or services! But it can be used, for instance, when you are going on vacation to store details of your itinerary, insurance, contact numbers, etc. Add a Word doc with these details to OneDrive and you will have access to them whenever you are online. There is even a Microsoft OneDrive app for iOS 11, so you can also access your Windows 10 files from an iPad or an iPhone.

### Letting OneDrive take the strain

Remembering to backup all of your important files on a regular basis can be a bit tedious. OneDrive is aware of this and offers some help in a way of an **Auto Save** function, which can be used to automatically save some types of content to OneDrive. To use this:

1. Right-click on the **OneDrive** icon on the Taskbar and click on the **Settings** option.

2. Click on the **Auto Save** tab at the top of the window.

3. Under **Choose where you want to save your documents and pictures**, click on the drop-down box, and click on **OneDrive**.

4. This ensures that documents and photos will be saved into OneDrive when they are created and then saved. However, they will not be saved to your PC or laptop file structure. This has to be done separately, using **Save As**.

5. Under the **Photos and videos** heading, check the **Automatically save photos and videos to OneDrive whenever I connect a camera, phone, or other device to my PC** to have photos and videos automatically saved into OneDrive when they are downloaded.

# Backing up an Android device

On an Android device, a range of apps can be set to have their data automatically backed up to Google. You have to be signed into your Google Account to use this, but once it is set up the apps will sync their data with the Google backup servers on a regular basis (at least daily).

CAUTION

The backup settings can only be specified by the main user on an Android device, i.e. the person who first set it up, not additional users who have been added subsequently.

To specify which items you would like backed up on your Android device:

1. Access Settings > Accounts and tap on the **Google** option.

2. Drag the buttons On or Off for the items that you want to sync with the Google backup servers.

3. To force an item to sync, tap the button Off and then On again, or tap on this button at the top of the window and tap on **Sync now**. All items that have new data on the Android device will be synced.

# Setting up Google Drive

For backing up and sharing files, the Google Drive app can be used on Android devices. This is the equivalent of iCloud Drive on a macOS or iOS device, or the OneDrive on a Windows 10 device. The Google Drive app is a pre-installed app on Android 8.0 Oreo devices (and numerous other devices) and gives you 15GB of free storage for your documents, photos, and other files. As with other cloud services, content within the Google Drive can be accessed from any online computer, smartphone, or tablet, providing there is online access. To use Google Drive:

1. Access **All Apps** and tap on the **Drive** app.

2. The Drive app opens at the **My Drive** homepage, which displays the content that has been added, or will be added.

Drive

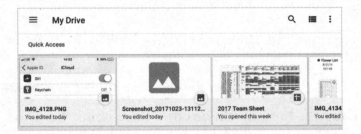

3. Tap on this button to search for an item within your My Drive.

4. Tap on this button to view files in a list or a grid.

5. Tap on this menu button to access options for sorting files, selecting them or viewing their details.

You can upgrade the 15GB of free storage for your Google Drive, to 100GB for $1.99 a month, or 1TB for $9.99 a month.

## Adding items to Google Drive

From within the Drive app on an Android device it is possible to add content from your device:

1. Click on this button.

2. Select what you want to add. This can be a new **Folder** into which content can then be placed; **Upload** an item from your Android device; **Scan** an item using the device's camera; or upload a Google **Docs**, **Sheets**, or **Slides** document, created with

Google's range of productivity apps, which are closely integrated with the Drive app.

3. For **Uploads**, navigate to the item on your Android device and tap on it to copy it to the Drive app.

## Accessing Google Drive files

Once items have been added to the Google Drive on your Android device, they can then be accessed online, edited, and shared with other people.

1. Go to the website at *google.com/drive* and click on the **Go to Google Drive** button.

2. Login with your Google Account details.

3. The contents of your Google Drive will be displayed. These should mirror the content on your Android device.

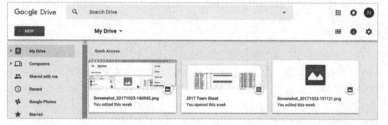

4. Click on the **My Drive** button to access options for creating the same range of items as on an Android device.

5. Right-click on an item to access its menu.

6. Click on the **Share** button.

7. Enter the email address of the person with which you want to share the item and click on the **Send** button.

8. Specify whether the recipient receives an **Invitation**, with which they can sign in with a Google Account and edit the item, or a **Link**, with which they can view the file, but not edit it, without a Google Account.

9. Click on the **Send** button.

---

**CAUTION**

If you send a link to someone to a file that has been created with Google Docs, Sheets, or Slides, the recipient will be able to view it online without the related app, but they will need the app if they want to edit it. There are app versions of Docs, Sheets and Slides for Android, iOS, and macOS. Microsoft Office apps can open the related Docs, Sheets, and Slides files.

---

# Checking your storage

As more items are added to a cloud service, it will start to use up the amount of available storage, particularly if you are backing up a lot of photos. In all services it is possible to check how much storage has been used, and how much is left.

## Storage in iCloud

To check your storage in iCloud:

1. Access Settings > Apple ID > iCloud.

2. The amount of used and free storage is displayed at the top of the window.

3. Tap on the **Manage Storage** button to view how much storage specific apps are using up. Click on the **Change Storage Plan** button to upgrade your iCloud storage.

## Storage in OneDrive

To check your storage in OneDrive:

1. Right-click on the **OneDrive** icon on the Taskbar of your PC and click on the **Settings** option.

2. Click on the **Account** tab. The amount of used storage is shown at the top of the window.

## Storage in Google Drive

To check your storage in Google Drive:

1. Open the **Drive** app on your Android device and tap on the menu button to the left of the **My Drive** heading.

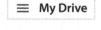

2. The amount of used storage is shown under the **Upgrade storage** heading. Tap on this button to view details about the amount of storage used.

# Dropping in with Dropbox

So far, all of the cloud services have been linked to specific operating systems (although the content can also be accessed from different platforms). However, there are also independent cloud services that are not linked to a specific operating system. The most widely used of these is Dropbox. This is a service that can be accessed on any platform or device and it is an excellent option for backing up and sharing your files. To use Dropbox:

1. Download the **Dropbox** app from the Apple App Store, the Microsoft Store, or the Google Play Store.

2. Create a user account with an email username and a password.

3. On a mobile device, access Dropbox by tapping on the app, or using your web browser and logging in at *dropbox.com*.

4. On a Windows 10 PC, a Dropbox folder is also created when you add a Dropbox account. Save or copy files here as you would with any other folder in File Explorer. Once a file has been added to the Dropbox folder on your PC, it will be available via Dropbox on any other devices or platform.

5. To access your files from the online Dropbox, go to *dropbox.com* and login with your username and password. The folders and files will be the same as if you access your account through the Dropbox app.

The standard, free Dropbox account provides 2GB of storage space. You also get an extra 500MB for anyone who you refer to Dropbox, once they create an account. There is a subscription option, which is 1TB of storage for $9.99 a month.

## Dropbox online

For the online version of Dropbox:

1. Click on the **Home** button to view the most recent activity in your account.

2. Click on the **Files** button to view the file structure in your Dropbox account.

3. By default, the folders in your Dropbox are not shared with anyone.

4. To share a folder, click on it to open it and click on the **Share folder** button.

5. Enter the email address for the person whom you want to invite to share the folder and specify their permissions, e.g. view only via a link, or view and edit.

6. Click on the **Share** button. The recipient will receive an invitation and, once they accept, it they will be able to access the content in the folder.

7. In the Files section, click on the **Upload files** button to add files from your computer.

8. Click on the **New shared folder** button or the **New folder** button to create one of these items within your Dropbox file structure.

9. Any changes that are made to the online version of Dropbox will be replicated in any other versions, e.g. when you open the Dropbox app, the changes will be displayed.

> **STAYING SECURE**
>
> There is no reason why you can't have your default cloud service, i.e. iCloud, and also use Dropbox. Save your important documents and photos into both for extra security and peace of mind.

# Using multiple cloud services

Since all platforms have their own dedicated cloud service, you may think that they do not allow any interactions between each other. But luckily, this is not the case and files can be accessed from different cloud services from a single device. For instance:

- On an iOS 11 device, you can download the Drive, OneDrive, and Dropbox apps and access content within them by logging into the apps. Even better, they also show up in the Files app (under the **Locations** heading) so you can access all of your cloud content (iCloud, Google Drive, Microsoft OneDrive and Dropbox).

- On Windows 10 PCs and laptops, you can download **iCloud for Windows** and access your iCloud content from this folder in the File Explorer. Go to *support.apple.com/en-us/HT204283* to download **iCloud for Windows**. Pin it to **Quick Access** to access it from here.

- On Android devices, you can download the OneDrive and Dropbox apps. For iCloud, there is a range of apps that can be used to access iCloud content (**Sync for iCloud, Sync for iCloud Mail,** and **Sync for iCloud Contacts**), although the process is not as straightforward as for other devices.

## Doubling up – creating a manual backup too

No matter how good your cloud backup service is (and they are very good) it is essential that you do not just rely on this for backing up your important documents. While it's unlikely that your computing device will crash at the same time as your cloud service is hacked and rendered unusable, anything is possible in the world of computing. If you plan for the worst and it doesn't happen, then that's a bonus. Plus, you can relax knowing that your content is backed up whatever happens.

Once your cloud service is set up and happily saving your documents and photos, look to creating a manual backup routine too:

1. The first step is to set a schedule for how often you want to backup your files and data, i.e. daily for newly created or edited files, and monthly for a full backup of your system. Use Settings > Backup for Windows 10, or Time Machine for macOS High Sierra.

2. For mobile devices, decide what to do with documents or photos that have been created on these devices. Since it is not as easy to create a manual backup, due to the lack of a USB port for connecting a backup device, it takes a bit more effort to do this, but it is worthwhile. One option is to email important files to yourself on a desktop PC or laptop and then manually back them up in the same way as for other files. Another option is to attach the mobile device to your computer using its USB cable. The device should then show up on your computer as an external drive, and you will be able to copy files from your mobile device and paste them into a folder on your PC or laptop.

## BRIGHT IDEA

If a mobile device does not immediately show up in the file management folder on your PC or laptop, try detaching and reattaching the USB cable a few times. Sometimes it takes a little while for the computer to recognize the mobile device.

3. To create a manual backup, use an external hard drive. Look for a hard drive with a capacity of 1TB, which will be more than enough. This can be attached permanently to your PC or laptop so that you can backup items whenever you want.

4. A USB flash drive is also a good manual backup option, particularly as it is easy to store it away from your computer, thereby giving you extra backup security. If your computer is stolen (and the connected external hard drive), you would still have your files on the USB flash drive. Keep it in your purse or wallet and have it with you wherever you go!

# 10  GETTING ONLINE

To say that we are all increasingly dependent on the online world is probably a bit of an understatement! From keeping in touch with emails, to shopping on the Web, to keeping up with family and friends on social media, there are few parts of our lives that are not touched by online access. This brings great benefits, and the world seems to shrink around us as we can reach out to all parts of the globe from our keyboards. However, there are risks associated with an online existence, both social and technological, so it is important to be fully aware of the potential, and the limitations, of the online world.

## Popular browsers

A Web browser is simply a window to the online world. Most things can be accessed from a browser: from your favorite social media sites, to your online Web mail, and a myriad of websites in between. Each platform comes with its own default Web browser:

- Microsoft Edge for Windows 10.

- Safari for macOS High Sierra and iOS 11.

- Google Chrome for Android (some individual manufacturers may use different default browsers on their handsets).

174

All of these browsers do an excellent job and should fully meet your online requirements. However, there are dozens of other browsers on the market, so there is no reason why you should restrict yourself to the default one that comes with your device. Some browsers, such as Chrome, can be used on more than one platform, while Microsoft Edge and Safari are only available on their default platforms.

# Downloading more browsers

If you want to expand your browser experience, you can download several browsers and see which one you like the best, and then use it as your main browser. On PCs and laptops, there is a default browser that will be used to automatically open Web pages. On mobile devices, just tap on the browser app that you want to use. Some browsers to look at are:

- **Chrome.** Although this is the default browser on a lot of Android devices, there are also versions for Windows, macOS and iOS devices. Try it by downloading the appropriate version at *google.com/chrome*, or download the app from your appropriate app store.

- **Firefox.** This is one of the most widely used browsers on the Web and comes in desktop and mobile versions. It has a range of security features and prides itself in protecting online rights. Try it by downloading the appropriate version at *mozilla.org* or as an app version.

- **Opera.** With versions for all platforms, this is a slick, well-designed browser that comes with a built-in ad blocking feature. Try it by downloading the appropriate version at *opera.com* or from your app store.

- **Internet Explorer.** An old favorite for Windows users, the last version of Internet Explorer was released in 2015. Although it is still provided with Windows 10 (type **Internet**

**Explorer** into the Search box to the right of the Start button), it is better to move on to Microsoft Edge, as this is the browser that will be supported and developed in the future.

---

**A CLOSER LOOK**

When you download a different browser to your device from the browser's website, it will recognize the type of device you are using and direct you to the correct version of the browser e.g. desktop or mobile. It is also possible to download the browsers from your device's app store.

---

# Setting a default browser

For desktop PCs and laptops, the default browser on your device is the one that opens automatically when Web content is accessed. For instance, if someone sends you a website link in an email, when you click on it the link will open in your default browser. If you have downloaded a different browser from the one that came with your device, you can change the default browser to the new one.

---

**CAUTION**

Never click on a website link in emails from people you don't know. In all probability, this will be the work of hackers or fraudsters trying to infect your computer with viruses or trying to persuade you to divulge private login or financial details.

---

### Windows 10

To change a default browser in Windows 10:

1. Access Settings > Apps > Default apps.

2. Under the **Default apps** heading, click on the **Web browser** option.

3. Click on another app to make it the default, or click on the **Look for an app in the Store** option to search the Microsoft Store for more suitable apps.

### macOS High Sierra

To change a default browser in macOS High Sierra:

1. Select System Preferences > General

2. Click on **Default web browser** option from the pop-up menu and select a default browser here.

# Home(page) is where the heart is

When you first open a Web browser on your device, it will open at the Web page that the browser's developer has chosen (homepage). This will inevitably be something that the browser's developer wants you to see, but you probably don't want to see it, particularly every time you open your browser. Instead, you can choose whatever Web page you want and set this as your homepage.

### Windows 10

To set a homepage with Microsoft Edge in Windows 10:

1. Open the **Microsoft Edge** browser and navigate to the Web page you want to use as your homepage.

2. Click on this menu button in the top, right-hand corner of the browser window.

3. Click on the **Settings** option at the bottom of the menu.

4. Click in the **Open Microsoft Edge** with box, and click on the **A specific page or pages** option.

177

5. Enter the website address that you want to use as your homepage in the **Enter a URL** box. This does not need to be the full address, e.g. enter *fca.com*.

```
Enter a URL                          💾
```

---

**BRIGHT IDEA**

The Edge browser contains a Home button on the top toolbar. However, if this is not showing, it can be displayed by accessing the Edge menu as above: select Settings, scroll down the page and click on the **View advanced settings** button. Drag the **Show the home button** to On, and specify a page for it to open, in the same way as setting a homepage.

---

**A CLOSER LOOK**

URL stands for Uniform Resource Locator, which is a reference to where an item is located on the Web. In most cases, it refers to the website address of a Web page.

## macOS High Sierra

To set a homepage with Safari in macOS High Sierra:

1. Open **Safari** and navigate to the Web page you want to use as your homepage.

2. Select Safari > Preferences from the menu bar.

3. Click on the **General** tab.

4. In the **Homepage** field enter the website address to use or click **Set to Current Page**, i.e. the currently active one in the browser.

```
●●●                            General
  [icons] General  Tabs  AutoFill  Passwords  Search  Security  Privacy  Websites  Extensions  Advanced

           New windows open with:  [ Top Sites              ⌄ ]
              New tabs open with:  [ Top Sites              ⌄ ]
                      Homepage:    [ http://www.apple.com/    ]
                                   [ Set to Current Page ]
```

## iOS 11

With an iOS device there is no facility for setting a specific home-page. However, you can add an icon to the Home screen that will open at your favorite Web page. To do this:

1. On an iPad or iPhone, open **Safari** and navigate to the page you want to use as a homepage.

2. Tap on this button (on the top toolbar on an iPad and on the bottom toolbar on an iPhone).

3. Swipe from right to left on the bottom line of icons and tap on the **Add to Home Screen** button.

4. Give the page a name and tap on the **Add** button.

| Cancel | Add to Home | Add |
| --- | --- | --- |

FC&A Publishing
https://fca.com/

An icon will be added to your home screen so you can quickly access this website.

5. An icon is added to your Home screen. Tap on it to open your favorite Web page in Safari.

## Google Chrome

To add an icon to the Home screen of an Android device.

1. Open **Chrome**, navigate to the page to use, and tap on the menu button.

2. Tap on the **Add to Home screen** option.

Add to Home screen

3. Enter a name for the page and tap on the **Add** button.

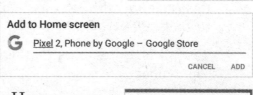

Add to Home screen

Pixel 2, Phone by Google – Google Store

CANCEL    ADD

4. An icon is added to your Home screen. Tap on it to open your favorite Web page in Chrome.

Say "Ok Google"

Pixel 2, Phone by Go...

> **BRIGHT IDEA**
>
> Tired of your homepage? Just find a new page on the Web and repeat the required process here.

# Adding favorites

Everyone has the same Web pages that they visit again and again. These can be for news, sports, lifestyle, finance, and hundreds of other topics, depending on your hobbies and interests. Rather than having to navigate to them by typing in a Web address each time, it is much easier to set them as a favorite (or a bookmark) so that you can access them in a couple of clicks.

## Windows 10 favorites

To add favorites in the Microsoft Edge browser:

1. Navigate to the required page and click on the star icon to the right of the address bar.

2. Select a name for the favorite (this can just be left as the default given by the Web page, but these can sometimes be quite long).

3. Select where to save the page.

4. Click on the **Add** button. Once a page has been added as a favorite, this is identified by the star icon turning yellow.

5. To view favorites, click on this button on the top toolbar.

6. Click on the star icon to view favorites that have been added. Click on one to go to that page.

7. To remove a favorite, right-click on it in the step above and click on the **Delete** button.

---

**BRIGHT IDEA**

Favorites can be added to the Favorites folder, as described above. However, they can also be saved to the Favorites Bar, which can then be displayed at the top of the Edge browser. To do this, select **Favorites Bar** instead of **Favorites** in Step 3 above. To display the Favorites Bar, select the main menu and click on the **Settings** option. Under the **Favorites bar** heading, drag the **Show the favorites bar** button to On.

---

## macOS High Sierra favorites

To add favorites (known as bookmarks) in the Safari browser:

1. Navigate to the required page and click on the **Share** button.

2. Click on the **Add Bookmark** button and select a folder for the bookmark.

3. Enter a name for the bookmark and click on the **Add** button.

4. Click on this button to show the Sidebar, from where the bookmarks can also be accessed.

## iOS 11 favorites

To add favorites (bookmarks) in Safari on an iPad or iPhone:

1. Navigate to the required page and tap on the **Share** button (on the top toolbar on an iPad, and on the bottom toolbar on an iPhone).

2. Tap on the **Add Bookmark** button.

3. Enter a name for the bookmarked page and select a folder under the **Location** heading.

4. Tap on the **Save** button.

5. To view bookmarked Web pages, tap on this button. (This opens three groups of bookmarked items.)

6. Tap on the left-hand button to view all of the bookmarked Web pages.

## A CLOSER LOOK

The two other options in the Bookmarks section are: Reading List, which is items that have been saved so that they can be read, even when you are offline; and History, which lists your Web browsing activity. Reading List items can be added from the **Share** button, and then tapping on the **Add to Reading List** button.

## Google Chrome favorites

To add a favorites (bookmarks) with Google Chrome on an Android device:

1. Navigate to the required page and tap on the star icon in the address bar.

2. Tap on the menu button to the right of the address bar and tap on the **Bookmarks** option.

3. Tap on a bookmark to go to that page.

4.  Tap on the menu button next to a bookmark to access options to **Select it, Edit it, Move it,** or **Delete it**.

5.  Tap on the **Edit** button to select a new name for the bookmark, or select a different folder to store it in.

6.  If you select to **Move** a bookmark (in Step 4), you can create a new folder for its location by tapping on the **New folder** button and typing a title for the folder. The new folder will appear under the **Mobile bookmarks** heading when you select **Bookmarks** from the Chrome menu.

# Tabbed browsing

What is better than having one Web page to look at in your browser? Having two or more Web pages that you can move between within the same browser window. This is known as tabbed browsing and is a common feature in all modern browsers. It is a great way to keep all of your favorite websites at your fingertips.

### Windows 10 tabs

To use tabs in the Microsoft Edge browser:

1.  Open the browser. It will open at its Start page, or a Homepage if this has been specified.

2.  Click on this button to open a new tab, or press Ctrl+T on the keyboard. (To specify what happens when a new tab is opened, go to Menu > Settings and under the **Open new tabs with** heading select what you want to appear when a new tab is created. The options are for **Top sites and suggested content**, **Top sites**, and **A blank page**.)

3.  Tap on one of the items on the new tab page, or enter a website address in the **address** search box.

4.  Open tabs are displayed at the top of the browser window. Click on one to make that the active page.

5.  If you feel you have too many open tabs, click on this button at the left-hand side of the top tab bar to shrink all of the open tabs, except the currently active one. This is known as setting them aside.

6.  Click on this button to view any tabs that have been set aside and click on the **Restore tabs** option if you want them to be visible again.

## macOS High Sierra tabs

To use tabs in the Safari browser:

1.  Click on this button on the top toolbar to add a new tab.

2.  In Safari, click on Safari > Preferences from the Menu bar.

3.  Click on the **Tabs** tab and make the required selections for how tabs operate.

## iOS 11 tabs

To use tabs in Safari on an iPad or iPhone:

1.  On an iPad, tap on this button on the top toolbar.

2.  On an iPhone, tap on this button on the bottom toolbar and then tap on this button.

3.  Select a page to open, or enter a website address in the address bar.

4.  Tap on this button to view thumbnails of all of the currently active tabs. On the iPad they are displayed in a grid and on the iPhone they are tiled vertically. On the iPhone, swipe on a thumbnail from right to left to close it. On an iPad, swipe a thumbnail to the top of the window to close it. On both devices, swipe up to view the bottom of the screen. This contains links to any tabs that are open on other Apple devices that you have.

**A** CLOSER LOOK

> To determine what appears when a new tab is first opened, go to Settings > Safari and tap on the **Favorites** option. This contains the folders that have been created for your favorite bookmarks. The default is **Favorites**, but click on another if you want it to appear as the option when a new tab is opened.

## Google Chrome tabs

To use tabs with Google Chrome on an Android device:

1. Click on this button to add a new tab.

2. The start page displays the Google Search box and recommended sites.

3. To view tabs that have been recently closed, tap on the menu button and tap on the **Recent tabs** option.

# Private browsing

Every time you visit a Web page, your browser keeps a record of it. This can be used to revisit pages that you have previously visited, but it can also let other people see a history of your Web activity. If you do not want other people to do this, you can perform private browsing, which does not collect any data about your browsing activity.

## Windows 10 private browsing (InPrivate)

To browse privately in the Microsoft Edge browser,

1. Click on the **Menu** button in the top, right-hand corner of the browser.

2. Click on the **New InPrivate window** option.

3. The private browsing is indicated above the Search box.

## macOS High Sierra

To browse privately in Safari on macOS High Sierra:

1. Select File > New Private Window from the Safari Menu bar.

2. A window using private browsing has a dark address bar with white text.

## iOS 11 private browsing

To browse privately in Safari on an iPad or iPhone:

1. Tap on this button (on the top toolbar on an iPad and on the bottom toolbar on an iPhone).

2. Tap on the **Private** option.

3. Tap on this button to access a new page in private browsing. This is indicated by a dark background for the address bar.

## Google Chrome private browsing (incognito)

To browse privately with Google Chrome on an Android device:

1. Tap on the **Menu** button to the right of the address bar at the top of the screen.

2. Select the **New incognito tab** option.

3. The incognito option displays the address bar on a dark background and displays this icon above it at the right-hand side. Tap on this button to toggle between incognito and standard tabs.

> **BRIGHT IDEA**
>
> If you use online banking or websites where sensitive financial details are entered, this could be a good time to use private browsing. This way, none of the sign-in details or pages visited will be stored by the browser.

# Managing history and cookies

Being able to determine how your browser deals with the history of websites and pages that have been visited is an important element of the online experience. Browsing data can be deleted, as can cookies that have been downloaded automatically from websites.

---

**CAUTION**

Cookies are small files that record browsing data for specific websites, such as pages visited and items accessed. It can be tempting to block cookies, since you don't always know what they are doing and they can be responsible for displaying targeted advertising through your browser. However, they also provide a useful service by remembering items such as login names and passwords for subscription sites and browsing preference. If you block or remove cookies it will take a bit more time to enter all of the required details on certain websites.

---

## Managing data and cookies with Windows 10

To manage these items in the Microsoft Edge browser:

1. Click on the **Menu** button.

2. Click on the **Settings** button.

3. Under **Clear browsing data**, click on the **Choose what to clear** button.

4. Check On or Off the items to clear and click on the **Clear** button.

5. In the main Settings section, click on the **View advanced** settings button (towards the bottom of the panel).

6. Under the **Cookies** heading (towards the bottom of the

panel) click in the drop-down
box and select how you want to
manage cookies. The options

are for **Block all cookies**, **Block only third party cookies**, and
**Don't block cookies**.

## Managing data and cookies with macOS High Sierra.

To manage these items in Safari on a macOS High Sierra computer:

1. Open **Safari** and select Safari > Preferences from the Menu bar.

2. Click on the **Privacy** tab.

3. Under **Cookies and website data**, check the **Block all cookies**
   checkbox On or Off as required.

4. To remove data and cookies that have been saved by Safari,
   click on the **Manage Website Data** button, and select a
   website to view items that it has stored and click **Remove** or
   **Remove All**.

## Managing data and cookies with iOS 11

To manage these items for Safari on an iPad or iPhone.

1. Access Settings > Safari

2. Under the **Privacy & Security**
   heading, drag the **Block All Cookies**
   button On or Off as required.

3. Tap on the **Clear History and Website Data** button to
   remove these items.

## Managing data and cookies with Google Chrome

To manage these items with Google Chrome on an Android device:

1. Open **Chrome** and tap on the **Menu** button.

2. Tap on the **Settings** option.

3. Select Privacy > Clear browsing data.

4. Check the items On or Off as required. These include: **Browsing history**; **Cookies and site data**; **Cached images and files**; **Saved passwords**; and **Autofill form data**.

| ← | Clear browsing data | | ❓ |
|---|---|---|---|
| | BASIC | ADVANCED | |
| Time range | | Last hour ▾ | |
| 🕘 | Browsing history<br>1 item (and more on synced devices) | | ☑ |
| ⊕ | Cookies and site data<br>From 44 sites | | ☑ |
| 🖼 | Cached images and files<br>2.7 MB | | ☑ |
| ⛬ | Saved passwords<br>None | | ☐ |
| ✎ | Autofill form data<br>None | | ☐ |

### BRIGHT IDEA

To see how cookies work, register on a new site with login details including username and password. Use the site for a period of time and then turn Off cookies to see how this affects the operation of the site. For instance, with cookies On you may see more information specific to you than if you have them Off. Also, it may be quicker to login to the site as some details will be saved and pre-inserted.

# To AutoFill or not to AutoFill, that is the question

Filling in forms and passwords is a common, if frequently tiresome, part of the online world. However, most browsers have an option whereby these details can be remembered and filled in automatically the next time you visit that site (AutoFill). This sounds like a great way of saving yourself the bother of remembering various login details and passwords, and it is. Or at least it can be. The potential problem is that if someone else gets hold of your device (particularly a mobile device, such as a smartphone or a tablet) they could potentially login to your online sites using the AutoFill function for your login details. Generally, for devices that just stay in your home, AutoFill is a useful and timesaving option. For mobile devices, it is best to think twice about where you want to enable this.

- To enable, or disable, AutoFill on an iOS 11 device, go to Settings > Safari > AutoFill and drag the required options On or Off. The available options are: **Use Contact Info**, which is useful for adding your own contact details into a form, including your address, phone number, and email address; **Names and Passwords**, which can be more sensitive as it would give access to secure sites; and **Credit Cards**, which is another item that should not be AutoFilled if you think there is the slightest chance that your device could fall into the wrong hands.

- To enable or disable AutoFill on an Android device, open the Chrome browser and tap on the menu button. Select Settings > Autofill and payments, and drag the **Autofill forms** button On or Off.

### STAYING SECURE

Always ensure your devices are locked with a passcode. This is the first line of defense if someone gets hold of your device that shouldn't. If there is no passcode, they would simply be able to access everything on the device.

## Using Gmail

Web-based email accounts have an obvious appeal:

- They are quick and easy to set up.

- They can be accessed from any Web browser, so your emails are always available (as long as you have access to Wi-Fi and the Internet).

- There are companion apps that can be used on mobile devices, so that you can access your account in one tap, without even having to access the Web.

There are dozens of Web-based email options, but Gmail (owned by Google) is a widely used one.

## Accessing Gmail

A Google Account is required for Gmail, which can be created when you first access Gmail. This is either done online at *gmail.com*, or the Gmail app can be downloaded for iOS 11 and Android devices.

For the online version of Gmail:

1. Click on the **Inbox** option to view your emails, which are displayed in the main panel.

   Inbox (6)

2. Click on an email heading to view its details.

   | | | | | |
   |---|---|---|---|---|
   | ☐ ☆ ☐ | Windows Insider Program | Thank you! - The latest news from the Window | 19 Oct |
   | ☐ ☆ ☐ | Club Carlson | Nicholas / Emma, save on your weekend sta | 17 Oct |
   | ☐ ☆ ☐ | YouTube | Butterfly Spanish: "Learn the top 26 phrases wi | 14 Oct |
   | ☐ ☆ ☐ | MyHeritage Notification | MyHeritage DNA: the perfect complement to | 13 Oct |

3. Click on the **Compose** button to create a new email.

   COMPOSE

4. Enter a recipient's email address in the **To** box, add a subject, then write the body text of the email.

5. Click on the **A** button on the bottom toolbar to access text formatting options.

   Sans Serif · ᴛᴛ · B I U A · ☰ · ☰ ☰ ☱ ☱ 99 Iₓ
   Send  A  ◌  ⬦  £  ▦  ⧉  ☺

6. Click on this button on the bottom toolbar to attach an item to the email from your computer, such as a photo or a file.

   🖇

7. Click on this button on the bottom toolbar to attach a photo from your Google Account photos.

8. Click on this button to access emojis to attach to the email.

   ☺

9. Click on the **Send** button to send the email.

> **A CLOSER LOOK**
>
> Emojis are small graphical symbols that can be added to emails, and text messages, usually for light-hearted purposes. There is a huge range available, and it is an area that is expanding rapidly.

Items in the Gmail Inbox can be managed in a variety of ways:

1. Click in the check-box next to an email heading to select it.

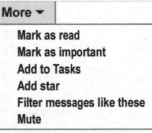

2. Click on this button on the top toolbar to **Archive** the item.

3. Click on this button to **Report spam**.

4. Click on this button to **Trash** the item.

5. Click on this button to **Move** to another folder.

6. Click on this button to add a **Label** to the item to make it more easily identifiable.

7. Click on the **More** button to access additional options, such as to mark an item as **Read** or **Important**, **Add star**, or **Filter messages like these** (whereby you can select certain actions for emails from a specific sender, or with certain words in the subject, to delete them or mark them as important).

More ▼

Mark as read
Mark as important
Add to Tasks
Add star
Filter messages like these
Mute

---

**A CLOSER LOOK**

Once you have a Google Account, you can also access some of the other services from Gmail. This includes **Contacts** for adding contact details for family and friends, and **Tasks** for adding notes about things to do. Contacts and Tasks can be accessed from the **Gmail** drop-down list above the **Compose** button.

## Gmail settings

To access a range of settings for Gmail:

1. Click on this button in the top, right-hand corner of the Gmail window and tap on the **Settings** option.

2. Click in this box to select how many conversations to display on a page.

   | Maximum page size: | Show 50 ⌄ conversations per page |
   |---|---|

3. Check On the **Enable Undo Send** checkbox and enter a time period, during which you can retrieve any email that you have just sent (this is a great option if you mistakenly send something that is embarrassing).

   | Undo Send: | ☑ **Enable Undo Send** <br> Send cancellation period: 10⌄ seconds |
   |---|---|

4. Check On the **Conversation view on** button to keep emails with the same topic heading grouped together.

   | Conversation View: <br> (sets whether emails of the same topic are grouped together) | ◉ Conversation View on <br> ◯ Conversation View off |
   |---|---|

5. Check On the **Signature** button and enter a signature that you want to appear at the end of all of your Gmail emails.

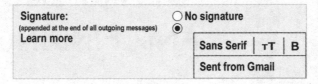

**A CLOSER LOOK**

Click on the Settings icon and select options for how the email headings are displayed in your Inbox. The options are **Comfortable**, **Cozy,** or **Compact,** and these determine how much space is included between each item.

# More Web-based email options

Some other Web-based email services are:

- Yahoo!
- Outlook.
- AOL Mail.
- GMX.
- ProtonMail.

**BRIGHT IDEA**

When you send an email to a family member or a friend, do you ever worry that it is has not arrived, particularly if you have attached a photo or a document? To give yourself peace of mind, copy it to yourself when you send it (enter your own email address in the **Cc** box, beneath the **To** box) and then you will know when it has been delivered through the system.

# 11 SEARCHING AND FINDING

## Making the most of Google

When your service becomes a generally accepted verb, i.e. "I'll just Google that," then you know that you have entered mainstream usage. Google has undoubtedly done that and it's the number one choice for a majority of people when they are looking for items on the Web. And there is good reason for this: the Google search engine is undoubtedly very good and will serve you well in all of your Web searching activities. However, Google is now a massive global company and there are a lot more arrows to its bow than merely searching. Here are 11 other uses for Google, all of which can be accessed directly from the Google Search page:

1. **Finding your way around.** Google Maps is an excellent option for finding locations and directions, whether it is near or far. Simply type a location, or a particular site, such as a tourist attraction, into Google and a map should be displayed in the search results. On the Maps page there will be a **Directions** button. Click on this to get directions to the location, either from your current location (which will be identified automatically by your device if GPS is On), or from a location that you enter into the **Choose starting point** box. The Google Maps app can also be downloaded for iOS 11 and Android devices.

2. **Translations.** Want to know how to say, "I would like some apples," in Spanish? Or translate something which has been sent to you from a friend overseas? Type the request into Google and the answer will appear on the translation page, complete with an audio button so that you can hear the spoken words. There are also two selection boxes for selecting languages as the source and the translation.

3. **Dictionary.** You need never be stuck for knowing the meaning of a word again. Type the word, followed by "definition," to see a Google dictionary definition.

4. **Math.** There is no need to be a math genius if you have Google at hand. In fact, you will quickly be able to appear like a genius yourself. Type a sum into the search box, e.g. "square root of 256," and the answer will be displayed, complete with a calculator for any calculations that you want to do manually.

5. **Tipping.** Working out the correct tip can be an awkward task, particularly if several people are splitting the bill. Google takes all of the hassle out of this: type in a sum, with the $ symbol, followed by "tip" to see the result. This displays the original bill, the amount of the tip, and the final total. The percentage amount for the tip can be adjusted in the **Tip** box.

6. **Unit conversion.** Converting units from one standard to another used to involve a lot of cards and charts, but no longer. Want to convert miles to kilometers? Easy. Centigrade to Fahrenheit? No problem. Pints to liters? Simple. Just type the required conversion, e.g. "27 Centigrade in Fahrenheit," and Google will do all of the hard work for you.

7. **Currency conversion.** Another useful conversion that Google can do is for currency, displaying the latest exchange rates for currencies around the world. But remember, if you are changing money for a specific currency, you will probably get a lower rate than quoted by Google, as this is not the rate for buying the currency. If you search, "how many Canadian dollars will I get for $100US," you will see the

official rate and also links to foreign exchange companies where you can change your money.

8. **Weather.** Google is an expert meteorologist and can give weather forecasts for locations around the world and also local forecasts for the current day and the week ahead. (There are also numerous weather apps that you can use on your smartphone – try different ones to see which is the most accurate.)

9. **Package tracking.** If you have a package being delivered and it has a tracking number, you can follow its progress simply by entering the tracking number into the Google Search box.

10. **Flight tracking.** Flights can also be tracked, using the flight number, e.g. "American AA 786 to Atlanta." The results will show the scheduled arrival time, any delays, the terminal, and gate number.

11. **Song lyrics.** Never wonder about the lyrics of your favorite songs again. Type "lyrics of" and the name of a song, and the lyrics will be listed.

## Refining your Google searches

Since Google does such a good job searching for items, it is easy to get a bit lazy when defining searches – sometimes Google even seems to know better than us what we are looking for, and can even correct any spelling mistakes and typos. However, there will always be times when what you are looking for is harder to find and does not immediately show up on the first page of search results. To make Google searches even more accurate, there are a few options that you can try:

- **Look for an exact phrase.** In a normal search, Google will look for all of the words in a search query. It does not give any one word prominence over another, and it does not search the words in a particular order. To search for an exact phrase, as it appears in its actual location, use quotation marks around the search words. This instructs Google to look for the exact phrase, rather than just any occurrences of the words.

- **Exclude items.** Sometimes a search query will result in some of the items that you are looking for, but in relation to something that you don't want. For instance, it may be linked to a geographic location that you do not want to include. To solve this, you can exclude certain words by putting a minus symbol (dash) in front of them. So if you do not want search results containing "Canada" to be included, enter "-Canada" at the end of the search query, e.g. "maple syrup -Canada."

- **Use Google's settings.** To refine the way that Google searches and displays results, use the Google settings. Select Settings > Search settings at the bottom right of the Google window. Check On the **Turn on SafeSearch** checkbox to prevent inappropriate or explicit material appearing in search results. Select how many search results to show on the results page (the fewer the number of results, the quicker the page will load) and check on the **Use private results** button to show content that Google thinks is relevant to you, based on previous searches and browsing history.

## It's not just about text

By default, Google searches return a mixture of content under the **All** tab. This is mainly the traditional links to related websites, including a summary of the site, and any related photos and maps.

However, when a search result is displayed, a toolbar below the Search box provides options for viewing specific items related to the search. These are:

- Videos.

- News.

- Maps.

- Shopping.

- More, which consists of Images, Books, Flights, and Personal.

So if you are searching for your favorite movie star, use these buttons to view a wider range of items for each specific category compared with on the **All** page.

---

**BRIGHT IDEA**

Google can also come to the rescue if you have a problem with your PC, laptop, tablet, or smartphone. In fact, it should probably be the first thing you do if something is not working. Enter the problem into Google and look through the results. It is almost certain that someone else will have had the same, or similar, problem and there will probably be a forum discussion somewhere about it. If there is not an obvious solution, try a slightly different search query.

---

## Searching by image

As well as being able to display a range of options from a text search, Google can also search for similar items based on an image. For instance, if you see a photo on the Web that looks familiar but you can't quite place it, you can ask Google to search over the image. You can also use your own images for the **Search by image** function. To use this:

1. Access the Google homepage and click on the **Images** button on the top toolbar.

2. The Google Search box is converted into the **Google Images** Search box. Click on the Camera icon.

3. Click on the **Paste image URL** option. To paste an image URL (its Web address), navigate to the image, right-click on it, and click on the **Copy image location** option (not available in all browsers). Right-click in the **Paste image URL** box and click on the **Paste** option.

4. Click on the **Search by image** button.

5. Google will provide what it thinks is a description of the image and links to other similar items.

6. To search your own images, click on the **Upload an image** button in the Google Images search box.

7. Click on the **Browse** button.

8. Navigate to an image in your file structure and click on the **Open** button to upload it.

9. A description, or best guess, of the image will be displayed and links to other images based on the description provided by Google Images.

---

> CAUTION
>
> The URL of an image is different from that of the website on which it resides. It will probably have the same first part of the address, but there will be an additional part that identifies the specific image and where it is stored on the Web. If an image is serving as a link to another Web page, the URL that will be copied will be the one to the page, not the image. Look for a link that ends with an image file format, such as .jpg or .png.

## Speaking your mind – voice searching

Digital voice assistants are the natural progression to being able to search the Web with text searches. Rather than having to type in a search query, a digital voice assistant lets you speak to your device instead, e.g. "Hey Siri, show me the weather for tomorrow," or "OK Google, show me the nearest Italian restaurants." These voice assistants can not only perform Web searches, they can also find items on your PC, laptop, tablet, and smartphone, so they can be used to open apps or play music on your device. Each major operating system has its own digital voice assistant:

- Cortana for Windows 10.

- Google Assistant for Android.

- Siri for macOS High Sierra and iOS 11.

When using a digital voice assistant, there are a few points that should be kept in mind:

- They usually take a bit of time to become trained to your voice. But as the technology becomes more sophisticated, they are becoming better at recognizing voices and accents.

- If you are using them in public, then people around you may become irritated if you are constantly talking to your device. Plus, they will be able to hear exactly what you are doing.

- On mobile devices, digital voice assistants can take up more battery power than if they are disabled.

Digital voice assistants are a great way to save typing, and they can be particularly useful on smartphones where the keyboards are smaller and so it can be harder to accurately type your search requests.

# 7 ways voice search can make your life easier

1.  **Opening apps.** Simply say to your digital voice assistant, "Open Calendar" or "Open Calendar app," and it should do the hard work for you.

2.  **Finding restaurants.** As long as Location Services are turned On on your PC, laptop, tablet, or smartphone, your device will be able to identify your current location and show you a range of services that are nearby. For instance, ask to show the nearest Japanese restaurant, and you should be presented with a list of options of matching places nearby, complete with directions, if needed.

3.  **Checking out the weather.** Just ask what the weather is like for your location to see the forecast. Refine the results by asking for a specific time or date.

4.  **Playing music.** Take the effort out of playing music on your device: just ask your digital voice assistant to play a certain track, and it will become your personal music presenter.

5.  **Sending text messages.** For digital devices, the voice assistant can be particularly useful for certain tasks when you cannot always access the keyboard. One of these is sending text messages with your voice rather than typing it. Ask your digital voice assistant to send a text message to a specific person. If they are in your address book they will be displayed. (If they have more than one number associated with them, you will be asked which one to use.) After you have spoken the message, it will appear at the top of the screen, with a prompt to send it. Just say "Send," and that's it, job done.

6. **Getting directions.** If you are out and about, getting directions to places is a few words away with your digital voice assistant. Ask for directions to a certain location and a map will be displayed with a route that can be followed. Tap on the **Go** button to start following the route, which changes as you progress along it, until you get to your destination.

7. **Random queries.** All digital voice assistants have their own "personality," depending on which company they have been produced by. In general, this has no affect on the search results, but some interesting results can be displayed if you ask random questions. For instance, ask a voice assistant about a product from a rival and it will remain loyal to its own brand, e.g. "Which is better, Apple or Google?" Voice assistants also show a certain sense of humor, depending on the question. Try asking them what they look like, or how old they are to get an idea of the particular personality for each voice assistant.

# Talking with Cortana

The Windows 10 digital voice assistant is called Cortana. To enable it to be set up properly, the language and region on the PC or laptop have to match, e.g. United States and English (United States), as does the speech language. To check this:

1. Access Settings > Time & language and click on the **Region & language** option in the left-hand panel.

2. Ensure that the **Country or region** option matches the one under **Languages**. Ensure the required language is set to **Windows display language**. If not, click on the required language and click on the **Set as default** button.

Region & language

Country or region

Windows and apps might use your country or region to give you local content

| United States | ∨ |

Languages

You can type in any language you add to the list. Windows, apps and websites will appear in the first language in the list that they support

+  Add a language

English (United States)
Windows display language

3. Access Settings > Time & language and click on the **Speech** option in the left-hand panel.

4. Set the **Speech** language as the same as for region and language.

Speech language

Choose the language you speak with your device

English (United States) ∨

## Checking the microphone

Before using Cortana, it is a good idea to check that the microphone on your PC or laptop is working properly. (This can also be done when you access Cortana for the first time.)

1. Access Settings > Time & language and click on the **Speech** option in the left-hand panel.

2. Under the **Microphone** heading, click on the **Get started** button.

Microphone

Set up your mic for speech recognition

Get started

3. Follow the microphone wizard to set up the device's microphone. This involves speaking a specific phrase to check that the microphone can hear you properly. (If there is an issue with the microphone, a **Troubleshooter** wizard will appear to try and resolve the issue.)

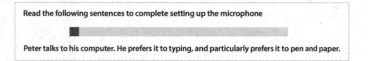

Read the following sentences to complete setting up the microphone

Peter talks to his computer. He prefers it to typing, and particularly prefers it to pen and paper.

## Getting started with Cortana

Once Cortana has been set up, it can be accessed from the Search box to the right of the Start button.

1. Click on the **microphone** button to activate the voice search function of Cortana.

Type here to search

2. Speak your query, e.g. "Open calendar," and the relevant app will open.

3. Cortana can also be used to search for items over your computer, e.g. say "Open documents folder."

4. Web related searches can also be done, in which case the Microsoft Edge browser will open with details for the requested item, or the item will be displayed in the Cortana search panel, e.g. "Show me today's news." Items in the search panel have links that can be used to access more details on the Web.

## Text searches with Cortana

Cortana is not just a digital voice assistant and has some powerful features that can be accessed using the mouse and keyboard.

1. Click in the **Cortana Search** box.

2. Type a text search in the Search box.

3. Click on these buttons to search over **Apps**, **Documents**, or the **Web**.

4. Click on the **I've got more for you** button to view a range of real-time information from Cortana. This includes the current weather forecast for your location, popular items currently on the Web, news headlines, and transit information.

5. Click on this button in the sidebar to access the **Notebook** area. This contains a range of widgets and also more useful functions performed by Cortana.

6. Click on the **Lists** button to add a new list, such as for groceries.

7. Click on the **Reminders** button to add a new reminder. Click on this button to create a new reminder, including the reminder topic and whether it is in relation to a **Person,**

**Place**, or **Time**. Enter the relevant details and click on the **Save** button. The reminder will appear as a pop-up box when the reminder criteria are matched, i.e. the time of the reminder.

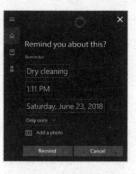

8. Click on the **Music** button to add a music service, such as Spotify or Groove Music, which can be managed through Cortana.

9. Click on the **Eat & drink** button to access options for receiving food, drink, and restaurant recommendations.

10. Click on the **Finance** button to include details from stocks that you are following. Under the **Stocks you're tracking** heading, click on the **Add a stock** button to include it in the results.

11. Click on the **News** button to access options for receiving news headlines.

12. Click on the **Packages** button to track a specific package that is on the way to you. Under the **Packages you're tracking** heading, click on the **Add a package** button and enter the tracking ID of the package.

Packages

See when your packages ship and track their progress as they get to you.

Package tracking cards

On

☑ Notification for your packages

Packages you're tracking

+ Add a package

13. Click on the **Sports** button to get results and news about your favorite teams. Under the **Teams you're tracking** heading, click on the **Add a team** button to include your favorite teams.

Sports

Spanning the globe to bring you the constant variety of sports. The thrill of victory and the agony of defeat. The human drama of athletic competition. This is Cortana's wide world of sports!

All sports cards & notifications

On

Score updates for your teams

On

Show upcoming games and matches

On

Teams you're tracking

+ Add a team

14. Click on the **Travel** button to access options for getting real-time flight details, set notifications for when you should leave for a flight and see what the weather is like for a destination that you will be traveling to.

Travel

Get up-to-date flight status, find out when to leave for the airport, see what the weather's like where you're going, and get other travel details for trips.

Travel cards & notifications

On

Flights

On

Trip plan

On

Hotel

On

# Interacting with Google Assistant

Google's digital voice assistant is called Google Assistant, and is activated with the "OK Google" voice control. It can be used mainly on Android smartphones and tablets. Google devices, such as the Pixel 2 smartphone or the Pixel C tablet, will work very well with Google Assistant and have more features than on some other Android devices. To get started with Google Assistant:

1. If Google Assistant is available on your device, just say "OK Google," or press and hold the Home button.

2. If Google Assistant is available, the **Listening** screen will appear.

3. Speak your query.

4. Google Assistant is designed to be conversational, so that you can ask several related questions, one after another, just as you would when talking to a person. However, each question has to be started with, "OK Google."

5. OK Google can be used to access and manage items on your Android device, such as opening apps ("Open Chrome"), viewing photos ("Show my photos from Hawaii"), or sending an email ("Compose an email to Sarah") – this is done by selecting a person from your device's address book app.

---

**A CLOSER LOOK**

Connected devices in the home is one of the areas that is being actively developed by a number of technology companies. This includes connected devices such as refrigerators, water heaters, laundry machines, and dishwashers. These devices interact with a digital device such as a smartphone, usually with an app that is developed by the connected device's manufacturer. The device can then be controlled through the connected device's app, e.g. you can set a time for your heating to come on or turn up the temperature on your refrigerator. Some of these devices can also be controlled by digital voice assistants, so you can control a device simply by giving a voice command such as, "Turn on the dishwasher." GE is one company that produces connected devices which can be used in conjunction with OK Google, although it requires going through a third-party device called Geneva Home. But if this is in place, you could turn up your oven by saying, "OK Google, ask Geneva Home to set the oven timer for 20 minutes." It may all sound a bit science fiction, but the future is here!

# Getting going with Siri

Apple's digital voice assistant is called Siri. Although it is available on macOS desktop and laptop computers, it is most effective on iPhones and iPads. There are a number of settings that can be applied for Siri, before you start using it.

1. Access Settings > Siri & Search.

2. Drag the **Listen for "Hey Siri"** button to On. This enables Siri to be activated simply by saying "Hey Siri" from any screen.

3. To maximize the accuracy of "Hey Siri" tap on the **Continue** button to complete the "Hey Siri" wizard.

4. Say, "Hey Siri" and repeat this two more times.

5. Say, "Hey Siri, how's the weather today?"

6. Say, "Hey Siri, it's me."

7. Tap on the **Done** button to complete the set up wizard.

8. On the Siri settings page, drag the **Press Home for Siri** button to On. This enables Siri to be accessed at any time by holding down the Home button.

9. Drag the **Allow Siri When Locked** button to On to access Siri even when the device is locked.

10. Tap on these buttons to make selections for the **Language**, **Siri Voice**, and **Voice Feedback** used by Siri.

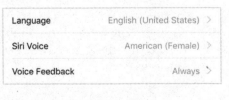

## Using Siri

Once Siri has been set up, it can be accessed by the methods specified in the Settings app, e.g. by saying "Hey Siri" or pressing and holding on the Home button. Both methods produce the Siri query screen.

1. Speak your query, such as, "Open the Mail app."

2. If no query is made, Siri offers some suggestions about what to ask.

3. For some items, Siri will ask questions about what to do next. For instance, if you ask to see unread emails, Siri will tell you how many there are and ask if you want all of them to be read. A certain degree of conversation can be used here; for instance, you can reply, "No, just read the most recent email."

4. If "Hey Siri" is not used, tap on the Siri icon at the bottom of the screen to make another query.

**A CLOSER LOOK**

On a Mac using macOS High Sierra, Siri can be set up in System Preferences > Siri and accessed from the Siri icon on the Dock.

# 12  SOCIAL MEDIA

Facebook is undoubtedly a phenomenon of the digital age. One of the original social networking sites, it has surpassed all of its close competitors to become the starting point for millions of people looking to keep in touch with family and friends online, share news, see what is happening around the world, and much more.

Like a lot of the best ideas, the concept of Facebook is a simple one: people register on the site for free at *facebook.com* (the tagline on the Facebook homepage is "It's free and always will be"), and then they have their own page on which they can post text, images, videos, and links to other parts of the Web. At the core of Facebook is the ability to connect with other Facebook users and become their friends. Once you have done this, anything that you post can be seen by your friends and vice versa.

## A CLOSER LOOK

To set up a Facebook account, you need to provide your first name, surname, cell phone number or email address, and a password. You are also asked to provide your date of birth, which is then used to alert your Facebook friends when it is your birthday so they can send you birthday wishes.

The idea behind Facebook may be simple, but it is executed with great clarity, efficiency, and power. For many people, it is their main means of communicating with family and friends and getting news updates.

## There's always a downside

As with anything that is very successful, there are undoubtedly some negative aspects about Facebook and the way people use it. These include:

- **Issues of social exclusion.** This is a particular problem for young people, but it can affect anyone. Facebook can sometimes appear like a competition, with people trying to get the most friends or most "likes" for a photo that they have posted. If someone has fewer friends than their peers or do not collect as many "likes" when they post something, it can lead to them feeling left out and excluded from their social circles. This may not be the actual case, but if someone feels this then it can lead to significant problems.

- **Facebook image.** A similar problem to social exclusion is that of people becoming too concerned about their own self-image on Facebook. This results from looking at photos of other people that appear to portray the perfect lifestyle, whether it is in relation to their own appearance or their personal success in terms of their job, their car, or their latest holiday. This type of portrayal may not always be accurate, but it can have a negative impact on some people if they feel their life does not match up to the Facebook image of their friends.

- **Online bullying or trolling.** Perhaps the biggest issue on all social media is bullying or trolling. It has always been in society, but it has become a lot more powerful through the instant nature of the Internet, and, in some cases, anonymity of the perpetrators. On Facebook it is not uncommon for individuals, or groups of people, to pick on individuals and subject them to terrible online abuse.

- **Overload of information.** The more that you use Facebook, the more you may realize that people have a lot to say. Added to this are items that your friends may have liked or shared. You may soon feel that you spend too much time just looking through the new items on your newsfeed timeline. Also, since Facebook is available on all mobile devices, it is easy to fall into the trap of regularly checking your Facebook timeline to see the latest posts and news. This can become very time consuming, and it can get to the point where the amount of information can be too overwhelming. To reduce this, consider how many friends you have on Facebook, and also limit yourself to checking it only at specific times of the day, perhaps once in the morning and once in the evening.

- **False and fake news.** False and fake news has become the scourge of modern communication. The Internet, and particularly social media, is the perfect vehicle for this type of information. False news on social media sites comes in two main forms: individuals simply posting false information about something and organizations promoting false news for their own purposes. Since a lot of this news is based on your own and your friends' preferences, it is easy to fall into the trap of thinking that everything you see on your newsfeed is correct and accurate. This is almost certainly not the case. Never rely solely on Facebook for your news, especially when there are major security alerts or natural disasters. During events such as these, there is a wealth of details posted on Facebook and other social media sites. Some of this is accurate, but a lot of it is false and includes items such as inaccurate reporting of fatalities, photos that relate to a completely different event, and reports of more additional incidents that have not happened. If you are looking to get information during a major incident, check the local or national TV news channels rather than just relying on social media.

> **CAUTION**
>
> A lot of the problems associated with social media have a greater influence on the younger generation, partly because they are the most prolific users of social media, but also because they can be more susceptible to these pressures. If you have grandchildren who may be affected by these issues, try to talk to them as it may be easier for them to talk to you, rather than talk directly to their parents, who may be too close to the issues. It can be a very sensitive and complex area though, so think carefully before you take any action.

# Setting your privacy options

Although it is tempting to dive straight into some of the exciting options that Facebook has to offer, the first stopping-off point should be the Privacy settings, which can be used to determine who gets to see your information on Facebook, and how people can interact with you. To do this:

1. Select the down-pointing arrow on the top toolbar and click on the **Settings** option.

2. Click on the **Privacy** button in the left-hand sidebar.

3. The Privacy section contains a range of options for how people interact with you, e.g. *Who can see my stuff? Who can contact me?* and *Who can look me up?*

**Privacy Setting and Tools**

| Who can see my stuff? | Who can see your future posts? | Custom | ✎ Edit |
|---|---|---|---|
| | Limit the audience for posts you've shared with friends of friends or Public? | | Limit Past Posts |
| | Who can see your friends list? | Friends | Edit |
| Who can contact me? | Who can send you friend requests? | Everyone | Edit |
| Who can look me up? | Who can look you up using the email address you provided? | Friends | Edit |
| | Who can look you up using the phone number you provided? | Friends | Edit |

215

4. For each item, click on the **Edit** button.

5. Click on the settings button for the selected item and choose the selection as required. In general, selecting **Public** is not a good option as it makes this item available to anyone, whether they have a Facebook account or not. If an item is public, it can show up in an Internet search and be accessible from there.

6. Go through all of the Privacy items and make selections accordingly (these can always be changed at a later date). If possible, limit access to most items to family and/or friends.

The more time you spend initially in the Privacy settings, the more time you may save yourself during your Facebook interactions.

---

**A CLOSER LOOK**

Other options on the Settings page include: **Timeline** and **Tagging**, which can determine who can post items on your timeline and who can tag you in their photos without you being aware of it; **Blocking**, which can be used to restrict what people see from your timeline and block messages from specific people; and **Notifications**, which can be used to determine how you receive notifications, e.g. just on Facebook or through email and text messages, too.

---

# Pick your friends carefully

When you first start on Facebook you may think that you will have roughly the same number of online friends as you do in real life. However, due to the power of Facebook, you will soon find that it's possible to have hundreds of friends that you never knew existed!

Finding your first friend is a relatively easy task:

1.  Type a name into the search box to view the matching entries.

2.  Click on the **Add Friend** button.

3.  The **Friend Request Sent** button is displayed. Once the person accepts your request, you have your first Facebook friend!

Even if you only have one Facebook friend, you will soon be sent suggestions for more potential friends. This is because Facebook will look through your friend's friends and automatically suggest that you may want to be friends with them, too. This works well with family members and close friends, and it is a good way to quickly find and add these people to your list of friends.

---

## CAUTION

As a general rule, don't accept a friend request from someone you don't know, and who isn't already a friend of one of your existing Facebook friends. Fraudsters and scammers operate within the social media world in the same way as in other online environments, with a view to conning money out of people or stealing their identity. Make sure you know who all of your friends are, and be careful about the type of information you make available on your Facebook page. Don't share items such as your home address or your mother's maiden name, as these could be used to impersonate you in an online financial transaction. Also, be careful of photos where sensitive information may inadvertently be in the background, such as a debit or credit card on a table behind someone you are taking a photo of.

---

Where suggestions of friends can get a bit out of hand is when you send requests to people you don't actually know, only because they appear as a suggestion. This can just end up as an overload of information — remember, you will see the newsfeed of all of your Facebook friends (if they have given permission for this to be seen by friends). Imagine if you had hundreds, or thousands, of friends in real life and had to keep up with them all. It would be exhausting. The same is very true of Facebook: in the real world you wouldn't ask to become friends with everyone you walk past, so why do it online? It's not a competition, and choosing your friends on Facebook is definitely a case of, "Less (or fewer) is more!"

---

### CAUTION

If there is one thing that you should never post on Facebook, it is the fact that you are going on vacation for a period of time, e.g. "Looking forward to the next two weeks away in Hawaii." This is like an open invitation to thieves, letting them know that your home will probably be empty for two weeks. Similarly, don't post vacation photos until you get back home — thieves do monitor Facebook, and knowing that you are on vacation could be like giving them the keys to your front door.

---

## It's not just about you – deciding how you want to use social media

The clue is in the name, but social media sites, such as Facebook, are designed to be sociable. This means that a lot of information about people is going to be made available online. Before you start using Facebook actively, it is worth taking a bit of time deciding how you want to use it and the type of information that you want to post. This does not just affect you, but also anyone else you include in your posts. For instance, if you have a new grandchild, speak to the parents before posting any photos, as they may want to restrict what is made available online. Similarly, if there is something including one of your friends that you are unsure about, ask them first before you post it to the Facebook community. Also be careful about wishing children of family members a happy birthday on social media — do you really want to broadcast the date of a child's birthday to anyone looking on Facebook? Remember, even the smallest piece of information can help fraudsters build up a profile of someone over time.

# Getting started

When you first start using Facebook, it can seem like an alien world of buttons, links, and icons. Therefore, it is worth taking some time to find your way around. A good starting point is your timeline. This is your own personal area where you can post content and add information about yourself. This is one of the areas to which you can restrict access using the **Privacy** settings. To get started with your timeline:

1.  Click on your account icon on the top toolbar.

2.  Your timeline homepage is displayed.

3.  Click on the **Profile picture** box to add or update your profile photo.

4.  Click on the **Add Cover Photo** button to add a main photo for your timeline.

5.  Click on the **Timeline** button to add posts for your friends to see.

6.  Click on the **About** button to update your profile information.

7.  Click on the **Friends** button to view the people you have become friends with on Facebook.

8. Click on the **Photos** button to view photos you have uploaded to Facebook.

9. To add a post, type in the top text box. Use the buttons below the text to add a background to the post and use the button below the background ones to add additional items, such as tagging other friends, so that the item is added to their timeline, too. Click on the **Post** button to add it to your timeline.

> ### Bright Idea
>
> The box to the left of the **Post** button can be used to specify settings for who can see a post, in the same way as in the Privacy settings. In this way, you can customize each post in terms of who can see it.

The option next to the **Timeline** button on the top toolbar is the **Home** button. This is where you can see all of the items that your friends have posted, including text, photos, and videos. You can also add comments to your friends' posts (if they have given permission for this), and this is a good way to have an online dialog with family and friends.

Home

The three icons to the right of the **Home** button are for:

- **Friend Requests.** This is where you can view and review friend requests that you have been sent. You can choose to **Confirm** the request or **Delete Request**. This will also include friend suggestions from your own friends and suggestions from Facebook for people you may know, based on mutual friends.

- **Messages.** These are messages that have been sent to you from your friends, either individually or via any groups of which you are a member.

- **Notifications.** This includes notification about your friends, such as if someone has changed their profile picture, or if they have posted something for the first time in a while.

## CAUTION

Whatever we do online we leave a record, known as a digital footprint. This may seem insignificant, but over time there can be a huge amount of information about us stored online. This is rarely an issue, but if there is something contentious that has been posted at any time — maybe years earlier — it could still be found and used against you or a member of your family, at a later date. A lot of employers now look through Facebook and other social media sites to check out the posting history of individuals. If you want to hide items from your own timeline, move the cursor over the **Settings** button below a post and under the **Who should see this?** heading, and make the required selection, such as **Only me**. However, this does not guarantee it will be hidden forever — if someone has already taken a screenshot of it then there is little control you have over how it may be used.

# Think twice, post once

There is an old adage for cutting timber, "Measure twice, cut once," and a similar approach should be used with Facebook: "Think twice, post once." This is particularly true if you are annoyed or angry about something someone has posted. It is easy and perfectly natural to want to post an immediate reply in the heat of the moment. While this may be temporarily satisfying, a much better approach is to take some time to consider a more measured reply. Or in some cases, no reply at all may be best. Whatever you do post will not only be seen by the original poster but also all of your friends. Getting into online arguments is known as a "flame war," and it rarely does anyone any good. If you do have an issue with an online post, contact the person privately, through a private message on Facebook or an email, and try and resolve it this way rather than in the full glare of the watching online public.

# Posting is permanent

Consider everything that you post on Facebook as potentially being available to a wider audience than just your Facebook friends — and also being around indefinitely. Even if you delete a post, someone could have taken a screenshot of it (an image of what is exactly on the screen at any given time) and keep it as an image file. It could then be posted online or sent in an email, so the post is always potentially in existence. There are almost daily accounts of public figures such as politicians and celebrities who have tried to delete inappropriate posts from social media, only for them to become widely available because someone had taken a screenshot of them almost as soon as they were published.

---

### BRIGHT IDEA

To capture a screenshot on a Windows 10 PC, press the PrtSc, or PrtScr, (print screen) button at the top of the keyboard, usually to the right of the F12 button; with macOS High Sierra use the Grab utility; on most iOS 11 devices, press the On/Off button and the Home button simultaneously; and on most Android devices, press the On/Off button and the volume down button simultaneously.

---

## What to do if you think your account has been hacked

Social media accounts are susceptible to hackers as they can be a goldmine for them in terms of direct contact with people and potential access to personal information. To try and ensure this doesn't happen, take a few security precautions:

1. Create a strong Facebook password with a minimum of eight characters, containing upper and lowercase letters, numbers, and symbols. Don't use easily guessed items such as family name or pets' names, and don't store your password online or somewhere it can be easily accessed.

2. Never answer emails or text messages asking for your login details, even if it appears to come from Facebook. This is known as phishing and is just a scam to try and steal your identify.

3. Log out whenever you finish using Facebook, particularly if you share the computer with other people.

4. Never click on suspicious looking items within Facebook itself, even if they appear to come from a friend. This could be a sign that their account has been hacked.

5. Set up extra security. This can be done within Settings > Security and Login. Under the **Setting Up Extra Security** heading, click on the **Edit** buttons for the required items.

| Setting Up Extra Security | | |
|---|---|---|
| 🔔 **Get alerts about unrecognized logins**<br>We'll let you know if anyone logs in from a device or browser you don't usually use | | Edit |
| ◉ **Use two-factor authentication**<br>Log in with a code from your phone as well as a password | | Edit |
| 👥 **Choose 3 to 5 friends to contact if you get locked out**<br>Your trusted contacts can send a code and URL from Facebook to help you log back in | | Edit |

If your account has been hacked, the first thing that you may know about it is if one of your Facebook friends gets in touch to say that strange things keep appearing on your timeline, such as inappropriate ads. (Similarly, if you see this on a friend's timeline, contact that person to let them know.) If you think you have been hacked, the Facebook Help pages can take you through a step-by-step process to identify and solve the problem. If possible, have the phone number and email address that is associated with the account on hand. Access the Help pages from the **Help** link on the bottom toolbar of any Facebook page. Under **Privacy and Safety** on the top toolbar, click on the **Hacked and Fake Accounts** option. The **Hacked and Fake Accounts** section has information about dealing with **Hacked Accounts, Impersonation Accounts, and Fake Accounts**.

| Privacy and Safety | Policies and |
| --- | --- |
| Your Privacy | |
| Staying Safe | |
| Keeping Your Account Secure | |
| Unfriending or Blocking Someone | |
| Hacked and Fake Accounts | |

## BRIGHT IDEA

If your account has been hacked so that you can't log in, or you can't log in for another reason, the Facebook Help Center can be accessed without having to log in, at *facebook.com/help*. Click on the **I can't log in** button on the homepage and follow the steps for trying to restore your account.

# Be a great Facebook communicator with Messenger

In addition to your timeline and homepage, Facebook also has its own built-in messaging app, Messenger. This can be used to send messages to individuals or groups, either through Facebook or by using the Messenger app on an iOS 11 or Android device. To use Messenger within Facebook:

1. Click on the **Home** button and click on the **Messenger** option in the left-hand sidebar.

   - Mark Scott
   - News Feed
   - Messenger

2. Click on this button to start a new message.

3. Select one of your friends to send a message to.

   | ⚙ | Messenger | ✎ |
   | --- | --- | --- |
   | 🔍 | Search Messenger | |

4. Type the message in the text box at the bottom of the screen and click on the **Send** button.

To: sa|

Contacts

Sara Scott

## Using live chat

Messenger also has a live chat feature, where you can communicate with your friends and see who is available. To use this:

1. The live chat panel is available at the right-hand side of any page within your Facebook account. Click on the **Turn on chat** option to activate it.

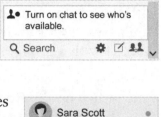

2. A dot next to someone's name indicates that they are online and available to chat.

3. Click on someone's name to start a new chat with them.

4. When you get a reply to a message, it appears as a notification at the bottom of the live chat window.

5. To turn off live chat, click on the **Settings** button at the bottom of the window and click on the **Turn Off Chat** button.

# Facebook is more fun with groups

Facebook is not only great for one-to-one communication, it is also excellent for group chats with family members and people with the same interests or hobbies. Groups can be easily set up and managed by any Facebook user:

1. Click on the **Home** button and click on the **Groups** option in the left-hand sidebar.

2. Click on the **Create Group** button.

3. Enter a name for the group in the **Name your group** box. Click on the **Add some people** box and type the names of Facebook friends that you want to include in the group. (These people have to accept the invitation before they

become part of the group.) Click on the **Create** button to create the group.

Once a group has been created, it can be used to communicate with the group members in a similar way as for individuals. To interact with a group:

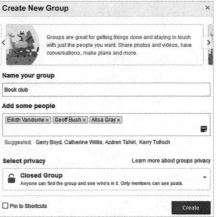

1.  Click on the **Home** button and click on the **Groups** option in the left-hand sidebar.

2.  Any groups that you have created, or joined, will be listed. Click on a group to view its details.

3.  Click in the text box to write a message to the group.

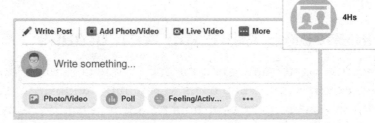

4.  Messages from group members appear in the group time-line, and each one appears in the Chat panel when it is posted.

Facebook etiquette is always important when you are posting messages, and perhaps more so when you are a member of a group. Try following some simple rules to ensure the group operates smoothly.

1.  Be respectful of other people's views and opinions. You may not always agree with them and while discussion and constructive debate is good, being negative or rude is not.

Always think about what you are posting and the effect it could have on other people.

2.  Be careful with humor. Something that you may think is hilarious may be offensive to someone else. If in doubt, don't post it.

3.  Be responsive to questions. If someone asks a specific question, such as, "What time shall we meet tomorrow?", it is polite to send some form of reply.

4.  Don't try and dominate the group – give everyone a chance to have their say and don't feel that you always have to have the last word.

## Don't always leave it to Facebook – using the personal touch

While Facebook has revolutionized the way that we communicate, it should not be allowed to take over our lives to the point where it is the only way in which we keep in touch with family and friends. Don't forget the old fashioned personal touch – perhaps a phone call or speaking to someone in person! One good example of this is the birthday function on Facebook. Whenever it is someone's birthday, you will get a reminder with a link to their timeline so you can wish them a happy birthday. While this can result in dozens of birthday wishes, it can end up feeling a bit impersonal, as if people are only sending their birthday wishes because they have been reminded by Facebook. Instead of doing this, or perhaps in addition, keep all important birthdays in your address book (online or hardcopy) and send a physical birthday card or even phone the person on their birthday and wish them a happy birthday. Social media can be great for keeping people together, but we should not let it take total control.

# Other social media options

Even though Facebook is the most widely used social media service (over 2 billion active users in 2017), there are several other options offering a range of functions:

## Twitter

Twitter is another very popular social media platform that enables users to post short messages (tweets) of up to 280 characters, including photos and videos. Popular topics become "trending" by adding hashtags (#) to posts. This is an excellent way for publishing views and opinions, but it can also be open to abuse in the form of online bullying and trolling.

## Google Hangouts

Hangouts is Google's version of Facebook but is handicapped somewhat because it can only be used with a Google Account.

## SnapChat

SnapChat can be used to share photos and video for short periods of time: they appear on the recipient's screen and then disappear (although they can be saved if the recipient takes a screenshot of the item).

## Pinterest

Pinterest is a sharing site where people pin notes about hobbies and interests on their own pinboards. Friends can then look at other people's boards to see what has been pinned. It is a good way to share information, such as recipes or reviews.

## Instagram

Instagram is a popular photo-sharing site: users post photos and other people can then follow them to see what they have published. It is particularly popular for following celebrities and their activities.

# Don't forget to log out

If there is one thing that you should always do whenever you finish a session using any social media service, it is to log out! If you don't, you are leaving yourself open to anyone being able to access your account and post information in your name. This can cause considerable anxiety and disruption, so make it part of your routine to know where the log out button is, and always click on it at the end of a session. (Also, make sure your devices are secured with a Lock screen password to stop people being able to access them in the first place.) For Facebook, the Log Out button can be accessed from the down-pointing arrow at the right-hand side of the top toolbar.

# 13 COMBATING ONLINE DANGERS

## Online threats

In terms of malicious online activity, the bad news is that there are numerous ways that hackers, fraudsters, and scammers can try to compromise your computing devices, steal money from you, or commit identity theft. However, the good news is that if you are aware of the dangers then you can take a range of security measures to combat these online dangers.

### Beware of the phishers

Unfortunately, online phishing is not something conducted on riverbanks with rods, although the perpetrators are equally intent on trying to hook their prey. Phishing is the act of trying to get people to divulge personal details of online accounts, such as usernames, passwords, and financial details, e.g. bank accounts. Once the fraudsters have these details, they can then access your account by pretending to be you.

Phishing is usually conducted via an initial bogus email stating that there is a problem with a certain type of account and asking you to click on a link in the email to fix the problem. These types of emails could include the following:

- A message from a cloud service, such as iCloud, saying that your account has been locked.

- A message from PayPal or eBay saying that your account has been suspended due to irregular activity on your account.

- A message from a bank saying that your account has been suspended.

- A message from a courier service saying that there is a problem with a delivery that they have for you.

The dangerous part of the email is the link that claims to be where you can verify your account details.

**Dear Customer,**

We have encountered a difficulty verifying your account information. Error code: (err21q86599)
Due to a random verification on our customer's accounts we have noticed that your password has been entered more than 5 times wrong. Please follow the link below to fix this issue and prevent account service suspension:

**Verify my account**
OR
https://www.paypal.com/cgi-bin/webscr?cmd=flow&SESSION=Gf82c6gPXL

If you have an account with the service mentioned in the email or are actually waiting for a delivery, then it can be worrying to think that your access has been blocked. However, whatever you do, don't click on the link in the email. No reputable company will ask for your details online in this way.

Before taking any action (which should just be to delete the email), there are a number of options to check the validity of the phishing email:

1. Do you actually have an account with the organization mentioned in the email? Phishing is not an exact science and millions of emails will be sent out, hoping that some will match the accounts of the people who receive them.

2. Check the sender's actual email address. When it arrives in your Inbox, it will probably appear only as the company's

name, e.g. PayPal, Apple, eBay etc. Click on the name (or right-click on it) to view the actual email address. This may be considerably different from what you would expect if it were actually from the company it claims to be.

3.  Check the language, spelling, and grammar in the email. Frequently, this is of a much lower standard than you would expect from a genuine email from these types of companies.

4.  Go online to look at the company's actual website. Do this by typing their website address into a Web browser, not by following any links in the email. If there is a genuine problem, then this may be highlighted on the company's website.

5.  Search the Web to see if other people have had the same email. There will undoubtedly be a lot of similar instances, often with information about what to do with the email, i.e. delete it.

6.  Check the US government website at *us-cert.gov* for up-to-date information about phishing and advice about what to do about it. It is also possible to report phishing emails to *phishing-report@us-cert.gov*.

---

**CAUTION**

It is worth repeating that no genuine organization will ask for login details or financial information via an email. Regardless of how worrying or urgent the details in a phishing email may seem, take a few minutes to assess whether it is genuine or not, and then take the appropriate action of ignoring and deleting it. Don't be tempted to reply to the email either. This will just encourage the phishers to contact you further as they will know that it is an active email address. Also, don't reply to any similar messages that you receive via text message on your smartphone, as this is another method used by phishers.

---

---

**A Closer Look**

No blame should be attached to any of the organizations that are mentioned in phishing emails. They have no more control over what is sent out in their name than the recipients do.

## Catching a virus

There is a range of malicious software that can infect your computing devices and compromise them in various ways. One of the original ones is the virus. This is a malicious software program that installs itself on the victim's computer without their knowledge. When it is opened (this is usually done automatically by the code within the virus itself, and sometimes it can be a considerable length of time after it has initially infected the machine), the virus then conducts its malicious mission. This can cause a range of problems, including:

- The operating system fails to start.

- All files of a certain type are deleted.

- Folders disappear without explanation.

- All contacts in an address book are sent random emails.

- Frequent, unexplained error messages.

- Slow performance and frequent crashes and freezes.

- Apps launch on their own.

Any erratic or unexplained behavior that suddenly starts happening regularly could be an indication that your device has a virus.

Viruses usually get onto devices through clicking on an infected attachment in an email or a link to a website containing the virus. If in doubt, don't click on links in emails from sources that you don't know. A virus could also be sent from your known contact, if it has already infected their device. If you suspect that this is the case, contact the person to confirm that they have sent the email that you have received.

> ### STAYING SECURE
>
> Some viruses can be spread through flaws in an operating system (Windows 10, macOS High Sierra, iOS, or Android), which can be exploited whenever the device is connected to the Internet. Because of this, it is important to install operating system updates whenever they are released, as they frequently contain fixes (patches) for any security issues that have been identified. This does not guarantee protection against all viruses, but it is the best defense in terms of your operating system.

## Worming their way in

Worms are similar to viruses but a bit more proactive. They operate by spreading themselves automatically from computer to computer over the Internet. They can perform similar destructive and irritating tasks to viruses. One of their specialties is to replicate — via email — by using the user's address book to send itself to all of the contacts. As with viruses, a strange email from one of your contacts could be a sign that they have a worm — don't click on anything in the email and contact the sender.

> ### STAYING SECURE
>
> Trojans are frequently hidden in innocent-looking apps such as games. In general, apps from recognized app stores, such as the Microsoft Store, Apple's App Store, and the Google Play Store, are subject to more checks than apps from third-party sites or those installed from CDs/DVDs. However, this does not mean that they are immune from Trojans, but it is better to download apps from a recognized store.

## Beware of the Trojans

Like the Wooden Horse of Troy that was presented as a gift but housed enemy troops inside, a computer Trojan is a seemingly innocent app that contains malicious software inside it. When the app is opened the Trojan is released. Trojans tend to have a different purpose to viruses and worms: they are more intent on gathering information from your device. For instance, they may copy all of the keystrokes used by the user, thus being able to find out usernames and passwords. They may also try and obtain your debit or credit card details by generating false advertisements for products, such as anti-virus software (which of course don't exist).

## Spyware is watching you

Similar to a Trojan, spyware tracks what you do on your computer and also on the Internet (known as keylogging). This information is then sent to the distributor of the spyware so that they can use it in various undesirable ways, such as sending you advertisements for products based on your Internet activity. Not only are the advertisements usually fake, they are also a means of obtaining debit and credit card details.

---

### A CLOSER LOOK

Another form of software attack is known as Denial of Service (DoS). This is when an organization's website is bombarded with so many page requests, i.e. people trying to access it, that it can't cope and crashes. This is computer hacking on an industrial level and is frequently targeted at high-profile companies and organizations. If your favorite website is suddenly unavailable, it may have been subjected to a DoS attack.

---

## Holding your data for ransom

A particularly nasty type of Trojan is known as ransomware. This involves the Trojan freezing some, or all, of the files on your computer so that you cannot access them. In some cases this may be certain types of files, such as word processing documents, but on occasions it could mean that you cannot log in at all. Once a ransomware attack has been performed, there will be a pop-up message to alert the user to what has happened and how they can unlock their device, usually by sending a payment to obtain a digital key to unlock the device. Frequently the key does not exist, and the payment is never seen again.

### A Closer Look

Ransomware is frequently targeted at large organizations where numerous computers are locked simultaneously and a fee is demanded for unlocking each device.

# Staying protected

So, with all of these nasty threats in the online world, how do we keep ourselves safe? The good news is that there are numerous companies who provide excellent anti-virus protection. However, the hackers and fraudsters usually manage to stay one step ahead of the good guys, and you can never be 100% safe all of the time. But with a robust security regime, you will give yourself the best chance of a safe and secure computing environment. Some general steps to take:

- Use anti-virus software to identify any malicious software on your device.

- Use a router with a built-in firewall to stop malicious items accessing your device over the Internet. (Check the specifications of the router before you buy it to see if it has a built-in firewall.)

- Use a software firewall on your computer for detecting malicious items trying to enter your computer via the Internet.

- Be aware of new viruses. Anti-virus software sites, such as McAfee and Norton, usually have news about the latest viruses.

- Never download apps from the Internet if you are unsure about their origin.

- Never follow links in emails from senders you don't know.

## STAYING SECURE

One way that fraudsters draw Web users into malicious websites is through the use of fake celebrity sites. These sites look as though they are related to celebrity names, but they are fake, and the links and images on them can contain viruses and other forms of malicious software. Every year, McAfee, the Internet security firm, conducts research into the top celebrity names that are used for these types of sites. Search "dangerous cyber celebrities" at their website *mcafee.com*, or perform the same search over the Internet. (Obviously, it is not the celebrities themselves that are dangerous, just the malicious activities done in their names.) Be particularly wary of any downloadable content on celebrity websites.

## Using anti-virus software

Anti-virus software is one answer to the computer hackers, but it is fighting a never-ending battle with the hackers frequently one-step ahead. Anti-virus software is installed on your device and then scans through your system looking for viruses, worms, Trojans, spyware, and ransomware. When it finds a malicious item, it will try to disable it and give you the chance to remove it. Scans can be set to be performed automatically at specific times, e.g. at 8:00 a.m. every morning, or they can be performed manually at any time. Some anti-virus software is free, while other options charge an annual or monthly fee. The reason for this is not only the initial cost of the software, but also for the updates it receives on a regular basis (usually at least once a day) to fight new viruses as they are released and identified. Some of the top anti-virus software includes:

**Paid-for**

- **McAfee** (*mcafee.com*) – A well established anti-virus brand that offers a range of several products.

- **Norton** (*norton.com*) – Another long-term anti-virus player.

- **TotalAV** (*totalav.com*) – Excellent value and products that cover Windows PCs, Mac, iOS, and Android.

- **Scanguard** (*scanguard.com*) – A range of products for Windows and Mac users.

- **BullGuard** (*bullguard.com*) – Separate packages for anti-virus and Internet security, or a premium option that combines both.

- **Kaspersky** (*kaspersky.com*) – Another well established operator in the anti-virus market, they have options for anti-virus, Internet security, or both combined.

- **AVG** (*avg.com*) – Provides a good range of products for Windows PCs, Mac, and Android users.

---
**CAUTION**

Only install and use one anti-virus product at a time. If you install two or more, they may try and compete with each other, causing inaccurate reporting and your computer to be less efficient and run slowly.

---

**Free**

- **Avast** (*avast.com*) – A long-term provider of excellent free anti-virus software.

- **TotalAV** (*totalav.com*) – A free version of the paid-for package, but powerful in its own right.

- **PCProtect** (*pcprotect.com*) – Another company that has a free version of their paid-for anti-virus software.

- **Panda** (*pandasecurity.com*) – A free trial version offers anti-virus software and also safe browsing, shopping, and banking on the Web.

> **CAUTION**
>
> Anti-virus software should be run every day on your PCs or laptops. However, this can sometimes slow them down, and it can get slightly annoying when they are performing a scan. Despite this, waiting a few minutes while your anti-virus software is checking your device is a lot better than the alternative of being infected by malicious software.

## Windows anti-virus with Defender

For Windows users, there is a built-in anti-virus option that also provides a free firewall to protect against malicious software accessing your PC. This is known as the Windows Defender. To use it:

1. Access Settings > Update & Security.

2. Click on the **Windows Defender** option in the left-hand panel.

   ⬢ **Windows Defender**

3. Click on the **Open Windows Defender Security Center** button.

   **Open Windows Defender Security Center**

4. The activity of Windows Defender is displayed.

5. Click on the **Virus & threat protection** option to view general details of the most recent scan.

6. Click on the **Scan history** button to view greater details about the most recent scan, including any current threats.

♡ Virus & threat protection

View threat history, scan for viruses and other threats, specify protection settings, and get protection updates.

🕲 Scan history

No threats found.

Last scan: 10/23/2017 (quick scan)

0      46686

Threats found    Files scanned

Quick scan

Advanced scan

⁰ₑ Virus & threat protection settings

No action needed.

ᘖ Protection updates

Protection definitions are up to date.

Last update: Wednesday, October 25, 2017 4:00 PM

7. Click on the **Virus & threat protection settings** option to determine how the virus checker works. Drag the **Real-time protection** button to On to ensure that Windows Defender checks regularly for viruses and malicious software.

⁰ₒ Virus & threat protection settings

View and update Virus & threat protection settings for Windows Defender Antivirus.

Real-time protection

Locates and stops malware from installing or running on your device. You can turn off this setting for a short time before it turns back on automatically.

 On

8. Click on the **Protection updates** button to see the last time that anti-virus definition files were updated. These are important because these are the files that look for the latest

Threat Definitions

Windows Defender Antivirus uses files called definitions to detect threats. We try to automatically download the most recent definitions, to help protect your device against the newest threats. You can also manually check for updates.

Threat definition version: 1.255.60.0
Version created on: 5:02:13 AM : Wednesday, October 25, 2017
Last update: Wednesday, October 25, 2017 4:00 PM

Check for updates

viruses – if the anti-virus definitions are not up to date then you may miss recent viruses, even if you scan your computer and it appears to be free of malicious software. Click on the **Check for updates** button to perform a manual check for new definitions.

9. On the main Windows Defender Security Center page, click on the **Firewall & network protection** option.

Firewall & network protection
No action needed.

10. The firewall options can be used to activate the Windows Defender Firewall, which helps protect your computer when connected to a network, e.g. when you are connected to the Internet via your home router.

**Firewall & network protection**

View network connections, specify Windows Defender Firewall settings, and troubleshoot network and Internet problems.

🖥 Domain network

Firewall is on.

👥 Private network (active)

Firewall is on.

🖳 Public network

Firewall is on.

11. Click on one of the options and ensure that the **Windows Defender Firewall** button is On.

Windows Defender Firewall

Helps protect your device while on a private network.

On

12. On the main Windows Defender Security Center page, click on the **Device performance & health** option.

**Device performance & health**

No action needed.

13. This lists any security or general issues related to your PC. If there are any issues, click on one of the items to view further details about it, including any action required to fix a problem.

💗 **Device performance & health**

Check that your Windows is up-to-date and if there are any issues impacting your device health. The Health report shows the status of the most recent scan.

📋 Health report

Last scan: 10/27/2017

✅ Windows Update
No issues ⌄

✅ Storage capacity
No issues ⌄

✅ Device driver
No issues ⌄

✅ Battery life
No issues ⌄

# What's the password?

Like taxes, passwords are a necessary evil that we need for our online activities, but they are a bit of drag to create, remember and keep secure. One option is a password manager (see page 242). But if you create your own passwords, it is important to make them as secure (strong) as possible, and also ensure that they don't fall into the wrong hands. Some tips to follow:

- Make passwords a minimum of eight characters long, preferably more.

- Use a combination of uppercase and lowercase letters, numbers, and symbols.

- Don't use obvious words or combinations, such as family names, pets' names, sports teams, and birth dates.

- Pick words at random. For instance, open a book at any page and use the first two words you see as the basis for the password, remembering to use numbers and symbols too. But don't use the words as they are: change the letters around and don't use single words as a password.

- Never share a password with anyone, even family members. Once a password has been shared, it could easily be distributed to a wider audience and fall into the hands of hackers.

- Use different passwords for different online accounts. If one is hacked and its password is compromised, the other accounts should still be secure.

- Try and change your passwords regularly in case hackers manage to compromise them. It is recommended that this is done every 90 days, but in reality if you do it once a year, this is probably more than most people. Do this for all of your passwords, e.g. those for locking your device, email accounts, online banking accounts, and social media accounts.

- Don't store a record of your passwords online – if a hacker gets into this, then they have easy access to all of your accounts.

- If you need to write down your passwords, store them away from your computer in a secure location such as a home safe.

## Let the manager take the password strain

Rather than remembering lots of different passwords, particularly if you have to change them for any reason, a great option is a password manager. This is an app that can be installed on your computer or mobile device, and it will remember all of your different passwords. All you need to do is remember one password for your password manager. The password manager stores your passwords and usernames for websites and online accounts and can also usually import passwords from other Web browsers that you use. The first time that you log in to an existing account with a username and password, the password manager should prompt you to remember the details so that this could be the last time that you have to enter them yourself. Also, when you create new online accounts, the password manager should offer to create a new, very strong password and store the details for whenever you go back to that site.

Do some research into password managers at *cnet.com* or *pcmag.com*. You can also try LastPass at *lastpass.com*, Dashlane at *dashlane.com*, and 1Password at *1password.com*. Regardless of the password manager that you choose, look for the following features:

- Encryption. Make sure that the password manager encrypts your passwords and saves them securely so that even if the password manager site was hacked, your passwords will be safely encrypted.

- Cross-device compatibility. Choose a password manager that will work on different browsers and different devices, i.e. make sure it will work on your iOS 11 iPhone and also your Windows 10 PC.

- Does the password include a password generator? This is used by the manager to create very complex and secure passwords, which it duly remembers for you.

- How much information does the password manager store? Is it just passwords and usernames, or does it include personal information, such as addresses and phone numbers, for use in auto-filling online forms?

- Does the password manager have a free version that can be used to test its features? (Most password managers require a fee to access all of their features.)

# Dealing with identity fraud

Identity fraud is the fraudulent practice of using someone's name and personal details to perform criminal activity while pretending to be the person whose identity they have stolen. It is not confined to online activity, but the Internet has undoubtedly made it easier for criminals and fraudsters to obtain individuals' personal details and then use them online for fraudulent purposes.

The type of information that identity fraudsters are interested in obtaining are:

- Name

- Birth date

- Address

- Social Security number

- Driver's license number

- Utility bills information

- Financial details, such as online banking login details and PIN numbers

- Credit card numbers

- Online usernames and passwords

Although certain pieces of information on their own may seem insignificant, the more the fraudsters can obtain, the more convincing they can be when they pretend to be someone else. Identity fraud can be very distressing for its victims and time-consuming and complicated to fix once it has been identified.

## Preventing identity fraud

The key to preventing identity fraud is to keep your personal information as secure as possible, whether it is online or in the real world. As long as you have a robust security routine, then it will make it much harder for the identity fraudsters and unlikely that you will be held responsible if you do fall victim to this crime. Some steps to take to secure your personal information include:

- Use a micro-shredder to shred all sensitive documents that you are discarding. Identity thieves have been known to go through the trash to find personal documents and can some-times put pages back together if they have been cut up or put through a standard shredder. A micro-shredder can cut paper into strips 6 times smaller than a standard shredder and some models can also shred old credit cards.

- Check your credit score regularly with a credit reporting website. These sites give you a free assessment of your credit rating. If you check it regularly, you will be able to see if there is any unexplained change to it, which could be an indi-cation of identity theft. Three credit reporting websites to look at are Experian at *experian.com*, Equifax at *equifax.com* and Trans Union at *transunion.com*. And you can also get a full, free report of your credit rating once every 12 months from the website *annualcreditreport.com*, which provides reports from these three credit reporting companies. For a monthly fee, these companies also offer more advanced identity theft protection.

- Ensure that your Social Security number is one of your most protected items, as this can open up numerous opportunities for criminals. Don't carry it around with you and don't write it down on any documents except essential official documents.

- If you are buying anything online or performing an online financial transaction, make sure that the website address starts with "https", as this indicates that it should be a secure site. Also, look for a locked padlock icon, as this contains details about the site's security. Click on the padlock to see security details about the site.

  🔒 https://

- Never respond to unsolicited requests for any of your personal information.

- Keep an eye on your utility bills. If any of them are late or do not appear, this could be an indication of identity theft.

- Keep an eye on bank and credit card statements to see if there are any suspicious or unexpected transactions. If there are, contact your bank or credit card provider immediately.

- Don't leave mail unattended for long periods of time. If you are going on vacation, ask a neighbor to pick it up or put your mail delivery on hold.

- Use anti-virus software and a firewall on your computer to keep the information held on it as secure as possible. Also, make sure you always download the latest updates (definitions) to your anti-virus software.

- Keep your digital devices locked with a secure password for the Lock screen.

- Use passwords that are as secure as possible – a minimum of 8 characters with a mix of uppercase and lowercase letters, numbers, and symbols.

- Never use public Wi-Fi hotspots for conducting financial transactions or anything involving usernames and passwords.

- Ensure that any old computing equipment that you get rid of has had all data wiped from its hard drive or reset to its original state for a smartphone or tablet.

- Store any sensitive details in a secure place, such as a home safe.

## Reporting identity theft

If you fear that you have been a victim of identity fraud, it is vital that you take action immediately. Any delay will give the criminals more time to perform transactions in your name, and you may be liable for some of the costs if you suspect identity theft but do nothing about it. The two main things to do are:

1. Report the issue to your local police in case the criminals are known to you and are conducting their fraudulent business in the local area.

2. Report the issue to the Federal Trade Commission (FTC) using their website at *identitytheft.gov*. They will be able to assess your case and, if necessary, issue you with an identity theft report and a recovery plan.

The government website *usa.gov/identity-theft* also has information about dealing with identity theft.

---

**CAUTION**

One way in which you can help keep your personal information private when you are online is to use a browser extension to monitor cookies and trackers that are following you on specific websites. You can then block these to help make your online activity untrackable when online. One of these extensions is Privowny, which can be downloaded to your browser from their website at *privowny.com*.

---

# Online banking security

Online banking gives you greater flexibility in conducting financial activities. However, with this technological flexibility comes the inevitable risk posed from fraudsters trying to steal your money or your financial details. Some areas to be aware of when you have signed up for online financial services include:

1. Never, ever, give out your personal online banking details (username, password or any other login details) to anyone. This is usually done through a fraudulent email that may claim that your account has been compromised or by a phone call from someone pretending to be from your bank. Your own bank should never ask for these details over the phone – unless you have phoned them, in which case they should just ask for certain letters or numbers of your password, e.g. "Could I have the second and fifth character of your password?"

2.   Never engage with a phone call when the caller claims to be someone from a technical support company or a computer company and tells you that they have identified a fault with your computer. They may say that you can buy some software to solve the problem and then ask for your bank and/or credit card details. This is simply a scam to obtain your financial details and, on occasions, to obtain remote access to your computer and compromise your data.

3.   Ensure you have a strong password for any online financial accounts you have. This is true for all computer passwords, but particularly so when there is money directly at stake. The tips in the **What's the password** section should also be used for passwords for online banking.

4.   Ensure that the bank or financial organization has an Online and Mobile Banking Security Guarantee, which should ensure that you are protected from a financial loss if money is fraudulently taken from your account. Make sure that you read this guarantee so that you know the exact details.

5.   Always log out of your online banking account once you have finished using it. Most apps and websites will log you out after a period of approximately 5 minutes, but this could be plenty of time for someone to get hold of your phone or tablet and access your account. (Even if there is a security guarantee, this type of incident may not be covered if it was deemed to be your fault.)

6.   Keep an eye on your account to ensure that there has not been any unusual activity or items that you cannot remember purchasing. Your bank will also monitor the account automatically for unusual activity and may contact you from time to time if they think there has been a suspicious transaction.

It's always good to be a bit cautious and suspicious if anyone contacts you in relation to online banking: if it doesn't feel right then it probably isn't, so hang up or walk away. As with many things in life, if it sounds too good to be true, then it probably is.

---

CAUTION

Investment scams are another area targeted by fraudsters. This is generally done through a phone call or email offering a new, exciting investment opportunity, promising excellent returns and low risk. Even if you decline the offer during the initial call, they may persist and call numerous times. Never undertake any investments as a result of this type of approach and, ideally, try to ignore any calls like this – if you have voice-mail, let it pick up the call.

# Surviving an email hijacking

One way that hackers try and obtain your personal details is by hijacking your email account. If they do this, they could then be able to follow links to items such as your bank accounts and health records, with potentially devastating consequences. To take steps to prevent this from happening, or if you think it has already happened:

1. Run your virus checker and a malware-removal app to identify any malicious software that is on your device. If so, remove it.

2. If you can't log in to your account, this is probably a sign that the hacker has changed the password. Contact your email provider immediately to ensure they are aware of the situation. This also helps ensure that you are not liable for any fraudulent activity conducted by the hackers – the sooner you alert someone, the more protected you will be.

3. If you can log in, change your password immediately. If your account has been compromised, this could prevent the hackers gaining access again, although the damage may already have been done.

4. Check in your **Sent Mail** folder to see if there are any messages there that shouldn't be.      | **Sent Mail**

5. Gmail users can also check recent account activity, which may give you an idea of what has been happening with your account. At the bottom of the Inbox, click on the **Details** link to view recent activity on your account.

Last account activity: 9 minutes ago
Details

**Recent activity:**

| Access Type [ ? ] (Browser, mobile, POP3, etc.) | Location (IP address) [ ? ] | Date/Time (Displayed in your time zone) |
|---|---|---|
| Browser (Edge) Show details | * United Kingdom | 12:04 (0 minutes ago) |
| Authorised Application (445112211283- Show details | United States | 11:53 (11 minutes ago) |
| Authorised Application (450232826690- Show details | United Kingdom | 8 Nov (19 hours ago) |
| Mobile | United Kingdom | 7 Nov (2 days ago) |

6. Send a message to all of your contacts (preferably not from the email account that may have been compromised) to alert them to the situation, suggesting they disregard any messages that claim to come from you until you can confirm that the problem has been resolved.

## STAYING SECURE

Fake email warning messages relating to viruses and malicious software can be very disruptive and time consuming to deal with. For instance, you may receive an email along the lines of, "Hi, I got a weird email from you that I don't think you really sent. Perhaps your email has been hacked and there is unauthorized access to your Inbox. Please email all of your contacts to let them know." As a result of this, you may do as they ask and also change your email address to solve the problem. In reality there is no such problem, and it is just an attempt to disrupt people's online experience. If you receive a message like this or about a specific virus, search the Internet to see if there is mention of this specific problem. There are numerous websites dedicated to reporting on genuine scams and also fake ones. Two sites to try for email scams and a whole host of myths and urban legends about the Internet are *scambusters.org* and *snopes.com*.

# Disposing of old devices

With the pace at which technology moves, it is only natural that hardware devices become obsolete reasonably quickly, or people simply want to upgrade to the latest device. Rather than just throwing them away, there are some better options for disposing of old devices (but there are also some security concerns connected with this, see *Wiping the hard drive* in this section):

- **Sell them.** Online auction sites, such as eBay, are ideal for selling old PCs, laptops, tablets, and smartphones. Make sure you post an accurate description of the device and ensure that it is in good working order.

- **Trade them in.** A number of websites will quote you a trade-in price for your device. Two to try are *wireflytradeins.com* and *nextworth.com*. You may get less from one of these sites than selling it privately, but it takes a lot of the hassle out of it. It is also possible to donate the value of the items to charity.

- **Recycle them.** Numerous companies will take old gadgets off your hands so they can refurbish them and sell them. You will probably receive some payment for your device, and you will know it is being reused rather than going to a landfill. Look at the Expert Environmental website at *environmental-expert.com* and search for "computer recycling" to find the nearest company in your area.

- **Give them to family and friends.** There may be members of your family or friends who could use your unwanted devices. Just ask around, send a group email, or post a group message on Facebook offering what you have.

- **Donate them to charity.** Several charity organizations use old computing equipment for training adults and young people in need. One organization to try is the National Cristina Foundation at *cristina.org*. Click on the **Donate Now** button on their homepage to find charities and schools near you who would be pleased to accept used computers and other technology devices.

## Wiping the hard drive

However you decide to dispose of your old devices, the most important task is to make sure that all of your data has been wiped from the hard drive. If you delete apps and files in your file manager, there will still be a digital footprint that can be accessed by hackers or fraudsters. The most secure option is to wipe the hard drive completely using software that is specifically designed for this. Some to try are:

- Active@KillDisk, free from *killdisk.com* – Use with a Windows PC or laptop.

- DBAN hard drive eraser & data clearing utility at *dban.org* – Another Windows option that can also remove viruses and spyware that may be lurking on your hard drive.

- ShredIt from *mireth.com* – A file shredder and hard drive eraser that can be used for Windows and macOS.

---

**A CLOSER LOOK**

macOS High Sierra also has a utility app that can be used to erase a hard drive. To use this, click on the **Launcher** icon on the Dock and click on the **Utilities** folder. Double-click on the **Disk Utility** app and click on the **Erase** button in the main window. Select a disk in the left-hand panel and click on the **Erase** button.

---

## Resetting devices

For mobile devices, one option is to reset them to their original factory default condition. This will delete anything that has been added to the mobile device, including documents and downloaded apps:

- To reset an iOS 11 device, select Settings > General > Reset and tap on the **Erase All Content and Settings** option.

- To reset an Android device, select Settings > Backup & reset and tap on the **Factory data reset** option.

## The low-tech approach

If you don't want to go with the software approach, you can take matters into your own hands and physically destroy the hard drive (or do both to be doubly sure). Use a hammer, thick nails, a block of wood to put the device on, and safety glasses to protect yourself from any flying pieces of plastic.

---

### BRIGHT IDEA

When you delete something from a PC or laptop (using the Delete key or by right-clicking on it and clicking the **Delete** option), it's gone from the device for good, right? Wrong. Delete only places a file into the **Recycle Bin** (or Trash on a Mac). To get rid of it permanently, right-click on the **Recycle Bin** icon, which should be on the Desktop, and click on the **Empty Recycle Bin** option (Finder menu > Empty Trash on a Mac). To bypass the Recycle Bin altogether, select the item in File Explorer and press Shift+Delete. Click **Yes** in the dialog box to remove the item permanently. However, even when something has been deleted in this way, it can still sometimes be retrieved by specialist software recovering companies. This is why hard drives should be wiped clean before devices are disposed of.

---

# Keeping grandchildren safe online

One of the greatest worries about the Internet and online activity is the adverse effect it can have on children. If you have grandchildren that may use your devices when they visit, this can be a particular concern, and the two main areas to consider are:

- Grandchildren accessing inappropriate content.

- Grandchildren being befriended by undesirable people through social media.

There are ways to limit the possibility of both of these things, but before you do this on your PC, laptop, tablet, or smartphone, it is important to discuss the dangers with your grandchildren and let them know any restrictions that you are putting in place. Hopefully they will have heard this from their own parents and also at school, but it doesn't do any harm to repeat the message.

## Restricting access with Windows 10

All platforms have their own options for children using their systems. For Windows 10 devices:

1. Access Settings > Accounts and click on the **Family & other people** option in the left-hand panel.

2. Click on the **Add a family member** button.

3. Check the **Add a child** checkbox On and click on the **Next** button.

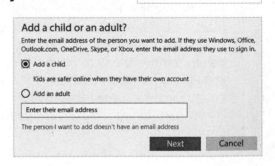

4. Add an email address for the person and click on the **Confirm** button in the next step. An email invitation will be sent to them. Once they accept it, their account will be activated, and they will be able to sign in with their own username and password.

5. Once a child account has been set up, click on it on the **Family & other people** settings page.

6. Click on the child's account and click on the **Manage family settings online** option.

7. The online options enable you to manage a child's account for a variety of activities. Click on the **Recent activity** button to request a weekly report about the child's computer use.

> Recent activity
> Web browsing
> Apps, games & media
> Screen time

8. Click on the **Web browsing** button to restrict the websites that the child can access. Drag the **Block inappropriate websites** button to On.

> Block inappropriate websites
> ⬤ On

9. Click on the **Apps, games & media** button to restrict inappropriate apps and games and set an age range for the type of content that can be accessed.

> Block inappropriate apps and games   We already block kids from mature films and games.
> ⬤ On
> Applies to:
> ▪ Windows 10 PCs & Mobile    ▪ Windows Phone 8
> ⊗ Xbox One
> Limit apps, games and media from the Store
> Child can buy and then download or stream content from stores in Windows and Xbox appropriate for:
> Any age (no restrictions)              ⌄
> Manage what your child can buy in Purchase & Spending
> Ratings
> 18+  Apps For ages 18 and over    18  Film For ages 18 and over    18  Games For ages 18 and over

10. Click on the **Screen time** option and drag the **Set limits for when my child can use devices** button to On. Then select times for each day for when you want the child to be able to access the device.

> Set limits for when my child can use devices
> ⬤ On
> Daily allowance & allowed time
>
> | | Daily allowance | 12 AM | 4 | 8 | 12 PM | 4 | 8 |
> |---|---|---|---|---|---|---|---|
> | Sunday | 5 hrs ⌄ | | | | | | |
> | Monday | 2 hrs ⌄ | | | | | | |
> | Tuesday | 3 hrs ⌄ | | | | | | |
> | Wednesday | Unlimited ⌄ | | | | | | |
> | Thursday | Unlimited ⌄ | | | | | | |
> | Friday | Unlimited ⌄ | | | | | | |
> | Saturday | Unlimited ⌄ | | | | | | |
>
> ▪ Allowed                                    Set a time limit

## Restricting access with macOS High Sierra

To restrict access on Macs with macOS High Sierra:

1. Access System Preferences > Users & Groups.

2. Click on the padlock icon to enable a new user to be added.

    Click the lock to prevent further changes.

3. Click on this button to add a new user. +

4. Enter the details for the new user and click on the **Create User** button.

5. Click on the new user under the **Other Users** heading.

   Current User
   Mark Scott
   Admin

   Other Users
   Sara Scott
   Standard
   Meredith Scott
   Standard

6. Check On the **Enable parental controls** checkbox and click on the **Open Parental Controls** button.

   ☑ Enable parental controls    Open Parental Controls...

7. Click on the **Apps** button to restrict certain apps that can be accessed.

   Apps

8. Click on the **Web** button to restrict or allow specific websites.

   Web

9. Click on the **Stores** button to set age ranges for the type of content that can be downloaded from the App Store, the iTunes Store, or the iBooks Store.

    Stores

10. Click on the **Time** button to set time limits for when the Mac can be used.

     Time

## Restricting access with iOS 11

To restrict access on an iPad or iPhone with iOS 11:

1. Access Settings > General > Restrictions.

2. Tap on the **Enable Restrictions** button.

3. Create a passcode for changing the restrictions (different to any passcode that is used to lock the iPad or iPhone).

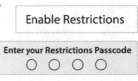

4. Drag the button to Off for any app that you do not want to be available. The app's icon will disappear from the Home screen, and it will not be able to be accessed until the restrictions have been changed.

## Restricting access with Android

To restrict access on Android devices:

1. Access Settings > Users and tap on the **Add user or profile** button.

2. Tap on the **Restricted profile** option.

3. Tap on the **Set Lock** button and enter a method for unlocking the Lock screen, e.g. password, PIN, or pattern.

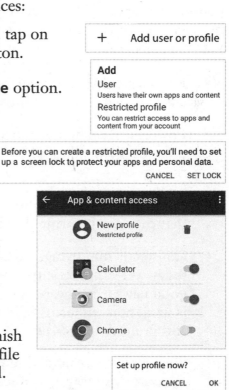

4. Tap on the new profile and drag the buttons On or Off to enable or disable the relevant apps.

5. Tap on the **OK** button to finish setting up the new user profile with the restrictions applied.

257

# 14 KEEPING IN THE PICTURE

## Smartphones vs digital cameras

Digital cameras have truly revolutionized the world of photography and have been so successful at being accepted into the mainstream consumer market that they have virtually replaced their analog predecessors. It is not hard to see why digital cameras have become so popular:

- Photos are instantly available for viewing. No more waiting days or weeks to see photos once they have been developed.

- Powerful. The functionality of digital cameras provides even the most demanding photographer with all of the features they need.

- Good quality. The quality of digital photos is now so good that they can be printed at large sizes with exceptional clarity.

- Constantly improving. What is a state-of-the-art digital camera today will easily be surpassed in a year's time. This may not be good news if you want to always have the best model, but it is great news in terms of bringing improvements to cameras and printing processes.

- Flexibility for using digital photos. Digital photos can be used in a variety of ways: produced as prints, printed on novelty items such as mugs and calendars, sent to family and friends via email, or shared online with social media.

---

## A Closer Look

Digital photos are made up of pixels, which are digital dots that have different colors assigned to them when a photo is captured. The total number of pixels in a photo is calculated by multiplying the dimensions of the photo (height x width). For instance, if the height of a photo has 3500 pixels in it and the width has 4000 pixels, the total number of pixels in the photo is 14,000,000. This is also known as 14 megapixels (MP), and this is frequently the terminology used by manufacturers when they are advertising their products. However, a higher pixel count does not always guarantee a superior photo: the quality of the pixels is also important, and this is determined by the image sensors. This is the element onto which the pixels are captured, and the better the sensor, the more color information can be stored for each pixel, giving a better overall image quality for the photo. The best image sensors are found in digital SLR cameras, and compact cameras tend to have better image sensors than those found in smartphones.

---

The first choice to make in terms of digital photography is whether to use a digital camera or the camera on a smartphone. Both of them have advantages:

## Digital cameras

- **Better quality.** Because digital cameras are mostly larger than smartphone cameras, they have bigger image sensors for capturing better quality photos.

- **More functionality.** Digital cameras often have more features in terms of menu options. This is useful, but it is important to check out these options before you start using a digital camera.

- **More pixels.** Digital cameras usually have a higher pixel count than cameras on smartphones. Pixels are the colored digital building blocks that make up digital photos. The more pixels the larger the photo.

- **Optical zoom.** An optical zoom is one that actually moves the lenses in the camera to enlarge a subject, while retaining the same quality. This is different to digital zoom, which just increases the size of the pixels in the image, in the same way as zooming in on it on a computer screen. A digital zoom is of an inferior quality to an optical one. A lot of digital cameras have both options, but the optical zoom should be used if possible.

---

## A Closer Look

The most powerful type of digital camera is a digital SLR (DSLR) camera. (SLR stands for Single Lens Reflex and refers to how the lenses in the camera operate.) This type of camera has a detachable lens so that you can use different lenses with the camera, e.g. a close-up lens or a zoom lens. DSLRs have a considerable range of functionality so that you can have complete control over the photos you are taking. They can also be used on automatic so that the camera determines the required settings. DSLRs are more expensive than compact digital cameras and are manufactured mostly by traditional camera makers, such as Nikon and Canon.

---

## Smartphone cameras

- **More convenient.** Since most people have their smartphones easily accessible at most times, using its camera can be easier than getting a digital camera out of a bag or camera case.

- **Digital options.** Since smartphone cameras don't have the same range of menu options, they often make up for it with an increased range of digital options, such as image filters that can be applied before a photo is taken.

- **Ease of use.** Smartphone cameras are the definition of "point and press" photography. A lot of compact digital cameras are the same, but there is nothing simpler than tapping on your camera app and tapping the shutter button.

- **Easier to upload photos.** One of the great advantages of smartphone cameras is that photos can be shared almost instantly. Want to share a photo of the latest family member that has just been born? No problem. Take a snap on your smartphone camera, open it in the photos app, tap on the Share button, and select how you want to share it, e.g. email, instant message, or on social media.

## Settings for your camera

Just like using a computing device, it pays to get to know the settings on your digital camera, or smartphone camera, before you start snapping away. Some of the general settings that can be found on most digital cameras and some smartphone cameras are:

- **Flash.** By default this is on automatic, so it is activated when the camera considers the light to be dark enough to need the flash. However, the flash can also be set to On, so that it is fired for every shot, or Off, so that it is never fired.

> **BRIGHT IDEA**
>
> If you are taking a portrait photo of someone outside and the sun is behind them, turn the flash to On, so that it fires when you take the photo. This may seem odd on a sunny day, but it will have the effect of ensuring that the subject's face is well lit, as opposed to being in shadow, which is what would happen without the flash and the sun behind them. This technique is known as fill-in flash.

- **Red-eye reduction.** This is a function that helps reduce the chance of subjects having red eyes in a photo as a result of the flash. It works by using a flash just before the photo is taken, so that the subject's eyes are accustomed to the light. The flash fires again shortly afterwards when the photo is taken.

- **Self-timer.** This can be used if you want to include yourself in a photo. Select the self-timer and select a time period, e.g. 10 seconds. You then have this amount of time to position yourself in the photo until it is automatically captured.

- **White balance.** This is the method by which a digital camera determines the appearance of white, and all other colors are then produced in relation to this. By default, white balance is set automatically, but it can also be set manually for specific lighting conditions, such as indoors or a cloudy day.

- **Filters.** Some digital cameras, particularly on smartphones, can apply filters to photos once they have been taken or, in some cases, before a photo is captured. These are similar to effects that can be applied in photo editing software.

- **Panoramas.** This is a feature that enables the camera to take several photos that create a panoramic view and stitch them together to create a single image. This is usually done by moving the camera slowly through the panorama, and images are captured automatically at different points. The overlapping parts of each image are then combined and the panoramic photo is created.

---

**A CLOSER LOOK**

A lot more effects can be added to a digital photo using photo editing software. This can be simply to improve the lighting or as advanced as removing unwanted items from a photo.

---

# Taking photos like a pro

Photo editing software that can be used to manipulate digital photos is a wonderful thing, as it allows photos to be enhanced and improved in a range of ways. However, this does not mean that you should not try and take the best photo that you can in the first place. A few tips for turning your snaps into photos that the professionals would be proud of:

- **Think about the time of day.** Good lighting is essential for photography, and the best type of light is natural daylight. However, this does mean that a sunny day is always ideal for photography. At midday, when the sun is usually at its highest, the lighting can be too harsh, and there is not enough contrast to get really good photos. The best times of day for taking well-lit photos are an hour after sunrise and an hour before sunset. In photography terms, this is known as the Golden Hour: since the sun is at a much lower angle in the sky, it generates a much richer, more textured light, which is ideal for getting exceptional photos. Sometimes you may have to get up a bit earlier in the morning to make the most of the Golden Hour, but it will be worth it.

- **Be patient.** Sometimes it pays off to wait a few extra minutes in order to get the perfect shot. It could be to wait until the clouds clear and the sun comes out to light up a subject, or when you have set up a shot for a moving item to appear in it, such as a train or car. When looking to capture the best photos, patience is definitely a virtue.

- **Use a grid for composition.** A lot of times when people take photos, they position the main subject in the middle of the frame. This can produce a perfectly acceptable photo, but it will probably not stand out from the crowd. An alternative is to position the main subject in different segments of the frame. Do this by imagining that there is a 3 x 3 grid over the frame and position the subject at one of the intersection points of the gridlines. This is known as the Rule of Thirds. This could result in the main subject being positioned in the top-right sector, or the bottom-left sector. One of the beauties of digital photography is that you can experiment with several photos of the same subject in different

positions, and then review them immediately to see which is the most effective. Some digital cameras and smartphones even enable you to put your own grid over the frame to position your subjects. (On the iPhone and iPad camera, this can be done in Settings > Camera and drag the **Grid** button to On.)

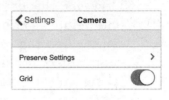

- **Use foreground objects.** A photo of a building or a land-scape can be impressive, but what can take it to another level is by including another object in the foreground. This adds an extra element of interest, and foreground elements can also be used to frame the main subject. For instance, a tree could be used in the foreground of a location, usually at the left-hand or right-hand side, and its branches could be used to frame the main subject. Street lights are another good option as foreground objects.

- **Change the perspective.** Instead of standing directly in front of a subject and taking a photo, try changing your position to capture a different perspective. For instance, get down low to look up at a tall building to emphasize its height, or take a photo at an angle to a subject to give it a different appearance.

- **Count down from 5.** Portraits of people can be one of the most rewarding types of photo, but also one of the most frustrating, as they can be ruined by someone blinking at the wrong time, or a fixed-expression takes away the naturalness of the photo. To overcome this, ask your subject to look down at the ground, as you count backwards from 5. Ask them to look up when you get to zero, and take the photo just as they look up. This should result in a more natural photo as they will not be so self-conscious about staring at the camera lens for several seconds.

---

### BRIGHT IDEA

Some smartphones, including iPhones and several models of Samsung smartphones, have a useful feature that enables you to take a photo using the volume button on the body of the phone. Open the camera app, compose the photo, and press the volume Up or Down buttons to take the shot. This is particularly useful if you are taking a "selfie" (a self-portrait with the camera facing towards you) as you can hold the camera away from you with one hand and still easily take the photo.

---

# Getting photos onto your computer

Once you have captured photos on your digital camera or smartphone camera, it is important to download them onto a computer. This enables you to back them up, edit them, and share them with other people. There are several options for downloading photos:

- Connect your camera or smartphone to your computer using a USB cable. This should be provided when you buy the device. For smartphones, the USB charging cable can be used in this way. When the camera or smartphone is connected, it will show up as an external drive in your file manager. Double-click on it to view the photos, and copy them into a folder on your computer. If you have a photo editing app, it may recognize the fact that a camera or smartphone has been connected and offer to download the images automatically.

- Using a card reader. This is a device that connects to a computer using a USB cable, or directly into the computer's

USB port. The camera's memory card is inserted into the card reader. This can be simpler than having to connect your camera each time.

- Bluetooth. If your computer is Bluetooth-enabled, it should be able to communicate with a smartphone or digital cameras that support Bluetooth. This enables the transfer of files wirelessly over short distances. Both devices have to have Bluetooth turned On and be "paired" with one another so that they can recognize each other.

- Uploading photos to a cloud storage service. Photos that have been uploaded to a cloud service (usually from a smartphone) can then be accessed on a computer and downloaded by accessing the same cloud service.

CAUTION

Because of the capacity of digital camera memory cards and smartphone storage, it is possible to store literally thousands of photos on a single device. However, it is a good idea to delete the photos from the camera once they have been downloaded onto a computer (but make sure they are backed up too, either with a USB flashdrive, or an external hard drive or a cloud storage service). This will make the number of photos more manageable, and you won't feel that you are being swamped by the photos on your camera.

# Sharing photos

All PCs, laptops, tablets, and smartphones have options for sharing photos that have been downloaded.

### Sharing with Windows 10

To share photos from a Windows 10 PC or laptop:

1. Open the **Photos** app.

2. Select a photo or photos.

3. Click on the **Share** button on the top toolbar.

4. Click on a method for sharing the photo(s).

### Sharing with macOS High Sierra and iOS 11

Sharing photos from macOS and iOS devices uses the same process:

1. Open the **Photos** app.

2. Select a photo or photos.

3. Click on the **Share** button.

4. Click on a method for sharing the photo(s).

### Sharing with Android

To share photos from an Android device:

1. Open the **Photos** app.

2. Select a photo or photos.

3. Click on the **Share** button.

4. Click on a method for sharing the photo(s).

# Editing photos

One of the best things about digital photos is that they can be edited, enhanced, and changed using a photo editor. The default Photos apps on Windows 10 PCs, macOS High Sierra devices,

267

iOS 11 devices, and Android devices all have a range of editing options for making your photos even better. In addition, there are several photo editing apps that can be downloaded for all platforms. Some functions to look for in a photo editing app are:

- **Auto-enhancements.** This is usually a one-click or one-tap function that will attempt to enhance all color elements in a photo at the same time, e.g. contrast, brightness, exposure, and lighting. If you don't like the final effect just undo it, either with the Undo button or by pressing Ctrl+Z (Command + Z on a Mac) on the keyboard.

- **Color enhancements.** These functions give you greater control over the color editing in a photo. It is possible to edit elements such as brightness, contrast, highlights, and shadows (areas in a photo that are too light or too dark), while leaving other elements of a photo untouched. For maximum control, functions such as Levels can provide precision editing.

- **Cropping.** Most photos benefit from some form of cropping. This is where the main subject is selected and the background is removed, giving the subject more prominence. The **Crop** tool is usually the same in most photo editing apps. Click on the **Crop** tool and drag it over the area of the photo that you want to keep.

- **Selection.** Some photo editing apps enable you to select areas within a photo, so that editing effects can be applied to this but nothing else in the photo. Selections can be made as a regular shape, such as a rectangle or a circle, or as a freehand selection.

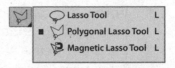

- **Filters.** Most photo editing apps have a range of filter effects that can be applied to photos, e.g. a sepia effect to give the photo an old fashioned appearance or more extreme effects to give an abstract appearance.

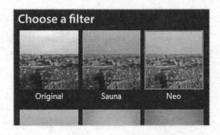

- **Red eye removal.** If photos suffer from people having red eyes, this can be removed by photo editing apps. The red eye area is selected and then replaced with a more natural looking color. A lot of apps have a step-by-step process for this.

- **Special effects.** These can be fun photo effects, such as superimposing rabbit features on someone, or combining photos of two people. Some apps also have special effects wizards that can guide you through step-by-step processes, such as removing an item from a photo, replacing the background, or turning someone's frown into a smile. Other apps specialize in creating collages from your photos.

# 7 free photo-editing apps

- **Adobe Photoshop Express.** This is a slimmed down version of the best-selling photo editing app, Adobe Photoshop. Photoshop Express is designed for use on mobile devices and has a range of powerful editing features including Auto-Fix, blemish removal, color correction, and over

45 special effects. It also has a collage feature for combining all of your favorite snaps.

- **Fotor.** This app not only has a good range of editing features, such as **Enhance** and **Scene effects**, but it also enables users to connect with other Fotor members to collect and share photos in creative ways.

- **Photo Editor** (Axiem Systems, macOS and iOS). For Mac and iOS users, this photo editor offers editing tools and also options for applying special effects, adding stickers to photos, and creating collages.

- **Photo Editor** (Aviary Inc, Windows). For Windows users, this is an easy-to-use and effective photo editor with a good range of editing tools and special effects.

- **PicsArt.** An excellent app for creating fun effects on photos and eye-catching collages. There is a collage maker, drawing tools, and a huge number of stickers that can be added to photos – users can contribute their own stickers, resulting in a massive selection.

- **Pic Collage.** One of the collage-making photo editing apps that is available. This one uses attractive templates and grids, to which you can add your own photos and create impressive photo collages.

- **PhotoFunia.** Another collage-making app, this one has features for adding your photos to famous backgrounds, such as in art galleries or notable landmarks, or adding fun costumes.

---

### CAUTION

Some photo editing apps create copies of your photos when you start editing them. Others use the originals and ask if you want to save the editing effects once you have finished with the process. To ensure that you always have your original photos, make copies of them before you start editing, and use the copies for the editing functions.

# Managing photos

One of the downsides of digital photography is that it is all too easy to collect thousands of photos on your digital devices, and it can then become hard to find specific items. To avoid the equivalent of a digital box of photos, it is important to look at a few management options for your photos.

1.  **Create folders.** Whenever you download new photos from a digital camera, create a new folder and store them here. Give the folder a relevant name, such as "Dad's 90th." On smartphones, folders can be created with the Photos apps, and photos can be moved here by selecting them in the main photos section and then sharing them to folders or albums.

2.  **Add tags or labels to photos.** A lot of photo editing apps have a feature for tagging photos. This involves selecting the relevant photos and then tagging them with relevant titles, e.g. Food. The tags can then be used to find photos within the app's search facility, e.g. type "food" into the search box of a photo editing app, and it will display all of the items that have been tagged with this keyword. It is possible to add numerous tags to photos, which enables more specific searching, e.g. you could search for "food, tortillas" to find photos that only have both of these keywords.

3.  **Delete photos.** Don't be afraid to delete photos. In any batch of photos there are always some that are perhaps not exactly in focus or feature someone with their eyes closed or with the top of their head cropped out. If you are sure you will not use a photo for anything, just delete it to save space.

4.  **Use the app's management options.** Some apps, particularly those on mobile devices, have options for creating automated selections of your photos, based on what the app thinks are the best ones. In the iOS 11 Photos app, this is the **Memories** function, which creates collections of photos based on criteria such as date, location, and people. These can then be viewed in a slideshow, from the **Memories**

button in the Photos app. The Photos app on an Android device sorts photos into categories such as **Places and Things**.

# Printing photos

Due to the number of ways digital photos can be shared online, the need to print them out is not as urgent as it has been with photos in the past. However, it is still popular to have printed photos around the home and there are several options for this:

- **Use a home printer.** This is convenient but can be relatively expensive because of the cost of photo-quality paper and printer ink.

- **Use an online printing service.** There are several online companies that enable users to upload their photos so that they can order printed copies at a range of sizes. Online printing is quick, cost effective, and offers a range of options for gifts and items such as photo books.

- **Use an in-store photo kiosk.** Photo kiosks can be used to print your own photos from a digital camera or smartphone, either by connecting it using a USB cable, inserting a memory card into the kiosk, or using Bluetooth to download your photos. Kiosks do not usually offer the same range as online printing services, but they are a good option for obtaining quick, standard prints.

# Animating photos in one tap

Using the iPhone 8 and iOS 11, it is possible to create your own short animated video clips, simply in two taps. This is known as a Live Photo, and it is activated by tapping on this icon at the top of the camera window. Then, take the photo as normal, ensuring that there is some form of motion, such as someone throwing a pile of leaves. Access the photo in the Photos app and press and hold on it. The photo will play as a short animation. This is done by the iPhone camera recognizing that it is in Live Photo mode and automatically recording everything for a couple of seconds before and after the shutter button is tapped. The result is known as an animated GIF, or Live Photo in Apple-speak.

┌─ **BRIGHT IDEA** ─────────────────────────────

When viewing a Live Photo in the Photos app, swipe upwards to access its editing options. These include Bounce, which plays and rewinds the clip continuously, and Loop, which repeats the clip continuously.

# 15 MUSIC, MOVIES, AND BOOKS

The digital revolution has affected the music industry as much as any other, perhaps more. The introduction of MP3 music players and digital music stores, such as Apple's iTunes Store, has ensured that the music industry has become firmly focused on the online world. This presents a range of options for how we can now listen to music: stream it from an online streaming service; download it from an online music store; or convert music CDs onto our computing devices.

## Streaming services

Streaming music is an increasingly popular way to listen to our favorite artists and songs. Streaming does not download any music onto your device: it enables you to listen to music being played over the Internet from the source company's computer (server). When the tracks ends, it is not available on your device, although you can always stream it again. There are several streaming services, and most of them offer a free option, in addition to paid-for subscriptions. Most of the paid-for options have a free trial period, usually 30 days. (The free options frequently have ads that appear before and after songs are played.) Some streaming services also allow you to download music to your device, so that you can play it when you are offline. This is usually only available from a paid-for service.

---

**HIGH-TECH HEALTH**

However you obtain your digital music, use a pair of good quality headphones if you are listening to it around other people. Also, make sure that the volume is not too high; partly for the benefit of anyone near to you, but also for the sake of the health of your ears.

---

## Spotify

This is one of the most popular streaming services and is not tied to one of the big technology companies, i.e. Apple, Amazon, or Google. Spotify provides a range of genres of music, and you can also create playlists based on types of music, artists, or for a particular mood. It also enables you to connect with friends on Facebook and share and compare music this way.

## Apple Music

With access to the massive iTunes Library of music, this is an excellent option for Apple users. There is a three-month free trial for Apple Music, and then you can choose a subscription option, from **Individual, Family or Student**.

**MUSIC**                          Cancel

**Choose a plan**

Individual

Family  Up to 6 people

University Student

Plan automatically renews monthly.

Join Apple Music

## Google Play Music

If you have a Google Account, you can sign up for a 90-day free trial of the Google Play Music service. Similar to Apple Music, it offers millions of songs, and you can take out an **Individual** or a **Family** monthly membership.

### Amazon Music Unlimited

This is one of the services that is provided with an
Amazon Prime subscription. This is an annual service, which
entitles you access to a range of Amazon's online content and also
ensures next-day delivery for your qualifying Amazon purchases.
There is a 30-day free trial for all Amazon Prime services.

### Pandora

This is another independent streaming service where users
can specify their likes and dislikes and then have personalized playlists created based on these preferences. Users can also
listen to playlists based on specific genres of music, or listen to
playlists created by other people.

## Downloading music

All of the major technology companies have their own online
stores where music can be bought and downloaded. This is different to a streaming service, as music is bought as an individual
item, rather than having access to millions of tracks. Some of the
online music stores are:

### iTunes Store

Apple's iTunes Store was one of the first online music
stores, and it continues to be one of the leaders in the
market. If you have an Apple ID,
you can access it from the iTunes
app on your Mac computer or
mobile device. Search through the
Music section of the iTunes Store
and review the songs and albums.
Tap on the price button next to an
item to buy it. This can then be
accessed from the iTunes app on a
Mac computer or the Music app on
a mobile device.

## A CLOSER LOOK

By default, music on an iOS 11 device that has been bought in the iTunes Store is stored in this location and played on your device by streaming, i.e. over the Internet. To download it to your device, access it in the Music app and tap on the cloud icon next to it.

## Microsoft Store

The Music section of the Microsoft Store has a good range of music available through genres or collections.

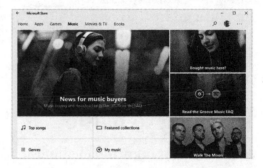

Once music has been downloaded, it can be played with the Groove Music app on a Windows 10 PC or laptop. A Microsoft Account is needed to access the Microsoft Store and the music within it.

## Google Play Store

For Android users, the Music section of the Google Play Store is a good option for downloading music using a Google Account. This can also be accessed online at *play.google.com/store/music* through any Web browser. This means that you can access music that you have bought on an Android device and any music you buy from the online site as well. Music that has been bought from the Google Play Store can be played on the Play Music app on an Android device, and this can also be used

to access the Store (tap on the main menu and tap on the Shop button to start shopping in the Store).

## Amazon

In addition to its streaming music service that is included with Amazon Music Unlimited, individual tracks and albums can be downloaded from the Amazon website. Use the Amazon Search box to find music from your favorite artists and buy it using the MP3 Download option.

Music downloaded in this way can be listened to using the Amazon Music app – when you make an MP3 purchase you will be able to enter a cell number or an email address to obtain a link for downloading the app.

# Listening to music

Once you have downloaded music to your PC, laptop, tablet or smartphone, you can then start listening to it. This is done using a music app and each platform has its own version:

- Windows 10 uses the Groove Music player.

- Apple devices use iTunes (Macs) or the Music app (iOS 11 devices).

- Android devices use the Play Music app or a music player provided by the manufacturer of the Android phone.

MONEY-SAVER

When digital music first became popular, it was played on MP3 music players such as the Apple iPod. Although these are still available, smartphones and tablets are so proficient at playing music that you don't need to worry about buying another device.

## All music apps work in a similar way.

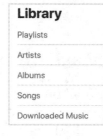

1. Select the music you want to play from within the music app's library. Content will be arranged according to different criteria, e.g. Albums, Artists, Songs, and Playlists.

2. Click or tap on an item to play it. If it is a single song, this will play and stop. If it is an album, all of the tracks on the album will be played.

3. As a track is playing, the music controls are available. These include a volume control, the pause/play button, and options for fast forwarding to the end of a track or rewinding to the beginning.

4. Most music apps also have menu options for specific tracks, which enable you to download a track, delete it from your music library, or add it to a playlist.

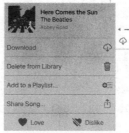

---

**A Closer Look**

A playlist is a collection of music that is selected by the user to create their own custom collections. It is a good idea to create playlists with specific themes, e.g. a relaxing playlist, a workout playlist, or a party playlist. Playlists can be created by selecting the Playlist option and clicking or tapping on the + button. Give the playlist a name and then select tracks to add to it.

---

# Music around the home

Smartphones and tablet are excellent for listening to music when you are on-the-go. However, when you are at home, there are options for how you listen to your music:

- **Docking station and speakers.** This is the same as a docking station that can be used to charge a smartphone, except it has additional speakers. When the smartphone is connected to the docking station, music can be selected from the music player, and this will be played through the speakers.

- **Wireless speakers.** These can be placed anywhere in your home (as long as they are in wireless range), and music can be streamed from your smartphone or tablet. Versions such as the HomePod from Apple and the Google Home speakers work with iOS and Android smartphones respectively; but other brands, including Sonos and Bose, can be used with both versions.

# Watching movies and TV

As with music, it is possible to watch movies and TV shows on any of your digital devices. The three main options for this are:

- **Buying a DVD or a Blu-ray disc.** These can be used in a DVD drive on your PC or laptop to watch the content. (If there is not a built-in DVD drive, an external one can be used with a USB cable.)

- **Streaming.** This is usually done through a subscription to one of the major streaming services such as Netflix, Amazon Prime Video, Sling TV, and Hulu. For a monthly fee you will get access to their library of new and old movies and TV shows. Apple also has their own TV service, called Apple TV, which is accessed using a separate Apple TV box. Once the box has been bought, it can be used to access content in the iTunes Store and also a wide range of streaming services.

- **Downloading.** The iTunes Store, Google Play Store, and Microsoft Store all have sections where you can buy or rent movies and TV shows. If you rent them, you usually have 30 days to start watching them. Once you have started watching a rented movie or TV show, you have 48 hours to complete it.

---

### BRIGHT IDEA

Another option for watching movies and TV shows is to combine a hard copy disc and the online version. One company that specializes in this is UltraViolet at *myuv.com*. If you buy a DVD or a Blu-ray disc with the UltraViolet logo on the case, you can use the code to obtain an online version of the content on the disc.

## Save money on cable

Do you want to watch movies and TV shows on your computing devices? Do you want to watch them for free, without paying for expensive cable? Ditch the cable subscription and try streaming content to your TV. This is done through a Wi-Fi connection, so you are watching your movies and TV shows over the Internet. The main streaming services (Netflix, Amazon Prime Video, and Hulu) charge a fee for this service, but it's also possible to get movies and TV shows for free. The range is not as great as for the paid-for services, but it is still reasonably extensive, and it's free! Some of these to look at include Crackle at *crackle.com*, Popcornflix at *popcornflix.com*, and Snagfilms at *snagfilms.com*. Some of the paid-for services also offer free trials – but remember to cancel at the end of the free-trial period.

Streaming services play on PCs, laptops, tablets, or smartphones, and you can also play them through your TV using an HDMI cable.

Also, the websites (and apps) of the major TV networks have episodes of TV series that you can stream to your devices. Look at the sites at *abc.go.com*, *nbc.com*, *cwtv.com,* and *cbs.com*.

---

### A CLOSER LOOK

Also known as connected TVs, Smart TVs enable content from the Internet, streaming services, and cable and satellite TV channels to be viewed directly on a flat-screen TV. This type of content is usually accessed using a set-top box. Much of it can be interacted with on-screen, in a similar way to using Web pages on the Internet. A huge range of content can be accessed in this way, and it is an area that will develop considerably in the future, as it gives users the option to access all of their online and TV content in the same place.

---

# Page turners with ebooks

When they first appeared, it was suggested that ebooks and ebook readers (e-readers) would be the death knell for hard-copy books. This has not been the case, partly because people still want to feel paper in their hands when they read a book. However, ebooks still fulfill a very useful purpose, particularly if you are traveling and want to have access to a lot of books without the weight and bulk of carrying them around.

Dedicated e-readers and tablets are the best options for reading ebooks on digital devices. Their combination of size and portability means that the screen is large enough to contain a good amount of text, and they can easily be slipped into a bag or a large pocket.

The Amazon Kindle was one of the first mainstream e-readers, and it was a natural fit with the huge catalog of ebooks on the Amazon website. Kindle continues to dominate the ebook market, with several different models available. Another option is the Kobo Aura e-reader.

As you would expect, ebook readers are designed specifically for reading ebooks and generally do little else, but they do it very well. (The Kindle Fire can be used to perform a range of general computing tasks, but this is a tablet with an ebook reader included, rather than a dedicated e-reader.) They use e-paper and e-ink technology to produce as similar an experience as possible to reading on paper. Most e-readers have some form of lighting, but this generally comes from the side, which does not produce as much glare as a back-lit device like a tablet. The original Kindle is one e-reader that does not have any lighting, and this is still preferred by some people.

## HIGH-TECH HEALTH

When buying an ebook reader it is important to physically test one, rather than buying it online without getting your hands on it first. This is because of the lighting of the screen. Since you will probably be looking at the screen for a long time, it is essential that you find the lighting relaxing. Different models have slightly different methods of lighting the screen and you may find some preferable to others.

### ebook reader or tablet

When tablets first appeared, it didn't take long for them to include ebooks apps – **iBooks** on iPads and **Play Books** on Android tablets. ebooks can be downloaded from the relevant online store and read on the tablet using the ebooks' apps. This means that you can have all of your digital content on one device. Another great benefit of an ebook reader is that the battery life is considerably longer than for a tablet and can last for several days. The one potential draw-back is that, since tablet screens are back-lit, it can be more tiring on the eyes when reading ebooks.

---

CAUTION

ebooks can be read on smartphones, but in general the screens are too small to make it a comfortable experience over a pro-longed period of time.

---

## Downloading ebooks

ebooks are downloaded in the same way as other digital content: go to the required online ebook store, browse to the required item, and download it. The main options for acquiring ebooks are:

- **Amazon Kindle Store.** This a section on the Amazon web-site dedicated to ebooks that can be downloaded and read on the Kindle. There is also a Kindle Unlimited option, which is a monthly subscription service that gives you access to over a million ebooks, magazines, and audiobooks. There is a free 30-day trial, after which the subscription is $9.99 a month and continues until it is cancelled.

- **iBooks Store.** Part of Apple's iTunes Store, this can be accessed from the iBooks app, and downloaded items can be read on an iPad (or on an iPhone if you don't mind the smaller size).

- **Google Play Store.** For Android users, the Play Books app can be used to access the Google Play Bookstore, where titles can be downloaded and read on an Android tablet or smartphone.

- **Microsoft Store.** Books can be downloaded from the Microsoft Store, but you are then limited to reading them on a Windows PC or laptop, using the Microsoft Edge browser.

- **Kobo Store.** If you have a Kobo e-reader, content can be downloaded from the Kobo Store at *kobo.com*. There are over 5 million titles to choose from and also a range of audiobooks.

- **eBooks.com** at *ebooks.com*. This is an independent store, and they have their own ebook reader app that can be downloaded to a tablet or smartphone and used to read *ebooks.com* titles. Their books can also be read in a Web browser on a Windows 10 PC or a Mac.

- **Project Gutenberg.** This is a tremendous resource for free books, with over 55,000 titles. Although the selection is small compared with the likes of Amazon, Apple, and Google, there are numerous classic titles such as Adventures of Huckleberry Finn by Mark Twain and Great Expectations by Charles Dickens. These titles are free, as the period of copyright has expired, and each year more books will become eligible to be added to the Project Gutenberg catalog. Visit the website at *gutenberg.org* to find out more about this excellent project.

- Most major bookstores also have ebooks on their websites.

---

### A CLOSER LOOK

Most ebook stores produce content in the ePub format, which is the industry standard for ebooks. However, Amazon uses their own AZW format, which is the only one that can be used on an Amazon Kindle. Therefore, ebooks in the ePub format cannot be used on the Kindle, but ebooks in the AZW format can be used on other devices if the Kindle app has been downloaded.

---

It is also possible to download the Kindle app to an iPad or an Android tablet. If you have an Amazon account, this can then be used to connect to any books that you have bought for the Kindle and make them available on your tablet using the Kindle app, not the tablet's ebook app.

# Reading an ebook

Regardless of the type of e-reader that you use and where you download your ebooks from, the process for reading them is similar.

1.  Tap on the ebook in your e-reader's library or within the appropriate app on a tablet, e.g. the **iBooks** app or the **Play Books** app.

2.  Swipe left and right to move between pages or tap on the left-hand or right-hand side of a page to move in that direction.

3.  Tap in the middle of the page to access the reading controls.

4.  Tap on this button to access the table of contents and any bookmarks or notes that have been added.

5. Tap in the top, right-hand corner to bookmark a page.

6. Tap on this button to select options such as text size, screen brightness, and screen background color.

7. Swipe on this slider to move through the book.

8. Press and hold on a word to select it and activate options, such as looking up a definition of the word.

# 16 SHOPPING ONLINE

## Buying items safely online

Shopping online is one of the favorite pastimes on the Web. However, there are a few security concerns that should be considered before looking for your latest online purchases:

- Create an online shopping email address, other than the one you use for family and friends. Use a Web-based service, such as Gmail or Yahoo!, whenever you register for a new online shopping site. (Most sites require some form of registration when you actually want to buy something, but this is partly so that they can get your email address for marketing purposes.) Then, when the retailer sends you an email asking for feedback about your online experience with them or news of their latest offers, the email will go into your shopping email Inbox, leaving your regular one free for more important messages from family and friends.

- Don't reply to any special offers in an email, unless you are sure the email is from the retailer it claims to be (click on their email address to see if the details seem accurate). Fraudsters use fake special offer emails to try and get people to divulge their personal details and even bank account details. If in doubt, go to the retailer's website and see if the special offer is listed there. If so, access it from their website.

Fake special offers also occur on social media sites such as Facebook.

- Keep your anti-virus and firewall software up-to-date. Also, make sure you have downloaded the latest version of your device's operating system as this will include the latest security updates. This is important, as online shopping involves giving out sensitive financial details, such as your credit card details.

- When you are paying for items using a credit or debit card, make sure that you are doing so on a secure site, i.e. one that has security features, such as encryption, to make sure that your card details are safe when you enter them at the check-out. The indicator that an online shopping site is secure is the *https* prefix at the start of a website address. This is used instead of the *http* prefix – the additional "s" stands for "secure." There should also be a lock icon at the bottom of the page or in the address bar to indicate that there is security software protecting the site.

- If you are accessing an online retailer from a Wi-Fi hotspot, i.e. not your own home network, don't select to save your card details at the checkout as this could mean someone could get access to your device in public and use these details. In fact, it is best not to enter any financial details when using a hotspot, as it is not a secure form of connection.

- Stick with online shopping websites that you have used before or are major names. If you do use a new site, conduct an Internet search to see if there are any issues connected with it, and read the reviews from other users.

- Even when there are a lot of positive reviews on a site, this sometimes has to be taken with a grain of salt. Even though it is illegal, some companies populate their sites with fake reviews to make their products look more popular. Look for reviews that seem to stand out from the rest in terms of the language used to identify fake ones.

---

### A CLOSER LOOK

Most modern day browsers do not always show the full website address in the address bar. Frequently they are condensed to just the name of the company, e.g. *Amazon.com*. If the full address is not showing, it can be hard to check if the site is secure or not. To overcome this, click in the address bar and the full website address should be revealed, with the *https* prefix at the left-hand side of the address (and the lock icon).

# Finding a bargain

Everyone likes a bargain, and this should be no different when shopping online.

## Haggling

You do not have to be in an overseas market in order to haggle for goods. Even in your local stores, it is worth trying to knock a few dollars off your purchases. Ask the sales assistant if they can take some money off the price, and perhaps mention that you have seen the same item for cheaper in another store. Even if they don't take any money off, they may offer you a free accessory. Whatever happens, you won't lose anything by asking.

## Refurbished and trade-ins

For computing equipment, some companies offer refurbished PCs and laptops on their websites. Some also offer trade-ins on older models. Look at the websites for the following companies, and use the Search box for **Refurbished**, **Trade in**, or **Trade up**:

- *apple.com.*

- *dell.com.*

- *hp.com.*

- *ibm.com.*

Independent resellers also offer refurbished computers. Two to look at are:

- TigerDirect at *tigerdirect.com*.

- Newegg at *newegg.com*.

---

**CAUTION**

Be careful when buying refurbished computer equipment: check that it has been wiped clean of any previous content; the specifications meet your needs; and also check if there is a warranty and a returns policy.

---

### eBay

eBay is a natural starting point if you want to buy a wide range of items. This can be done either through an online auction or from one of the online stores that now populate eBay. (See section on Buying and selling with eBay on page 293.)

# Researching

The Web is ideal for researching products that you want to buy. This can be on the site where they are being sold or using a general Web search. Online shopping sites should include the details of a product and also reviews from people who have bought it. With a general Web search you may find a wider range of information and, if there are any issues with a product, these may show up from the general search.

# Price comparison sites

Price comparison websites are a great option for looking at the prices across a range of different websites. Some price comparison sites to look at are: pricegrabber at *pricegrabber.com*;

Shopping.com at *shopping.com*; Shopzilla at *shopzilla.com*; and Become at *become.com*. To use a price comparison website:

1. Items can be searched for in the site's Search box, or they can be found through the categories listed on the site.

2. Review the results, and click on an item you want to buy. This will take you to that site where you can buy the item.

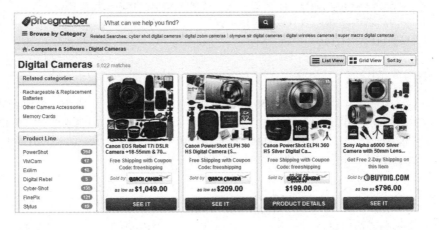

## MONEY-SAVER

Even better than doing price comparisons before buying something is being able to do them while you are actually going around a store. The Shop Savvy Barcode Scanner app can be used on the iPhone and Android smartphones to compare prices as you are shopping. Scan an item with your smartphone's camera, and then the Shop Savvy app will show price comparisons using other brick-and-mortar stores and online ones. The app is also able to display sales in your local area and online shopping sites. Make sure that your smartphone has **Location Services** turned On, so that the Shop Savvy app can determine your location and display results in relation to it. Retailers are not fans of the Shop Savvy app, but it could help save you hundreds of dollars.

# Try before you buy

Some things can be bought online without trying them first, but with many purchases, it is good to try them first. This could be for items such as perfume, a laptop (to test the keyboard), or clothing. Before you dive into your online shopping experience, go down to your local stores and try out the items that you are thinking of buying. This could save you the time and hassle of having to return items once they have been delivered.

> **CAUTION**
>
> Try not to only shop online. If local stores are always bypassed for online ones, then they may not be there for long. Online shopping is great, but we probably don't want to live in a world where this is the only option.

# Buying and selling with eBay

eBay was one of the first major successes of the dot-com era of the late 1990s. From a simple concept of getting sellers and buyers together in an online environment, it has expanded into a billion dollar business. In addition to the original eBay auctions on which the site was founded, there are now thousands of sellers and retail outlets, which sell goods at one price without the auction element. eBay can be used by anyone to buy and sell items, but there are a few useful points to follow to ensure you stay safe on eBay and make the most of the experience.

1. Although it is free to register for eBay, there is a small fee for listing items for sale and a 10% fee on the selling price of items.

2. When buying something in an eBay auction, look at the price that similar items are listed for or have been sold at. Auctions show the selling price once it has finished, which can be a good indicator of the value of something.

3. Decide on how much you want to pay for an item, and don't go over it. Being in an eBay auction can be an exciting experience, but don't get swept up in it and pay more than you want.

4. When buying items, read the feedback about the seller. If there have been any problems or issues in the past, think about looking elsewhere.

5. If you see an item that you think is a fair price, use the **Buy It Now** option rather than waiting to buy it in an auction.

6. If you are buying an item in an auction, wait until the final minute to make your last bid. Some people wait until the final seconds to make a bid, but don't leave it too long in case there isn't time for your bid to be registered.

    **Buy it now**

7. Look carefully at delivery charges. Each seller can set their own delivery charge, and sometimes a low selling price is compensated with a higher delivery charge.

8. Provide feedback whenever you buy something. eBay still relies on the sense of community on which it was founded, and it is important to let everyone else know about your experiences.

9. When selling items, be honest in your descriptions and accurate with any photos that are used. There is no point having an inaccurate description, as the item will probably be returned, and you may receive negative feedback from the purchaser.

10. Never send an item until you have received the money for it, even if the buyer says it is on the way.

11. If there is a problem with a seller, such as an item not being delivered, report it in the eBay Resolution Center or as a last resort, report it to the Federal Trade Commission at *ftc.gov*.

# Good online shopping habits

It is all too easy to get carried away when shopping online, partly because it is so easy. This can quickly have an adverse affect on your bank balance. There are two steps to ensure that your online shopping does not get out of hand.

1. Make a list of what you want, find it, buy it, and then stop shopping. Most sites have suggestions for buying more items, usually based on what you have bought, but don't be tempted by this. The site may show items bought by other people who also bought the same things as you. However, this does not mean that you have to buy them too. Stay focused and stick to your original list.

2. Think twice, click once. As with posting items on social media sites, it's always best to pause before you complete the transaction. If in doubt, a lot of online shopping sites have an option to create a wishlist, where you can add items you may want to buy but are not sure. You can place items here, and then return later to review your earlier choices.

# Never pay full price again

We all like a bargain, but imagine if you could get a bargain every time you went shopping. Well imagine no longer because it is possible with the Ebates app. This app can be used to get cash back on purchases in over 2,000 stores, including Macy's, Target, and Walmart, and online websites including eBay and Groupon. They also have a wide range of coupons, gift cards, promo codes, and offers on everything from hotels to home improvements. Use **Location Services** on your smartphone to let the app know where you are so that it can tailor the best offers to your location. If used wisely, the Ebates app could save you large amounts of money.

## MONEY-SAVER

Coupons for online purchases and in-store purchases can be obtained from several websites and also by typing a store name or a product and the word "coupon" into a Search engine. Some sites to look at for getting paper coupons, digital coupons, or coupon codes are: Coupons.com at *coupons.com*; CouponCabin at *couponcabin.com*; Coupon Craze at *couponcraze.com*; and CouponAlbum at *couponalbum.com*. Remember though, even with coupons, something is only a bargain if you wanted to buy it in the first place. Don't buy items just because they have a money-off coupon.

## Returning items

Make sure that you read the returns policy on any online shopping site. For items such as clothing or shoes, it is hard to know exactly if they will fit, so it is important that you can return them easily. Check a site's return policy for the following:

- What is the time limit for returning items?

- Are there certain items that cannot be returned?

- Who pays the postage for returns?

- Do you receive a full refund for the item, or store credit?

Some sites provide return labels that can be printed from their site, and they sometimes include free postage. Keep the original packaging that an item comes in until you are happy that you want to keep it. If you do have to return something, it is better to use this packaging than having to use your own or buy more.

## BRIGHT IDEA

When buying clothes and shoes online, find a retailer whose items you like and use them regularly for your online purchases. This is because sizes vary in all stores, so if you find a good option that fits well, then you can be confident that subsequent purchases will be the same.

# 17 TRAVEL AND TECHNOLOGY – THE PERFECT COMBINATION

## The joy of travel

Travel is one of the great joys in life, and the huge amount of travel-related information that is online in the form of apps and websites has only made this better. There are several areas where the online world can enhance your traveling experiences.

- **Review sites.** These are apps and websites that offer reviews from fellow travelers covering a huge range of locations, hotels, restaurants, and excursions. TripAdvisor is one of the best options for this, and it offers a community environment for those with itchy feet.

- **Booking sites.** Need a hotel? A flight? A car rental? Whatever you need for your vacation, there is an app that can help you. Some specialize in one area, e.g. *Hotels.com*, while others provide the full range of elements for a perfect vacation. Expedia is one of these companies, but there are dozens of them, each with their own online presence.

- **Inspirational sites.** Some apps and websites just show you amazing places and incredible things to do. Some of these sites have titles, such as "101 Amazing Things To Do Before You Die" or have a range of articles and reviews about specific places and activities. One website to look at is *roadscholar.org*.

- **Specific interest sites.** Want to take a cruise to Alaska? Take a walking holiday in the Rocky Mountains? Take a wine tour in the Nappa Valley? Don't worry, there's an app for it covering everything from how to book, to how to get there, and what to do.

- **Travel health sites.** Staying healthy on vacation is just as important, or more so, than when you are at home. Use travel health apps and websites to find out about specific health issues in the places that you want to visit. Try the website at *wwwnc.cdc.gov* for official U.S. Government health advice for traveling.

---

**BRIGHT IDEA**

When you are on vacation, use your smartphone camera to take photos of bus and train timetables. This way you will always have them with you.

---

# The one trick travel companies don't want you to know

Online travel sites are an excellent option for booking vacations: they offer reasonable prices, and you can book flights, hotels, car hire, and excursions all in one place. However, be careful how you book these, as sites can offer different prices for exactly the same package depending on the type of device you are using to access the site. In a lot of cases, if you are using a mobile device, you will be redirected to the mobile version of the website which may have different prices. Experiment by looking up the same vacation on at least two different devices: the price may be the same, but in some cases, there may also be a difference. In general, prices are cheaper from Windows 10 PCs and laptops than mobile devices.

If you register for an airline's Frequent Flyer program, you not only get points towards discounts when you book flights, you can also use their retail portals to gain points when you buy items from a range of popular stores. Click on a retailer's icon on the airline's website, and then make your purchases on the retailer's website. The value of the purchases will be converted into Frequent Flyer points, since you have accessed the site from the airline's website.

# Always have your boarding pass in your pocket

Vacations and traveling always require a certain amount of paperwork: passports, insurance documents, boarding passes, etc. However, it is now possible to convert one of these into a digital version. Smartphones have apps that can download boarding passes and store them for use at airports. iPhones use the Wallet app for storing these, and Google Feeds can be used for this on Android devices. To download a digital boarding pass, use the online check-in facility for your flight and select to download the boarding pass once you have checked in. If the airline supports this function, it will display the required option. Click on this to have your boarding pass downloaded to your smartphone.

Even though it can save paper to download your boarding pass to your smartphone, you may still want to print off a hard copy, just in case your smartphone decides to stop working at the crucial time when you arrive at the airport. If this happens, the airline can still print another boarding pass, but it is best to have a backup, just in case.

# Knowing your destination before you go

The Internet offers options like never before for researching virtually any destination around the world. It is possible to find out detailed information about somewhere, view maps, see photos, and even watch videos. However, there are some factors that it are good to know before you set off:

- **Time differences.** It is always useful to know the time in your proposed destination. This can help you to adjust to any jet lag, and it is also helpful when getting in touch with family and friends back home – knowing the time difference could mean that you do not call them when it is the middle of the night back home. The Clock app on the iPhone or an Android phone can display times for hundreds of locations around the world, and also the time at home.

- **Money.** Understanding the local currency is useful for working out the relative price of items. It is important to know if credit cards are widely accepted and if you can withdraw money from ATM machines. If you are going to be using your credit card abroad, it may be worth mentioning this to your bank so that they do not view any purchases as unexplained uses of the card. Download a currency convertor app from the App Store or the Google Play Store to show how much you get for your dollar in foreign currency.

- **Local customs.** When traveling overseas, make sure that you are aware of the local customs and traditions. In some cases, following these will be polite, in others it will be the law. For instance, in some countries there are certain rules about the way people dress. Hand gestures can also be confusing: our positive interpretation of a "thumbs up" is not the same around the world, and in some countries, it can be viewed as a derogatory sign.

- **Weather.** Predicting the weather for a vacation is never an exact science, but you can view a forecast for your destination using a weather app or an online weather site.

## Finding locations

The Internet has truly shrunk the globe, and it is easy to find any location around the world. All you need is Google Maps or Apple's Maps app. The world is then at your fingertips:

1. Open the app, or access **Google Maps** through a Web browser, and enter a location into the Search box. This can be a city, a zip code, a significant feature (such as Yosemite National Park), or even a business.

2. Suggestions appear as you type. Click or tap on one to view that item.

3. The location is displayed on a map.

4. To the left of the map is an information panel that provides general information about the location.

5.  Maps can be viewed in map view, and also in satellite view.

6.  If you zoom in, you can view a location in great detail, which can be particularly effective in satellite view. There is also a 3D option in Google Maps and Apple Maps.

## A CLOSER LOOK

Google Street View is a great way to travel virtually through locations. The location is displayed at street level, and you can navigate through the streets using the on-screen arrow.

# Setting up GPS

The Global Positioning System (GPS) is a navigation system based on satellites in space. It is operated by the US Air Force and provides accurate global location identification for any device that has a GPS sensor. Luckily, this is now standard in most smartphones, so you can take full advantage of this powerful technology for getting around, both at home and on vacation.

To use GPS on your smartphone, Location Services have to be turned on, so that the GPS satellites can communicate with the GPS receiver on your phone.

To turn on **Location Services** for an iOS 11 device:

1.  Access Settings > Privacy.

2. If **Location Services** is Off, tap on it.

3. Drag the **Location Services** button to On.

4. Since the Maps app is one of the most important in terms of using GPS, tap on the **Maps** option.

5. Tap on the **While Using the App** option so that the check icon is showing, which enables GPS when using the Maps app.

To turn on **Location Services** for an Android device:

1. Access Settings > Location, and drag the **Location** button to On.

2. To turn **Location Services** On for a specific app, e.g. the Maps app, select Settings > Apps, and tap on the required app.

3. Tap on the **Permissions** option.

4. For **Location**, drag the button to On.

## Using GPS for getting around

Once Location Services have been turned on for the smartphone and the Maps app, it can be used to find your way around from wherever you are. This can be done in two ways:

- Follow a route suggested by your Maps app.

- Find your own way, using a marked destination and your current location.

**To follow a route on your smartphone (using Apple's Maps app or Google Maps):**

1. Open the **Maps** app.

2. Enter an address into the Search box. (If the Search box is not showing, swipe up from the bottom of the Maps app.)

3. Select the required address.

4. Tap on the **Directions** button.

5. The route is shown on the map.

6. Tap on the **Go** button to start the route.

7. Follow the on-screen instructions. This includes audio directions – make sure your phone is not on mute, otherwise you won't be able to hear the audio directions.

8. Your location is indicated by the blue circle. As you move along the route, the circle should move along the route on the map.

9. The map will change as you work your way along the route.

10. Tap on the **End** button, and then the **End Route** button to finish.

**To follow your own route:**

If you choose not to follow a specific route, you can still use GPS to find your way to a location.

1. Open the **Maps** app and enter an address in the same way as for following a route.

2. Tap on the address but don't tap on the **Directions** button.

3. Your location and the selected destination are shown on the map.

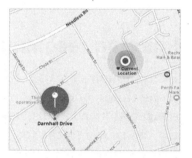

4. Start walking or driving. The blue circle (indicating your location) will move in the direction that you do. If it is not towards your intended destination, turn so that the blue circle is moving in the right direction.

# Finding recommendations

Guidebooks have been around as long as mass tourism, but they have one main drawback in that they can become dated quickly. So, if a recommended restaurant changes ownership and deteriorates in quality, the information cannot be updated until the next printed version of the guidebook. This is where the Internet comes into its own: travel sites can display the very latest information, particularly reviews from people who have just been there.

TripAdvisor at *tripadvisor.com* is the largest travel review site, with over 500 million reviews of hotels, restaurants, cafes, excursions, and activities. To find a certain item, enter it into the TripAdvisor Search box and select the required result. Take some time to look through reviews for things in which you are interested, including negative reviews and the response from the owners, if there is one. TripAdvisor is an excellent resource for finding the best places to eat and visit, but remember, everyone else is probably looking up the same things so you may need to book in advance, particularly for restaurants.

Even once you have found what seems like a good recommendation on TripAdvisor, do a bit of cross-referencing to ensure that it is accurate. Try the trusty guidebook and also do a search online for individual establishments to see what the wider community has to say about them.

## Ignoring recommendations

Even though sites like TripAdvisor are excellent for online research for a new destination, it is sometimes beneficial to ignore the recommendations, and do your own thing. Rather than following the crowd to the top-ranked, nearby restaurant, go somewhere that you may have passed during the day and liked the look of. Taking a chance on something unknown could result in an uninspiring experience, but it could also be one of the best things you have ever done. Travel is partly about taking risks and trying new things. If it doesn't work out well, you always have TripAdvisor to fall back on for the next day.

## Organizing your travels

There are plenty of apps that can be used to help organize different aspects of taking a vacation:

- **Packing apps.** Take the stress out of packing for vacations with an app that keeps a record of what is needed and enables you to check it off once you have packed it. Search the App Store or Google Play Store for "vacation packing list."

- **Itinerary apps.** To keep track of what you are doing on vacation, itinerary apps can be used to create a day-by-day schedule. Search the App Store or Google Play Store for "travel itinerary."

- **Places visited apps.** App stores have travel apps that can be used to mark countries and places that you have visited around the world. Search the App Store or Google Play Store for "places visited".

- **City guides.** Most major cities around the world have apps dedicated to them. These contain historical and current information about the city, hotels, places to eat and drink, and also city maps. Search the App Store or Google Play Store for the required destination.

- **Transit apps.** For some destinations around the world, there are apps for the local transit systems, e.g. buses, trains, trams, and metros. Search the App Store or Google Play Store for the city name plus "transit."

- **Flight tracking apps.** These can be used to follow flights online in real-time so you always know when a flight is due and if it has been delayed. Search the App Store or Google Play Store for "flight tracker" or "flight scanner."

---

**BRIGHT IDEA**

Note-taking apps are also excellent for creating packing lists for traveling. Look for one with radio buttons, so that you can check off items as you pack them, and put your mind at rest.

# Love it or loath it – the most divisive item of travel tech

The gadget industry is alive and well for smartphones, but one item divides opinion like no other: the selfie stick. This is a pole with an attachment on the end, into which you place your smartphone. There is a button on the handle of the selfie stick that enables you to take a selfie (self portrait photo) from a greater distance than you would be able to do by just holding the phone. Some people love this as it enables them to capture more impressive selfies, mainly for posting on their social media sites. However, other people hate them as they think they are intrusive and unattractive. In fact, some venues and locations have banned them altogether on the grounds of health and safety. But it is an individual decision at the end of the day, so dive into the great selfie stick debate!

# Keeping in touch

We are so used to being permanently online that we expect Wi-Fi access wherever we go. In general, this expectation will be met in most corners of the world so that you can keep in touch with family and friends at home with email, text, or video chatting.

To find out where you can connect to Wi-Fi when you are on vacation, use a Wi-Fi finder app to find the nearest options. (A great number of hotels worldwide now have Wi-Fi.) There are several Wi-Fi finder apps available, and three to look at are: Avast Wi-Fi Finder; WiFi Map; and Boingo Wi-Finder. (There are iOS and Android versions for these three apps.)

# 18 ENHANCING MIND AND BODY

## Health & fitness

There is no reason health and fitness should be seen as a chore – the range of apps for conducting workouts, monitoring your overall fitness, and giving you encouragement, has transformed the ways in which we keep fit. Some types of apps are:

- **Tracking app.** These are used to measure how far you have walked/run/cycled for a specific workout. They can also display your average speed, maximum speed, and number of calories burned during the activity. The route is displayed on a map, and you can save routes to compare times whenever you complete the same route.

- **Diet and calorie apps.** These not only provide healthy eating advice, recipes, and diet plans, they also let you add your calories for each meal to build up a profile of your eating habits. You can also enter in details of any exercise that you do.

- **Workout apps.** These usually have accompanying videos or animations that you can follow for your workouts. They can track your progress and reward you with virtual prizes when you reach a target. These apps cover a range of workouts, from gym routines to yoga and pilates.

- **Mindfulness apps.** These look at the health of the mind and body together, covering areas such as meditation, relaxation, and getting a good night's sleep.

---

### BRIGHT IDEA

If you develop an unusual ache or pain, you do not have to immediately go to the doctor. Instead, check the symptoms online with the website *webmd.com*. Enter your age and gender, then use the body model to identify the part of the body that is painful and select the options for symptoms related to that part of the body. However, regardless of the information provided here, or any other online medical website, always go to see your own doctor if the symptoms persist.

---

# Carry your smartphone and lose weight

Carrying a smartphone may not initially seem like a good way to lose weight, but if you use one of the built-in health apps you will have a health companion right in your pocket. On the iPhone this is the Health app, and on Android smartphones there are a range of health apps provided by the manufacturers of the Android handsets.

One of the simplest tasks that a health app performs is to count the number of steps that you take each day. As you walk, the sensors in your smartphone recognize the type of movement and record steps accordingly. This in itself will not transform your health and weight, but if you use it to establish and meet targets, then it can be an effective way to measure your progress. For instance, measure how many steps you take in an average day (do this over a few days and calculate the average) and then set a target above this. Make it realistic, such as 10% more, and work towards this. Once you have achieved it, move the target up again. Seeing your progress in the health app is a good way to keep motivated and push yourself to greater achievements.

# Keeping track of your exercise

As well as just keeping count of the number of steps that you take each day, apps on your smartphone can also be used to track workout routes that you do for walking, running, or cycling. They log your route on a map and calculate the distance, time, average speed, and number of calories burned. The route can then be saved so that you can do it again and compare the statistics each time you complete the route. Some exercise tracking apps (available in the Apple App Store and the Google Play Store) to look at include:

- Runkeeper.

- MapMyRun.

- MapMyWalk.

- Strava.

- Runtastic Running & Fitness Tracker.

All exercise tracking apps operate in a similar way:

1. Open the app and tap on the **Start** or **Start Workout** button.

START WORKOUT

2. As you follow a route, it will be displayed on a map. This is done using GPS on your smartphone to identify your location. (Ensure **Location Services** are turned On for the tracking app so that it can follow your route.)

3. Once you have completed the route, it is displayed on the map.

4. Information about the workout is displayed below the map.

5. If required, a route can be saved to use again in future.

311

---

A CLOSER LOOK

Most exercise tracking apps have an audio commentary that offers encouragement as you are performing the workout and notifies you about milestones in terms of distance covered and calories burned.

## Let your smartphone count the calories

Apps on your smartphone can also count calories to assist with a weight-loss program. Calorie counting apps calculate your calorie intake based on the foods that you enter into the app, and then they offset this against the amount of exercise you have done. The final daily figure shows whether you have consumed more or fewer calories than the target you have set in the app. Some calorie-counting apps (available in the Apple App Store and the Google Play Store) to look at are:

- MyFitnessPal.

- Lose It!

- My Diet Diary Calorie Counter.

- MyPlate Calorie Counter.

- Lifesum.

To use a calorie-counting app:

1. Initially, you have to register with the app. Enter your date of birth, gender, height, and weight to create your health profile on the app.

2. Enter your goal weight and how quickly you want to work towards it. (It is generally better to aim for a slow and steady weight loss. If you lose weight too quickly, there is more

chance that you will put it back on quickly too.)

3.  The app will create a weight-loss plan, detailing how much weight to lose, and the target number of daily calories to achieve this.

4.  Enter an email address and a password to create an account with the app.

5.  Once the app has been setup, enter what you have eaten for various meals. Use the Search box to find items within the app.

6.  For each item there is a list of options (together with the number of calories). Tap on one to select it.

7.  Detailed information is shown for each item. Tap on the **Add** button to include it in a meal.

8.  Once you have added all of the items for a meal, tap on the **Done** button.

9.  Details of the meal are displayed, including the number of calories consumed, the target number, and the remaining amount of calories for the day.

313

10. To add details of exercise taken, tap on the **Exercise** option.

11. Select a type of exercise.

12. Enter details for the amount of exercise taken and tap on the **Add** button.

13. The target figures are updated to include the calories burned during exercise.

14. Complete the details for the rest of the day to collate the final figures.

---

**A CLOSER LOOK**

A lot of calorie-counting apps have a function to use a smart-phone's camera to take a photo of an item of food and identify it from this. Cameras can also be used to scan barcodes on packaging to get the calorie information.

---

# Taking the strain out of exercise

The App Store and the Google Play Store both have a dedicated category for Health & Fitness. Many of the apps help make the idea of exercising less daunting and help you get started and stay motivated. Some to look at include:

- Seven – 7 Minute Workout.

- 5 Minute Home Workouts.

- Sworkit – Workouts & Fitness Plans for Everyone.

- Weight Loss Fitness.

- Daily Workouts Fitness Trainer.

- Dog Down: Great Yoga Anywhere.

- Daily Yoga – Yoga Fitness Plan.

- 5 Minute Pilates.

Most exercise apps have videos or animated tutorials that take you through the workout step by step. It is possible to pause the tutorials, so that you can go at your own pace. Don't be put off by the title of a workout app. If it says it is a 7-minute workout, don't feel you have to do it in this time. If you want to pause as you go along, then do this and focus on finishing the workout without overdoing it.

---

A CLOSER LOOK

Both the iPhone and Android smartphones have pre-installed apps for keeping track of the number of steps you take and entering details of physical activity and nutrition. On the iPhone the Health app is used for this, and on Android smartphones it is the Google Fit app (if this is not pre-installed, it can be downloaded from the Play Store).

# 9 amazing things to do with Apple Watch

The Apple Watch is a smartwatch that can be used for a number of tasks other than telling the time. The earlier versions, Apple Watch Series 1 and 2, had to be used in conjunction with an iPhone to enable the full range of functionality; but the latest version, Apple Watch Series 3, can connect to your cellular network so that it can be used independently from your iPhone. Uses for the Apple Watch include:

1. **Keeping an eye on your heart rate.** The Heart app can display your heart rate using the sensors on the back of the Apple Watch.

2. **Tracking your workouts.** The Workout app can be used to record details of workouts for a range of different activities. The app records the type of workout, the duration of the activity, the number of calories burned, and average heart rate during the activity.

3. **Setting daily targets for moving, exercising, and standing.** Use the Activity app to record your activity during the day. It will even give you reminders to stand every hour to ensure you don't sit down for too long during the day.

4. **Viewing your text messages.** The Messages app displays your latest text messages, and you can reply to them with a voice message.

5. **Making and receiving calls.** The Phone app enables you to take calls and also make them to people in your address book. (Since the Apple Watch 3 is waterproof, you can make and receive calls while you are swimming, if you feel inclined to do this.)

6. **Finding your way around.** The Maps app can be used to show directions from your current location.

7. **Using your own photos as a clock face.** The Apple Watch clock face can be customized with numerous different faces, and you can even use a photo on your iPhone and transfer this as a new clock face.

8. **Listening to your favorite music.** Music can be streamed to the Apple Watch, which can be a great companion during a workout.

9. **Asking Siri.** Just say, "Hey Siri", and speak your request to see what Siri can do for you. (This is more limited than on an iPhone as you can't access the Web from an Apple Watch.)

# Fitness bands to keep you going

In addition to the Apple Watch, there is a range of other smartwatches and fitness bands that are available. They contain a range of features, but they will all do a great job in tracking your exercising activity. Some fitness bands to look at are:

- Fitbit Charge.

- Fitbit Flex.

- Nokia Steel.

- TomTom Spark.

- Garmin Vivosport.

# Taking time to breathe

We all take breathing for granted, and it is seldom thought of as an important part of an overall good health regime. However, taking a few minutes every day to concentrate on breathing deeply can have many beneficial effects in terms of helping to reduce stress and promote relaxation. There are health apps that can help you with this by encouraging you to take the time to breathe. There are also plenty of apps for meditation and mindfulness techniques, which are good for lowering stress.

# Embracing targets and rewards

A lot of health apps enable you to set targets, and then you get virtual rewards such as virtual stars or stickers or a confetti shower when you meet a target. Although these can seem a bit gimmicky at times, it can be a good motivator, and you may be surprised how pleased you are when your app awards you a new virtual gold star.

# Keeping your medical records together

Keeping track of all of your medical records can be a tiresome process, especially if you have moved around and had several different doctors. However, it is possible to keep them altogether using the HealthVault app. The app can be used to store all of your personal health records wherever they come from. You can then access them whenever and wherever you want and share them with anyone, too. So, if you go to a new doctor, you can show them your complete medical history on your smartphone or tablet.

HealthVault can also be used with a range of health and fitness devices, such as smartwatches, activity trackers, blood pressure monitors, blood glucose monitors, and weight scales. It is also possible to add an emergency profile that can be used by first responders in the case of an accident.

HealthVault is a Microsoft product, and you need to have a Microsoft Account to sign up for it. It can be downloaded from the Microsoft Store, the Apple App Store, and the Google Play Store. It is free to sign up for HealthVault.

---

### BRIGHT IDEA

If you can't get to a doctor in person, help is at hand on the Internet. At *HealthTap.com* there are over 100,000 doctors available to give free medical advice. The wait time for an answer is usually between 24 to 48 hours. There is also a HealthTap app for the iPhone. If you want a quicker or more personal consultation, there are paid-for options for video chat or private-messaging communications and a prime service where you should get a response in approximately two minutes.

---

## One step to better sleep

Getting a good night's sleep is essential for good health, and it should not be underestimated when thinking about your overall health regime. One of the simplest things that you can do to try and achieve this is to turn off your smartphone or tablet before you go to bed. This will ensure that your sleep is not interrupted by any sounds or notifications or by your phone lighting up in the middle of the night.

## Healthy habits with your devices

When using your PC, laptop, tablet, or smartphone, the most important thing is not the hardware, the operating system, or the apps that you use. The most important thing is you! Avoiding any health issues when you are using computers and technology is essential to ensuring that you have a comfortable and productive relationship with the devices that you use. With two simple steps, you can ensure that you develop healthy habits when using your computing devices:

1. **Step away from the screen.** It can be easy to get engrossed in whatever you are doing, whether it is watching a movie, writing an email to a friend, or catching up with social media. However, this can lead to poor posture and eye-strain as you stare at the screen for prolonged periods. Instead, make sure that you take regular breaks from the screen. This does not have to be for long, but it gives you a chance to stretch your limbs and lets your eyes have a screen break. This also has the benefit of giving your mind a bit of a break, as well as your body.

2. **Seating position.** When PCs were pretty much the only computing story in town, it was straightforward in terms of how you sat: the PC was on desk, and you sat in front of it. Now, with laptops and other mobile devices in all shapes and sizes, we can view our devices wherever we like. This has the benefit of mobility, but it can play havoc with posture. For instance, using your laptop in bed or in an armchair may seem like a relaxing option, but once the laptop is in a suitable position, your body may not be in the best position for using it, particularly if you are going to be using the keyboard for typing. When using a PC or laptop, try to ensure it is on a flat surface and your eyes are in line with just below the top of the screen. Use a comfortable chair that supports your back and make sure that your arms are level with the height of the keyboard. If you start to feel any aches or pains when using a digital device (particularly in your hands, wrists, or arms), look at your seating position and adjust it as required.

## HIGH-TECH HEALTH

One online aid to improving monitor lighting is f.lux from *stereopsis.com*. This is free software that adjusts the brightness and tint of your monitor, based on the lighting at a specific time of day. For instance, during the day the lighting is appropriate for the surrounding light, and at sunset the color becomes gentler and easier on the eyes. It is available for Windows, macOS, and iOS devices.

# 19    GETTING ORGANIZED

Using social media, browsing the Web, looking at photos, watching movies, and listening to music are some of the fun things that can be done on computing devices. However, as with most things in life, there will be times where we have to do more mundane tasks. Luckily, modern digital devices are fully equipped to make all day-to-day organization as easy as possible, with a range of apps and productivity suites to help keep us up-to-date and fully in control.

## Address books

Having an up-to-date address book is a great way to store all of the contacts that we accumulate. All devices have their own pre-installed address book apps:

- People app (Windows 10)

- Contacts app (macOS High Sierra and iOS 11)

- Google Contacts app (Android)

There is also a wide range of address book apps that can be downloaded from a device's linked app store. Enter "address book" or "contacts" into the Search box to view the available options.

All address book apps work in a similar way.

1. Open the app and select the **Add** option.

2. Enter the details for a contact, including name, address, email address, and cell number.

3. Once a contact has been entered, start typing their name as the recipient of an email or a text message. As you type, their name should appear. Click on their name and select the appropriate item, e.g. their email address for an email or cell number for a text message.

# Calendars

Calendar apps can be used to add entries for important events and occasions. Reminders can also be added and other people can be sent invitations for specific events. The main pre-installed calendar apps are all called Calendar in Windows 10, macOS High Sierra, iOS 11, and Android.

**Adding an event in Windows 10**

1. Open the **Calendar** app and click on the **New event** button.

2. Enter details for the event, including **Event name**, **Location**, and **Start** and **End** times, or check the **All day** option.

3. Click in this box to select a time for a reminder for the event.

4. Click on this icon to select options for a repeat event, such as a birthday.

5. Once an event has been added, double-click on it in the calendar to view its details.

## Adding an event in macOS and iOS 11

1. On a Mac, open the **Calendar** app and click and hold on a date. Then click on the **New Event** button. On an iOS 11 device, tap on the plus button.

2. On both platforms, add the **Title** and **Location** for the event.

3. Select the **Starts** and **Ends** options to add a start and finish date and time or check the **All day** option.

4. Select the **Repeat** option to add a repeat event, such as a birthday.

5. Select the **Invitees** option to invite other people to an event. This can be a good option for something like a party.

6. Select the **Alert** option to specify a time at which an alert for the event will be displayed.

## Adding an event on an Android device

1. Open the **Calendar** app and tap on this button.

2. Tap on the **Event** button.

3. Add a title for the event.

4. Tap on the date and time options to specify these or drag the **All-day** button to On.

5. Tap on the notification options to specify a time and type of notification for the event.

6. Tap on the **Invite people** option to invite other people to an event.

7. Tap on the **Save** button to add the event to the calendar.

# Reminders

Reminder apps work in a similar way to adding an event to a calendar. Enter details for the reminder and set a date and time for when the reminder appears. On a Mac and an iOS 11 device, this is done with the Reminders app.

On a Windows 10 PC it is done from the Cortana Search box.

1. Click in the **Search** box.

2. Click on the **Notebook** button.

3. Click on the **Reminders** option to add details for the reminder.

There are no universal default reminders apps on Android devices, but there are numerous options in the Play Store: enter "reminders apps" into the Search box.

# Notes

Notes apps are a great way to write down short items such as shopping lists, to-do lists, or participants for a party. They are designed to be used with shorter amounts of text than a word processing app, but there is still a range of formatting options with most notes apps. One feature to look for is a checkbox that can be added and then checked once the item has been completed.

### Notes on Windows 10

The pre-installed notes app on Windows 10 devices is OneNote. This is a powerful note-taking app that also can be used to sync notes with the cloud service OneDrive. OneNote enables you to create a notebook, into which individual notes can be added. There are several formatting functions that can be used, such as text formatting, lists, and paragraph styles. These are accessed from the **Home** tab on the top toolbar.

The **Insert** tab can be used to insert additional content into a note, including a table, a file from your computer, a photo, a Web link, or an audio file.

The **Draw** tab can be used to draw freehand content into a note.

The **View** tab can be used to select viewing options for the notebook area.

## A CLOSER LOOK

The Sticky Notes app in Windows 10 can be used to create short notes that can be "stuck" to the desktop. This is a good option if you want to have a visible reminder about something.

Remember to feed the dog

## Notes on macOS and iOS

On macOS High Sierra and iOS 11 devices, notes are created with the Notes app. This is an iCloud app so, as long as Notes is turned On for iCloud (Settings > Apple ID > iCloud > Notes), notes created on one device will automatically be saved in iCloud and be available on other Apple devices.

## Notes on Android

Notes can be created on an Android device with the Google Keep app (if this is not pre-installed on an Android device it can be downloaded from the Play Store). As with OneNote, this provides a noticeboard onto which individual notes can be placed.

1. Tap on the **Take a note** button to create a new note.

   Take a note...

2. Enter content for the note. Tap on this button to access options for adding checkboxes, photos, or a voice recording.

3. Tap on this icon to pin a note to the top of the noticeboard.

4. Tap on this icon to add a reminder for the note.

5. Each note is added to the notice board, and the other notes move along to accommodate the latest note.

6. Swipe a note away from the noticeboard to remove it.

7. Go to the website at *keep.google.com* to access notes from any online device.

Several other notes apps can also be downloaded from a device's respective app store.

# Productivity suites

A productivity suite of apps is one that includes several productivity apps packaged together. If you buy or download the suite, it will include apps for word processing, spreadsheets, and presentations. It is also possible to obtain each app separately, rather than as part of a suite of apps. The main software player – Microsoft, Apple, and Google – all have their own suite of productivity apps.

### Microsoft Office (Word, Excel, and Powerpoint)

Microsoft Office is one of the longest established productivity suites of apps. The standard version costs $9.99 for a monthly subscription or $99.99 for an annual subscription. (The subscription renews automatically, so add a calendar event or a reminder if you want to cancel it at a particular time.) Microsoft Office contains the standard productivity apps:

- **Word.** The most widely used word processing app on the market, Word is a very powerful and sophisticated app that can produce documents to a high standard. For anyone doing a lot of word processing, Word should certainly be considered.

- **Excel.** For creating spreadsheets, whether it is for complex calculations or for working out household expenses, Excel is one of the best spreadsheet apps. There are templates that can be used as a starting point for a range of functions.

- **Powerpoint.** For anyone creating a presentation consisting of different slides with text and graphical content, Powerpoint has long been the go-to option.

---

**CAUTION**

If you are creating a Powerpoint presentation, whether it is to display your vacation photos to family and friends or for a club or society, the concept of "less is more" is very much the key. Don't include too much text on each slide and beware of too many different types of transitions between slides. These are the animated effects that can be added when one slide moves to another.

---

## Apple iWork (Pages, Numbers and Keynote)

Apple's version of Microsoft Office is known as iWork and contains a similar range of apps. While they are not as powerful as the Microsoft ones, they will do a good job for creating word processing documents, spreadsheets, and presentations. The iWork apps are:

- **Pages** for word processing.

- **Numbers** for spreadsheets.

- **Keynote** for presentations.

The iWork apps are compatible with iCloud and iCloud Drive, so you can create documents on one device and then continue with them on another device. All of the changes will be stored in iCloud and be available the next time the document is opened.

The iWork apps are free. If they are not pre-installed on your Apple device, they can be downloaded from the App Store.

---

**A CLOSER LOOK**

Historically, there were issues around sharing documents created on a Windows PC and a Mac. However, this is now a thing of the past, and productivity documents can be shared between both platforms.

---

## Google productivity (Docs, Sheets and Slides)

The Google productivity apps options are predominately online ones, and this is a great way to have documents at your fingertips at any time. The Google productivity apps are:

- **Docs** for word processing.

- **Sheets** for spreadsheets.

- **Slides** for presentations.

A Google Account is needed to use Docs, Sheets, and Slides. You can access the apps online or download them to your device from the Play Store.

### Using Google Docs

1. Go to *docs.google.com* and sign in with your Google Account details.

2. Select a template as the basis for a new document or click on the Blank option.

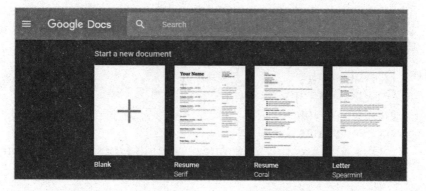

3. A new, untitled document is opened.

4. Create the content for the document.

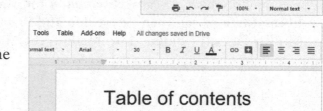

5.  Click in the **Untitled document** box.

6.  Enter a name for the document.

7.  Click on the Menu button at the left-hand side of the top toolbar to go back to the Google Docs homepage.

8.  The document is saved under the **Recent documents** heading.

9.  The document is also automatically saved to your Google Drive folder.

10. Download the **Google Docs** app for another option for accessing your documents, and creating new ones. Google Docs documents are also available via the Google Drive app.

The two other Google productivity apps can also be accessed from the *docs.google.com* website: *docs.google.com/spreadsheets* for Sheets, and *docs.google.com/presentation* for Slides. Spreadsheets and presentations can then be created and managed in the same way as for Docs (including downloading the **Sheets** and **Slides** apps for use on mobile devices).

---

┌─ A CLOSER LOOK ─────────────────────────────┐
│ If you use the Chrome browser you will also be able to use the │
│ Google productivity apps offline to edit and create content. │
└─────────────────────────────────────────────┘

# Apps for productivity and organization

Productivity work is frequently easier to do on a PC or laptop, but there are also several apps that can be used on mobile devices, for a range of organizational tasks:

- **Todoist.** A powerful list-making and organization app.

- **Evernote.** A note-tasking app with a range of impressive functionality for adding content and sharing notes.

- **Any.do.** A to-do list and calendar app for keeping everything up-to-date.

- **Wunderlist.** Ideal for creating lists and tasks that can be shared with family members. A shopping list can be created on a PC and then sent to a mobile device while someone is shopping in a store.

- **Doodle.** A planning app that can manage all of your social events, send invitations for events, and set up event chat groups.

- **2Do.** A personal planner that lets you organize your events and activities.

# 20 ACCESSIBILITY

Using computing devices should be as inclusive as possible, giving everyone the chance to use them to their full potential, regardless of any issues with sight, hearing, or motor skills. To address this, PCs, laptops, and mobile devices all have a range of accessibility options that can make computing devices easier to use for everyone.

## Zooming in

Deteriorating eyesight is generally a result of the aging process. Because of this, it is useful to be able to increase the size of what you are looking at on a computer screen. This can either be for a specific item, particularly text, or for everything on the screen.

### Zooming in with Windows 10

On a Windows 10 PC or laptop, there is an option for zooming in on areas of the screen, and it is also possible to change the magnification level:

1. Access Settings > Ease of Access and click on the **Magnifier** option in the left-hand panel.

2. Drag the **Turn on Magnifier** button to On.

3. This activates a window (lens) that magnifies everything it passes over. The window can be dragged around the screen to magnify items as required.

4. Click on the **Magnification zoom level** buttons to decrease, or increase, the amount of magnification used in the magnification window.

5. Set the required options for the Magnifier.

6. Click in the **Magnifier mode** box to select the type of magnification that is used. The options are for: **Lens**, which is the default option of the on-screen window; **Docked**, which inserts a bar across the top of the screen – everything the cursor passes over is magnified in this bar; and **Full screen**, which magnifies the whole screen.

7. Drag the sliders around the **Change lens size** window to alter the size at which the default lens appears over the screen.

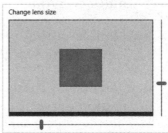

## Zooming in with macOS High Sierra

On a Mac, the zoom settings are within System Preferences:

1. Access System Preferences > Accessibility.

2. Click on the **Zoom** option in the left-hand panel.

3. Check On the **Use keyboard shortcuts to zoom** checkbox to activate the zoom function from these keys.

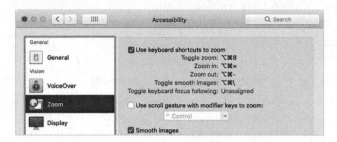

## Zooming in with iOS 11

On an iPhone or iPad with iOS 11, the zoom function is accessed within Settings:

1. Access Settings > General > Accessibility.

2. Tap on the **Zoom** option.

3. Drag the **Zoom** button to On.

4. The Zoom function activates a window that can be dragged around the screen, and it magnifies everything underneath it.

5. Double-tap with three fingers to zoom in and out. Drag the zoom panel with three fingers to move it around the screen.

6. Tap on the **Zoom Region** option.

7. Select whether to zoom using the zoom window or zoom on the whole screen.

8. Drag the **Maximum Zoom Level** slider to specify the amount of zoom used.

## Zooming in with Android

On an Android device, the zoom function is accessed within the Settings:

1. Access Settings > Accessibility.

2. Tap on the **Magnification gesture** button.

3. Drag the **Magnification gesture** button to On to enable zooming by tapping and swiping on the screen.
Triple-tap with one finger to zoom. Drag with two fingers to move around the screen. Pinch inwards with two or more fingers to adjust the amount of zoom.

4. In the main Accessibility window, tap on the **Display size** option.

5. Drag the slider at the bottom of the window to change the overall display size of the screen.

# Using narrators

For anyone with visual issues, having a computing device speak what is onscreen is a valuable feature, using the narrator feature. This usually covers the text that is on the screen and also the controls, such as buttons and checkboxes, keyboard strokes, and file management functions.

### To use the Windows 10 narrator

1. Access Settings > Ease of Access, and click on the **Narrator** option in the left-hand panel.

🖵 Narrator

2.  Drag the **Narrator** button to On.

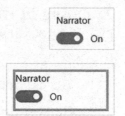

3.  The item that is being read is highlighted with a blue box, and the narrator gives a description of what it is, e.g. "On, Narrator, toggle switch."

4.  Use the Voice settings to specify a voice for the narrator, the speed of speech, the pitch, and whether there are pauses in the intonation.

## To use the macOS High Sierra narrator

1.  Access System Preferences > Accessibility.

2.  Click on the **VoiceOver** option in the left-hand panel.

3.  Check the **Enable VoiceOver** check-box On to enable the narrator.

## To use iOS 11 narrator

1.  Access Settings > General > Accessibility.

2.  Tap on the **VoiceOver** option.

3. Drag the **VoiceOver** button to On to enable the narrator.

4. Drag the **Speaking Rate** slider to specify the speed of the narrator.

5. Tap on the **Speech** and **Verbosity** options to specify these settings for the narrator.

6. To turn off **VoiceOver**, tap once on the **VoiceOver** button to select it and double-tap to turn it Off.

## To use Android narrator

1. Access Settings > Accessibility.

2. Tap on the **TalkBack** option.

3. Tap on the **TalkBack** button to turn it On.

4. To turn **TalkBack off**, tap on the **TalkBack** button to select it and double-tap to turn it Off.

# Dictating text

Another accessibility issue is using a keyboard: if people have problems with their hands, it may be painful to type for prolonged periods of time. To overcome this, content can be added by using dictation.

## Dictation with Windows 10

Windows 10 has a keyboard shortcut that can activate the dictation function.

1. In an appropriate app, such as a word processing app or a notes app, press the Windows key+H.

2. The dictation bar is activated.

3. Speak what you want to appear on screen. Punctuation can also be added by saying, "period", or "comma", and general commands can be given, such as "Select All." Say "Stop dictating" when you are finished.

> ### A CLOSER LOOK
>
> Voice commands can also be used with Cortana, the Windows 10 digital voice assistant, by clicking on the microphone icon at the right-hand side of the Cortana Search box next to the Start button.

## Dictation with macOS High Sierra

1. Access System Preferences > Keyboard and click on the **Dictation** tab.

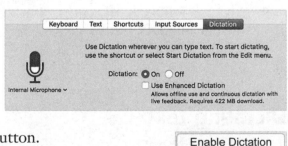

2. Check the **Dictation** checkbox to On.

3. Click on the **Enable Dictation** button.

4. To use dictation within a compatible app, select File > Start Dictation from the Menu bar.

## Dictation with iOS 11

On an iPhone or an iPad, dictation can be activated directly from the keyboard of a compatible app by tapping on the microphone key.

## Dictation with Android

On an Android device, dictation can be activated directly from the keyboard of a compatible app by tapping on the microphone key.

---

**BRIGHT IDEA**

If you are going to be doing a lot of dictation, it would be worth looking at a dedicated dictation app. For Windows 10, one option is the Dictation App that is available in the Microsoft Store. For Apple and Android devices, try Dragon Anywhere.

---

# Using closed captions

When watching movies, TV shows, or videos (such as those on YouTube), closed captions (a type of subtitle) can be a useful feature for people with hearing issues. Closed captions will only work on some apps – if it supports closed captions, there will be an option to turn this on within the app.

## Closed captions with Windows 10

1. Access Settings > Ease of Access and click on the **Closed captions** option in the left-hand panel.

2. Select the required closed captions settings. These will be displayed in an app that supports closed captions.

CC Closed captions

Closed captions
Preview

These are my caption settings

Font
Caption color

Yellow

Caption transparency

Default

Caption style

Default

Caption size

Default

## Closed captions with macOS High Sierra

1. Access System Preferences > Accessibility and click on the **Captions** option in the left-hand panel.

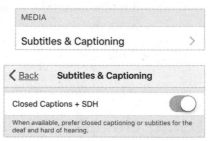

2. Check the **Prefer closed captions and SDH** checkbox to On to use closed captions rather than standard subtitles.

## Closed captions with iOS 11

1. Access Settings > General > Accessibility.

2. Tap on the **Subtitles & Captioning** option in the **Media** section.

> MEDIA
>
> Subtitles & Captioning          >

3. Drag the **Closed Captions + SDH** button to On to activate this, when using a compatible app that supports closed captioning.

> ‹ Back        **Subtitles & Captioning**
>
> Closed Captions + SDH          ◯
>
> When available, prefer closed captioning or subtitles for the deaf and hard of hearing.

## Closed captions with Android

1. Access Settings > Accessibility.

2. Tap on the **Captions** option.

> Captions
> Off

3. Drag the **Captions** button to On to activate this, when using a compatible app that supports closed captioning. Make appropriate selections for how the **Language**, **Text size**, and **Caption style** options operate by tapping on each item.

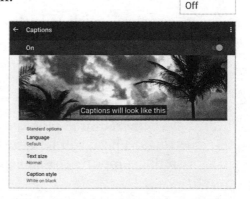

# Inverting the screen colors

Traditionally, computer screens display text as black on a white background. However, this does not suit everyone, and some people find it easier to read text on a different colored background. To help with this, it is possible to invert the screen colors on a computing device. On some platforms, it is also possible to change the overall color scheme to make elements easier to see.

## Inverting screen colors with Windows 10

1. Access Settings > Ease of Access and click on the **Color & high contrast** option in the left-hand panel.

2. Drag the **Apply color filter** button to On.

3. Click in the **Choose a filter** box.

4. Select a color filter. This will be applied to elements such as scroll bars, icons, Desktop, and menu bars.

5. Select the **Invert** option to invert all of the screen colors.

6. Click in the **Choose a theme** box under the **High Contrast** heading. (Turn **Apply color filter**, in Step 2, Off before applying a high contrast color theme).

7. Select a color theme and click on the **Apply** button.

8. The new color theme is applied according to the elements described in the selected option.

## Inverting colors with macOS High Sierra

1. Access System Preferences > Accessibility and click on the **Display** option in the left-hand panel.

2. Check the **Invert colors** checkbox to On. Make any other selections, as required, such as for **Use grayscale** or **Increase contrast**. Drag the **Display contrast** slider to determine the amount of contrast for the screen elements.

## Inverting colors with iOS 11

1. Access Settings > General > Accessibility.

2. Tap on the **Display Accommodations** option in the **Vision** section.

3. Tap on the **Invert Colors** option.

4. Select one of the options for inverting screen colors.

5.  In the **Display Accommodations** window, tap on the **Color Filters** option.

6.  Drag the **Color Filters** button to On and select which color to apply as the screen color filter.

7.  Drag the slider at the bottom of the window to determine the intensity of the filter.

## Inverting colors with Android

1.  Access Settings > Accessibility.

2.  Drag the **High contrast text** or **Color inversion** buttons to On to apply these features.

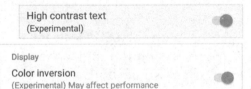

# Flash alerts

For anyone who is hard of hearing, sound alerts and notifications can be of limited use. To overcome this, there is an option for displaying screen flashes to indicate a new alert or notification.

## Flash alerts with Windows 10

1.  Access Settings > Ease of Access and click on the **Other Options** button in the left-hand panel.

2. Click in the **Visual notifications for sound** box.

3. Select an option for how the visual notification works.

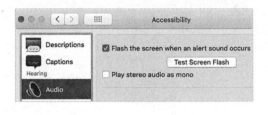

## Flash alerts with macOS High Sierra

1. Access System Preferences > Accessibility and click on the **Audio** option in the left-hand panel.

2. Check the **Flash the screen when an alert sound occurs** checkbox to On. Click on the **Test Screen Flash** button to preview the effect.

## Flash alerts with iOS 11

1. Access Settings > General > Accessibility.

2. Tap on the **LED Flash for Alerts** option under the **Hearing** heading.

3. Drag the **LED Flash for Alerts** button to On.

## Flash alerts with Android

For Android devices, the best option for flash alerts is to download an appropriate app from the Google Play Store. Search for "flash alerts" in the Play Store. These apps operate by using the device's camera to produce a flash alert when a sound notification is received.

# Accommodating hearing aids

For hearing aid users, the iPhone and iPad have some options that can help improve the sound quality. Check with the manufacturer of the hearing aid to see if they have any specific recommendations.

## Hearing aids with iOS 11

1. Access Settings > General > Accessibility.

2. Tap on the **MFi Hearing Aids** option under the **Hearing** heading to link your iPhone or iPad to a compatible Bluetooth hearing aid.

3. Drag the **Hearing Aid Compatibility** button to On to improve sound quality with compatible hearing aids (check with the manufacturer of the hearing aid).

HEARING

MFi Hearing Aids >

LED Flash for Alerts      Off >

Mono Audio

Phone Noise Cancellation

Noise cancellation reduces ambient noise on phone calls when you are holding the receiver to your ear.

L                                    R

Adjust the audio volume balance between left and right channels.

Hearing Aid Compatibility

# Keyboard and mouse settings

On PCs and laptops, there are accessibility options for customizing the keyboard and mouse to make it easier for users with motor issues or who find it painful to use a keyboard and mouse.

## Keyboard settings with Windows 10

⌨ Keyboard

1. Access Settings > Ease of Access and click on the **Keyboard** option in the left-hand panel.

2. Make selections for the keyboard as required. These include turning On the **On-Screen Keyboard**, which is a virtual keyboard that appears on the screen once it has been activated.

Keyboard

On-Screen Keyboard

Turns on the On-Screen Keyboard

Off

Sticky Keys

Press one key at a time for keyboard shortcuts

Off

Toggle Keys

## Keyboard settings with macOS High Sierra

1. Access System Preferences > Accessibility and click on the **Keyboard** option in the left-hand panel.

2. Make selections for the keyboard as required. These include the amount of time between when a key is pressed and the action is activated. Click on the **Accessibility Keyboard** tab at the top of the window for more options.

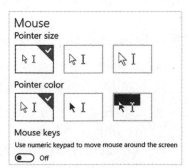

## Mouse settings with Windows 10

1. Access Settings > Ease of Access and click on the **Mouse** option in the left-hand panel.

2. Make selections for the mouse as required. These include changing the size and color of the pointer (cursor) and also enabling the numbers pad to be used to move the mouse pointer around the screen.

## Mouse settings with macOS High Sierra

1.  Access System Preferences > Accessibility and click on the **Mouse & Trackpad** option in the left-hand panel.

2.  Make selections for the mouse as required. These include controlling the mouse with the numbers pad and the speed at which a double-click action is activated. Click on the **Trackpad Options** button and the **Mouse Options** button for more specific options for these items.

# 21

# PROBLEM SOLVING AND TROUBLESHOOTING

## 10 ways to speed up your Windows PC

Even with the advanced operating system that is Windows 10, there may be times when your desktop PC or laptop is running slowly and sluggishly and generally not behaving as it should. There are a few options you can try to rejuvenate it and return it to its former glory.

1. **Clean up your disk.** This is a process whereby Windows will look through your files and identify ones that can safely be deleted to free up disk space and improve performance. Type "Disk Clean-up" into the Search box to the left of the Taskbar at the bottom of the screen. Click on the **Disk clean-up** option. The files recommended for removal by Windows 10 are checked in the **Files to delete** box, with the amount of space that will be saved below this. Click on the **OK** button to remove the files.

2. **Defragment your hard drive.** Also known as "defragging," this is a process that puts tiny bits of data back together on your hard drive. Whenever files are created, modified, and saved, bits of the file (which is just a collection of digital data) become detached and saved in different parts of the hard drive. When you access the file again, all of the pieces are reassembled so that you see the full file. However, the more that the file is fragmented, the longer it takes to reassemble the pieces. This is usually a very small amount of time, but as files become more fragmented, it can slow down your PC. This is where defragging comes in – it gathers together all of the pieces of data and puts them back where they should be. To do this, open File Explorer and right-click on the hard drive (C:). Select **Properties**, select the **Tools** tab, and click on the **Optimize** button under the **Optimize and defragment drive** heading. Select the C: drive and click on the **Analyze** button to see how fragmented the drive is, e.g. 12%. Click on the **Optimize** button to defragment the drive. (This could take several hours, depending on how fragmented the drive is.) Once this is completed your PC should run faster.

3. **Scan for viruses.** Viruses on any computing device can slow it down, and this is certainly true for Windows 10. The best way to avoid this is to enable the Windows Firewall (Settings > Update & Security > Windows Defender > Open Windows Defender Security Center and click on the **Firewall & network protection** option) and use one anti-virus software package. (If you use more than one they could causes conflicts with each other and both be less effective.)

4. **Turn off graphical effects.** Modern computers are very graphically impressive devices with vibrant colors and interesting displays and designs. However, this comes at a cost in terms of speed: your computer uses up a certain amount of its processing power and memory delivering all of these graphical elements, which can cause it to run slowly. It is possible to turn off some of the graphical elements in a bid to make your computer run faster. Type "adjust appearance" into the Search box next to the Start button and click on the **Adjust the appearance and performance of Windows** result. Click on the **Visual Effects** tab and check On the **Adjust for best performance** checkbox. There is also a **Custom** option, where you can enable or disable individual elements of the visual effects.

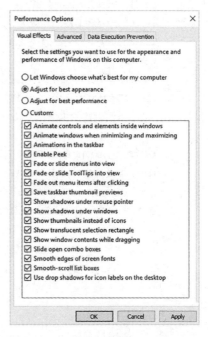

5. **Remove apps from the Startup process.** When Windows 10 boots up (starts) it can open a lot of apps to get them ready for use. However, this can take a lot of processing power and lead to the whole Startup process taking longer than you would like. A lot of the items in the Startup process can be disabled. To do this, right-click on the **Start**

button and click on the **Task Manager** button.
Click on the **More details** button, and click on
the **Startup** tab to view all of the items that
take place in this process. If an app has
Enabled next to it, click on it and click on the **Disable** button.

## A Closer Look

Having too many files stored on a PC's Desktop can also slow
it down. Instead, store files within an organized structure in
File Explorer. Also, Zip files can slow down a PC if too many
are stored. These are compressed files that are usually used to
send or copy large amounts of data – when the Zip file is
opened, the data is uncompressed for use. Once you have
done this with a Zip file, delete it to free up space on your
hard drive.

6. **Use Disk Check.** This can be used to check your hard
   drive for any problems or damage. Open File Explorer,
   right-click on the C: drive, and click on **Properties**. Click on
   the **Tools** tab and, under the **Error checking** heading, click on

the **Check** button (make sure that C: is showing at the top of the window, i.e. the selected drive to check). Once the drive has been scanned, a report will appear detailing any issues or stating that no errors have been found.

7. **Add more memory with ReadyBoost.** The one element that can most effectively improve the speed of your Windows PC is memory, also known as RAM. It is best to buy a PC with as much of this as possible, but you can add more memory by using a USB flash drive. The PC can then use the memory from the flash drive to help it perform quicker. To do this, buy a USB flash drive with as much memory as possible (a minimum of 16GB and ensure that it is "Enhanced for ReadyBoost"). Attach the drive to your PC and right-click on it in the File Explorer. Click on the **Properties** option, and click on the **ReadyBoost** tab at the top of the window. Select either **Use this device** or **Dedicate this device to ReadyBoost** (in which case it will only be used for this process and to ensure that no content is saved on the flash drive) and click on the **OK** button to use the memory on the USB flash drive as extra memory on your PC.

8. **Empty the Recycle Bin.** It is definitely good to recycle, but this has a slightly different meaning on your PC. When you delete something, it doesn't really go anywhere, except into the Recycle Bin. This can be useful if you want to restore it

at a later date, but it can also cause your PC to run slowly. This is because of the number of files in the Recycle Bin. To solve this, empty it by right-clicking on the Recycle Bin on the Desktop and click on the **Empty Recycle Bin** button (but only after you are sure that there is nothing there that you want to keep).

9. **Update Windows 10.** Keeping Windows 10 as up-to-date as possible ensures that you have the latest version of the operating system, which should also be the most efficient. To check for updates to Windows 10, go to Settings > Update & Security and click on the **Windows Update** option in the left-hand panel. In the main window under the **Update status** heading, click on the **Check for updates** button to see if there are any Windows updates waiting to be downloaded and installed.

10. **Turn off OneDrive syncing.** If you use OneDrive, the Windows cloud service for backing up and sharing files, this can slow down your PC, since it is regularly looking to sync the OneDrive on your computer with the online service. To turn this off, right-click on the OneDrive icon on the Taskbar and click on the **Pause syncing** option. Select the length of time for pausing the syncing process. (This is only limited to 2 hours, 8 hours or 24 hours, since part of the function of OneDrive is to sync items from your PC to the online site.)

# Sign in with a Local account

For Windows 10 users, if you are signed in as an Administrator, this gives you access to install new software and make changes to Windows 10. While this can be a good thing, it also opens up the opportunity for a hacker or a virus to perform destructive tasks on your computer. To limit the chances of this, it is possible to sign in with a Local account instead of an Administrator one.

1.  Make sure that anything that you have been working on has been saved and preferably closed.

2.  Select Settings > Accounts and click on the **Your info** tab on the left-hand side.

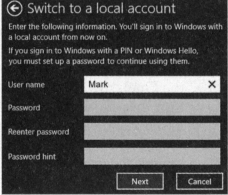

3.  Your account details will be shown at the top of the screen. If the word **Administrator** appears under your own name, look to change it to make your system more secure.

4.  Click on the **Sign in with a local account instead** option.

5.  Enter the current password for your Administrator account and click on the **Next** button.

6.  Enter a username, password, and password hint for your local account and click on the **Next** button.

7.  Click on the **Sign out and finish** button.

8.  The next time the login screen appears, use your newly created password to sign in to your Local account. (This will restrict access to some of the apps accessed through a Microsoft Account.)

# Keeping your email account safe from Wi-Fi hotspots

Online email accounts require a username and password in order to log in to them. However, if you do this using a public Wi-Fi hotspot, there is a chance that hackers could obtain these details and use them to access your email account. Anything in the account could then be used by the hackers, such as banking and financial details. Even if the Wi-Fi hotspot requires a password to access it, there is still a security risk from entering any sensitive details in these circumstances.

---

BRIGHT IDEA

When using a PC or Mac, it can be frustrating to access the same commands from menus for simple and repetitive tasks. Instead, there are some simple keyboard shortcuts that can be used (on a Mac, use the Cmd key, rather than the Ctrl key):

- Save a document – Ctrl+S
- Copy an item – Ctrl+C
- Cut an item – Ctrl+X
- Paste an item – Ctrl+V
- Undo the previous action – Ctrl+Z
- Redo an action – Ctrl+Y
- Close a document – Ctrl+W

Command key

---

# 7 tricks for saving battery life

One of the main complaints about mobile digital devices is that the batteries run down a lot sooner than we would like. But help is at hand, with a few handy hints for preserving battery power.

1. **Turn your mobile devices off at night.** Even on standby, smartphones and tablets still use up battery power. Although this is a lot less than when the device is being used, every little bit helps; and it also gives you the chance of a better night's sleep if your devices are turned off.

2. **Turn down the screen brightness manually.** Smartphones and tablets usually have an auto-brightness function, whereby the brightness of the screen is determined by the surrounding

ambient or natural light. This means that the device is constantly monitoring the lighting conditions and adjusting the screen brightness accordingly, using extra battery power. One way to save battery power is to set the screen brightness manually for smartphones and tablets. On an iOS 11 device, do this in Settings > Display & Brightness, and drag the **Brightness** slider. (The brightness can also be amended by accessing the Control Center, by dragging up from the bottom of the screen, and dragging on the brightness icon.) On an Android device, do this in Settings > Display > Brightness level and drag the slider. (**Turn Adaptive brightness** Off.)

3. **Activate the Lock screen sooner.** It is possible to specify the amount of time before the Lock screen is activated on a smartphone. This is when it is put into a state of sleep, and the screen becomes blank. The quicker the Lock screen is activated the more battery power that is saved. On an iOS 11 device, do this in Settings > Display & Brightness, tap on **Auto-Lock**, and select a period of inactivity before the device is auto-locked, e.g. 30 seconds. On an Android device, do this in Settings > Display > Sleep.

4. **Turn off Wi-Fi and Bluetooth.** Both Wi-Fi and Bluetooth use up battery power as they are regularly looking with their respective networks and connections. So, turn them off when you are not using them. If you need to connect to the Internet or a Bluetooth device, just turn them on when needed. On either an iOS 11 or Android device, do this in Settings > Wi-Fi/Bluetooth.

5. **Turn off Location Services.** On mobile devices, Location Services are used by several apps to determine your location. It is particularly useful for items such as maps apps to assess your location in relation to directions to other locations. However, Location Services uses a significant amount of battery power since it is regularly scanning your location using GPS. At times when you do not need it, Location Services can be turned off to save power. On an iOS 11 device, do this in Settings > Privacy > Location Services and drag **Location Services** to Off. On an Android device, do this in Settings > Location and drag **Location** to Off.

6. **Turn off background app refresh.** On mobile devices, apps can be instructed to update automatically in the background, usually when connected to Wi-Fi. This can be to install updates or send notifications. If this is turned off, more power will be saved. On an iOS 11 device, do this in Settings > General > **Background App Refresh** > Background App Refresh, and tap Off. (**If Background App Refresh** is On, the first screen for Background App Refresh has a list of all of the apps that can be updated in the background, and individual ones can be turned Off here.) On an Android device, to see which apps are running in the background, go to Settings > Apps and tap on an app. If you have not been using the app, but there is a figure for usage under Battery, the app could have been operating in the background. Tap on the **Force Stop** button to close it.

7. **On iOS 11 devices, turn off "Hey Siri."** This is the function whereby the digital voice assistant, Siri, can be activated from any screen simply by saying, "Hey Siri." Having this running uses up battery power, and it can be turned off in Settings > Siri & Search by dragging the **Listen for "Hey Siri"** button to Off.

A lot of the items here are automatically restricted if you put your device into Low Power Mode. This turns off items such as Location Services, and background app refresh. They are reinstated once **Low Power Mode** has been turned Off. On an iOS 11 device, do this in Settings > Battery, and drag the Low Power Mode button to On. On an Android device, do this in Settings > Battery > Battery saver and drag the button to On.

# Never put this in your will – your family will thank you

No one likes to think about dying, but it is inevitable, and it is always a good idea to have your affairs in order. This includes your digital affairs so that there are no unpleasant problems for your family. One important issue is to never put your passwords or usernames in your will, particularly if they relate to financial concerns, such as online banking. The reason for this is simple: a will is a public document, so anyone could, in theory, get hold of it, and then your online accounts and services could be compromised. Keep all of your important information, such as usernames, passwords, and online banking log in details in a safe place away from your computing device. A good option for this is a home safe. Look at *Safewise.com* for a range of reasonably priced home safes.

**BRIGHT IDEA**

One issue that can cause problems in the digital world is high cellphone bills. However, there are some options for trying to reduce this (in some cases you can cut it by half).

- Get rid of a long contract. If you have a contract for a year, or even two years, you could be locked into paying more than you need to for an extended period. Instead, look for a month-to-month plan.

- Find the right plan. Work out what you want to use your phone for (in terms of calls, texts, and data), and find the appropriate plan: don't pay for services that you won't use. Go to *whistleout.com* to compare cellphone plans.

- Watch your data usage. Most plans give you a certain amount of data each month for accessing the Web and online services. However, if you go over this you will be charged. Try to limit your data usage to just texts, emails, and browsing the Web. If you want to do more data-intensive tasks, such as downloading music or streaming movies, do this when you can connect to Wi-Fi.

# Save money on repairs

It is an undeniable fact that computers sometimes misbehave, stop working, or don't do what you want them to. Getting professional help to fix problems can be expensive, and a lot of the time you don't even need to do this – you can fix it yourself. Try these 5 simple steps to become your own IT technician and save yourself some money.

1. Turn it off and back on again. It is a cliché of the computing world, but a lot of the time it does work. Computers are complex devices, and sometimes they just need a chance to reorder everything and start again. If your computer is frozen, press Ctrl+Alt+Delete, and click on the Shut Down button in the bottom right-hand corner.

2. Similarly, if your computing device is not performing a task the way that you had hoped, just walk away and leave it for a few minutes to see if it can figure it out for itself, which it quite often will do.

3. Press the Esc key twice on the keyboard. This can sometimes remove a blockage that is preventing an app from working properly.

4. If still no luck, press Ctrl+Alt+Delete and click on the **Task Manager** option. This displays the currently open apps and background processes that are taking place on your PC. If an app has a "Not responding" message next to it, click on the **End task** button. If in doubt, do this for all open apps that you think may be causing a problem. (On a Mac, select Apple Menu > Force Quit, select an app, and click on the Force Quit button to force it to close.)

5. If your computer remains stubbornly frozen, hold down the **Power** (On) button for approximately 10 seconds. The PC should turn off. Press the Power button in the normal way to (hopefully) turn it back on again.

If none of this works, then you may need to seek professional help, although the troubleshooting settings for Windows 10 (Settings > Update & security > Troubleshoot) is another place to look.

# Stop annoying "robo-calls"

All technology has its own particular annoying traits, and for smartphones and cellphones, one of these is unwanted automated calls or texts, also known as robo-calls. These can not only be time-wasting, such as those from telemarketers, they can also be fraudulent, as part of a campaign to obtain sensitive financial information through an automated call or text. Help is at hand though, to try and block these robo-calls:

1. Register your smartphone or cellphone (and your home phone) with the National Do Not Call Registry at *donotcall.gov*. This is the official US government website for addressing the issue of unwanted calls. Once you have registered, this should limit the number of robo-calls that you receive.

2. On the National Do Not Call Registry website you can also report robo-calls, using the **Report Unwanted Calls** button.

3. Report robo-calls to the Federal Trade Commission (FTC) at their website *ftccomplaintassistant.gov*. This is the US government website for protecting consumers' rights, and there are several categories of complaint that can be selected. Click or tap on one of the categories on the homepage to access information about topics including **Unwanted Telemarketing**, **Text**, or **SPAM**.

| ▼ Select a category below: |
| --- |
| › Identity Theft |
| › Scams and Rip-offs |
| › Unwanted Telemarketing, Text, or SPAM |
| › Mobile Devices or Telephones |
| › Internet Services, Online Shopping, or Computers |
| › Education, Jobs, and Making Money |
| › Credit and Debt |
| › Other |

4. Forward robo-call text messages to 7726, which is a free service which will report the robo-call number to your cellular phone carrier.

5. Use an app on your smartphone or cellphone to help block the automated calls. Type "call blocker" into your app store's Search box and download one of the options to your phone.

---

**STAYING SECURE**

The FTC services cover a wide range of areas, including identity theft, scams and rip-offs, issues with Internet services, and online shopping. It is a good starting point if you have any problems with services relating to the online world.

# Encouraging an unresponsive app

Apps can be your best friends, but like any friend they can be annoying at times. Occasionally they won't work as you expected, or they will simply freeze and do nothing. But with a bit of gentle encouragement it is usually possible to win them around and get them working properly. Some things to try with unresponsive apps:

1.  Close them down and open them back up to see if this fixes the problem. If you cannot close them, press Ctrl+Alt+Esc on a Windows 10 PC to activate the Task Manager. Select the app and click on the **End Task** button. On a Mac, select Apple Menu > Force Quit, select the app and click on the **Force Quit** button to force it to close. On an iPad or an iPhone, double-click on the

    **Home** button to access the App Switcher window, and swipe the app to the top of the screen (iPad), or left or right (iPhone). On an Android device, tap on the **Recents** button, and swipe the app to the left or right of the screen.

2.  Turn off the device and turn it back on again. Make sure you have saved all of your work before you do this, and close down any other open apps, too.

3.  Uninstall the app, and then reinstall it from its related app store. Downloading a new version of the app could fix any bad habits that it has developed. It is free to download again, even if it had to be paid for the first time. To uninstall an app on a Windows 10 PC, right-click on it on the Start Menu, and click on the **Uninstall** button. To uninstall an app on a Mac, drag it over the Trash icon on the Dock. To uninstall an iOS 11 app, press and hold on it until it starts to wobble, and tap on

the **X** in the top, left-hand corner. To uninstall an Android app, press and hold on it, and drag it over the **Uninstall** button at the top of the screen.

4. If an app keeps misbehaving, there could be a bug or a serious problem with the app. If this is the case, look in the app store to see if there is an update for the app that could fix the problem.

# Dealing with monitor/screen problems

If there are problems with monitors or screens, these can be more or less serious, depending on the device that they are connected to:

- If there is a problem with a standalone monitor, i.e. one that connects to the hard drive with a cable, then, if the worst comes to the worst, you could buy a new monitor. These can be relatively inexpensive and tend to be used with Windows 10 PCs.

- If the monitor or screen is physically part of the computer, (such as an iMac or a laptop), this could have more serious consequences. For instance, if the screen of an all-in-one computer fails, then the whole computer will be affected and rendered unusable.

Monitor issues can be different, depending on the type of device involved. For a standalone monitor, some of the issues could include:

- Blank screen. If this occurs, check that the power cable is connected securely and that the cable from the monitor to the computer is also secure.

- The items on the screen appear blurry or the color is not represented correctly. Check the cables, as above, and use the monitor's control button to adjust its settings. The buttons are usually positioned at the bottom of the monitor and can be used to adjust items such as brightness and contrast, color temperature, and horizontal and vertical positioning. There should also be an **Auto-Fix** option. The monitor's menu may also have a **Factory reset** option, which returns the monitor to its original factory settings.

- Videos or graphics don't display properly. This could be an issue with the video card. Take your PC to a computer repair outlet and ask them if they can install a new video card.

If any of these problems occur with a laptop, it could be more serious, as the screen cannot be replaced on its own. Try the following if there are screen problems:

- Make sure that the laptop is charged or connected to a power socket.

- Make sure that the screen brightness is at a visible level.

- Connect the laptop to an external monitor to see if the issue lies with the laptop's screen or the hard drive.

- Check that the screen is connected properly to the body of the laptop. If the connecting hinge is loose or broken, this could affect the screen's performance.

- If the problem persists, take the laptop to a computer repair specialist rather than trying to fix anything inside the laptop yourself.

# Dealing with printer problems

When you want to print something, it can be frustrating if you click on the Print button for a document and nothing happens. However, there are a few steps to take to check what the problem might be:

1. Check that there is paper in the printer. If not, the printer display may be flashing or showing an error message. If the printer stops midway through a print job, then lack of paper is a likely reason.

2. Check for paper jams. Even the smoothest printers can experience paper jams when the paper does not move smoothly through the internal print rollers and becomes jammed within the mechanism. If this happens, turn off the printer. (The item will have to be printed again anyway, so you will not be losing anything, and it is unsafe to be delving inside a printer when it is on.) Remove the printer's cover and, if required, use a flashlight to look inside the printer to see if you can identify the paper jam. If you can reach the jammed paper, pull it slowly out of the printer. Close the cover and turn the printer on again. (If the cover is not closed properly, this will also stop the printer from working.)

3. Check the cables and connections. If a printer is physically connected to your computer with a cable, check that this has not become detached or is loose. If the printer connects wirelessly, check that your Wi-Fi is working properly, and that the network is working. (If you can connect to the Internet then the network is working.)

4. Check the print queue. When a file is sent to the printer, it resides in the print queue until it has been printed. This is fine if everything goes to plan, but if there is a problem, and the item doesn't print, it will remain at the front of the print queue. This means that any items that are subsequently sent to the printer will be stuck behind the first one in the queue. If there is a document pending to be printed, double-click on the printer icon on the Taskbar. The Printer dialog box displays the print queue. To remove an item from the print queue, right-click on it and click on **Cancel**.

---

BRIGHT IDEA

To avoid paper jams, fan the paper before you load it into the printer, load the paper tray to near the top, and ensure that the paper guides in the paper tray are fitted correctly around the sides of the paper.

# Things to try when you can't get online

One of the most frustrating computing experiences is not being able to get online. Before losing patience with your computing device, try a few of these steps first:

- Check that your device is connected to your Wi-Fi router (Windows 10, Settings >Network & Internet and click on the **Wi-Fi** option in the left-hand panel; macOS High Sierra, System Preferences > Network; iOS, Settings > Wi-Fi; and Android, Settings > Wi-Fi). If the router is showing as **Connected** this means that the problem lies with the connection coming into the router. Contact your Internet Service Provider (ISP) if the problem persists.

- If your device is not connected to your router, try moving the router to a different location to pick up the signal.

- If the router does not seem to be working properly, try resetting it. There is usually a small hole that can be accessed with a paper clip to reset the router. Push the paper clip firmly into the hole until you feel some resistance.

- On a Windows 10 PC, use the Network troubleshooter to identify the problem. Access this from Settings > Network & Internet. Under the **Network troubleshooter** heading, click on the **Network reset** option, which will return network components to their

⚠ Network troubleshooter
Diagnose and fix network problems.

View your network properties

Windows Firewall

Network and Sharing Center

Network reset

default settings. Use this if your device stubbornly refuses to connect to the Internet.

- On a macOS High Sierra computer or laptop, access System Preferences > Network and click on the **Advanced** button to identify any problems with getting online.

# Resetting – the solution of last resort

If there is a recurring problem with your PC, laptop, tablet, or smartphone, it is possible to reset it to an earlier state to see if this removes the problem.

---

CAUTION ————————————————————————

Before resetting any device, remember to backup all of your files to a USB flash drive, an external hard drive, or a cloud service.

---

There are various options for resetting devices.

### Resetting with Windows 10

To reset a Windows 10 PC or laptop:

1. Access Settings > Update & Security and click on the **Recovery** option in the left-hand panel.

2. Under the **Reset this PC** heading, click on the **Get started** button.

   Recovery
   Reset this PC
   If your PC isn't running well, resetting it might help. This lets you choose to keep your personal files or remove them, and then reinstalls Windows.

   Get started

3. Select whether you want to keep your files or remove everything. Initially, select **Keep my files**. (If this doesn't work, repeat the process and select the **Remove everything** option.)

   Choose an option

   **Keep my files**
   Removes apps and settings, but keeps your personal files.

   **Remove everything**
   Removes all of your personal files, apps, and settings.

4. Third-party apps that have been installed will be removed and will need to be reinstalled.

5. Follow the wizard to reset your PC or laptop to see if this improves its performance.

## Resetting with macOS High Sierra

Resetting a Mac with macOS High Sierra involves wiping the hard drive. (This is also useful if you want to sell your Mac.)

1. Access Applications > Utilities from the Finder or open the Utilities folder from the Launchpad.

2. Double-click on the **Disk Utility** icon.

3. Select the **Startup disk** (usually Macintosh HD) and click on the **Erase** button.

Disk Utility

Erase

| Internal | | Macintosh HD | | |
|---|---|---|---|---|
| ▼ Hitachi HTS5450... | | 317.09 GB Logical Volume Mac OS Extended (Journaled) | | |
| Macintosh HD | | | | |

| ● Used | Purgeable | ● Free |
|---|---|---|
| 166.95 GB | 10.38 GB | 139.76 GB |

| Mount Point: | / | Type: | Logical Volume |
|---|---|---|---|
| Capacity: | 317.09 GB | Available (Purgeable + Free): | 150.14 GB |
| Used: | 166.95 GB | Owners: | Enabled |
| Device: | disk1 | Connection: | SATA |

4. Select **Disk Utility** from the Menu bar and select **Quit Disk Utility**.

## Resetting with iOS 11

To reset an iPhone or iPad:

1. Access Settings > General > Reset (at the bottom of the window).

2. Select one of the reset options. Use **Reset All Settings** to retain your content and media. Use **Erase All Content and**

**Settings** to return your iPhone or iPad to its factory settings, e.g. delete everything from it. (See Chapter Seven for details.)

## Resetting with Android

An Android device can only be reset by the primary user of the device, i.e. the person who first set it up. To do this:

1. Access Settings > Backup and reset.

2. Tap on **Factory data reset** to remove all content and settings and return the device to its original factory settings. (If other users have been added to the device, they will lose all of their content and settings too.)

# 22

# THE FUTURE IS HERE

## Keeping pace with change

Predicting the future in the world of computing and technology is certainly not easy. Not only is the speed of change so fast, but the range of possibilities seems to multiply every time a new break-through is made. One thing that can be predicted with a reasonable amount of certainty is that all of the software and hardware we have today will be upgraded to newer versions within the next 12-18 months. There will be new versions of Windows, macOS, iOS, and Android and a range of new devices on which to use them.

In terms of some of the more seemingly far-fetched developments in technology, a lot of them are already upon us: headsets that enable us to immerse ourselves in 3D games; apps that can display rooms in your home, and show them with different décor; computers that can think for themselves, and adapt to tasks accordingly; and robots that can become our companions and assistants. The only thing that can be said with any certainty about the future of computing and technology is that it will move at breakneck speed.

## Virtual Reality (VR)

For a number of years, major technology companies, including Google, Microsoft, and Samsung, have been developing virtual reality hardware and software. A headset is worn by the user and this delivers the VR content, to create realistic but virtual images and environments. Some VR headsets also include physical elements, such as vibrations, which are delivered through the handset that is used to control the content. One of the main uses for VR technology to date has been for gaming, and there has yet to be a breakthrough development that has brought VR to a wider mainstream audience. But it is an exciting technology that offers a range of opportunities for exploring virtual worlds.

## Augmented Reality (AR)

Augmented reality is similar to virtual reality, except that it mixes real world images with virtual ones. For instance, an AR game on a smartphone could display your physical environment, such as your backyard. The elements of the game are then superimposed on the physical environment, i.e. augmenting your physical experience. The advantage of AR is that it can be viewed directly on smartphones or tablets. Apple's iPhone 8 and X have both been developed with support for AR apps, and this is an area that has the potential to deliver significant growth in the years ahead.

## Artificial Intelligence (AI)

Artificial Intelligence refers to computers' ability to learn from what they are doing, and "think" for themselves. This can be in relation to playing a game, such as chess, or for learning a language. Some of this is still rather hit and miss, but a lot of AI applications are highly sophisticated and powerful. AI is also beginning to be used in our computing devices. For instance, face recognition technology on some smartphones uses AI to work out differences in your appearance, such as if you are wearing a hat or glasses. A lot of AI development will go unnoticed by users, but used correctly, it should enhance our day-to-day computing experiences.

# The robots are coming

The idea of robots in society is probably one of the most identifiable, in terms of what we may have seen in science-fiction movies. However, they are no longer a thing of myth – they are well and truly part of society: from assembling cars to underwater exploration to remote surgery, robots play an increasingly significant role in daily life. This raises an important question: how should we use robots in society? For instance, should we replace all store assistants with robots just because we can? This is the kind of issue that will have to be confronted more frequently as robotic devices become increasingly sophisticated and their use more widespread.

# Top tip for keeping up with the changes

If you tried to keep up with all of the changes in computing and technology you would perhaps be overwhelmed by the amount of information out there. Instead, look out for the next edition of this book to keep you informed about all of the latest updates and developments in the ever-changing world of computing and technology.

# INDEX